THE POWER
AND BLESSING

The POWER

JACK W. HAYFORD

& BLESSING

*Celebrating the Disciplines
of Spirit-filled Living*

VICTOR BOOKS
A Division of Scripture Press Publications Inc.

Chapters 19–25 are taken from the book *Prayer Path* by Jack
Hayford, Tyndale House, 1984.

Unless otherwise indicated, all Scripture references are from
The New King James Version. © 1979, 1980, 1982, Thomas
Nelson, Inc., Publishers. Used by permission; other references are from the *Authorized (King James) Version* (KJV), and
the *New American Standard Bible* (NASB), © the Lockman
Foundation 1960, 1962, 1963, 1968, 1971, 1972, 1973,
1975, 1977.

Copyediting: *Barbara Williams*
Cover Design: *Paul Higdon*

Recommended Dewey Decimal Classification: 248.2
Suggested Subject Heading: CHRISTIAN LIVING
ISBN: 1-56476-199-1

1 2 3 4 5 6 7 8 9 10 Printing/Year 98 97 96 95 94

For information write
Victor Books, 1825 College Avenue,
Wheaton, Illinois 60187.

Acknowledgments

WHEN MY WIFE, ANNA, AND I set forth in public ministry over thirty years ago, we had no idea the day would come when we would be charged with so privileged a role in being called pastors and teachers to so large a congregation, or received so widely via radio, television, and printed media. But God, knowing what our future would require, arranged for a marvelous staff of people to surround and partner with us—giving us both the professionally trained as well as a host of equally dedicated lay people to enable the accomplishment of wonderful, Christ-glorifying enterprises.

None of this esteemed body of teammates has been a greater blessing to us than our personal aide, Janet Kemp. For over seventeen years she has "been there"—laboring with a tirelessness only explainable by reason of her devotion to Christ and His kingdom; doing so with a skill that is only explained by an unusual gifting, joined to remarkable earlier experience as part of the secretarial staff of the Attorney General and the Vice President of the United States.

As with at least a dozen books before this one, Janet's hard work and relentless effort is a key part in there being a well-finished product. For this, yet another evidence of our being blessed by her help, as well as for innumerable other instances of past and continuing attentiveness to duty, we both thank her.

Jack and Anna Hayford
Van Nuys, California
October 1993

Contents

III. PRAYER DISCIPLINES

IV. BEYOND DISCIPLINES

I

THE PILLAR
PRINCIPLE

"As We Start Together..."

It might strike you as a little romantic, but I have always taken a new book in hand with an unusual spirit of adventure. It could be such as the many musty volumes I've explored in so distant a place as Hay-on-Wye, the little English village on the border of Wales. Or perhaps a brand-spanking-new, brilliantly colored, graphically enriched piece from one of today's most creative publishers. But when I take hold of a book I feel I have something on the order of an ancient treasure map!

As you open to these first words, whether you share my above-described emotion or not, I'd like to offer some guidelines as we start together—something of a *chart*, mapping the way into a book I hope might become a gold mine of resource for you as a disciple of Christ.

The Power and Blessing is a four-sectioned book, which I've written in hopes that you will be encouraged and assisted in your quest of healthy, hope-filled Christian discipleship. By "disciple" I'm talking about you and me—people who know Jesus, care about His will and ways, and want to learn how to grow in solid, joyous patterns of living life effectively. By "discipleship" I mean the process of acquiring "disciplines," without their becoming burdensome baggage—and without you becoming a religious prude.

The four sections I've mentioned are a practical device to help make this book more easily used and digested. Section I starts here. It's titled, "The Pillar Principle," and you'll walk side-by-side with Simon Peter through seven great days of his life, finding—I hope—that you're there too.

The other two sections elaborate details of specific disciplines—general, fundamental ones for solid footing (Section II) and specific categories of prayer patterns for a fruitful devotional life (Section III). Section IV is a brief pair of chapters to close and focus the future in a way that will help keep you realistic about discipleship. Idealism is only as useful as it is to *summon* us forward. Pragmatism is only as useful as it is to keep us "real" with the *processing* of our ideals.

When you get to these later sections, I'll say a little more about them, but right now let's get going. To start, I'd like you to imagine your front door has been knocked on: there are two men present—Simon Peter and me. As you turn to the next page, open the door—OK? I'd like to introduce you to him.

Chapter One

The Pillar Principle

Simon Peter — as saint or sinner, as giant or dwarf — is a favorite to most everyone. He rises to the highest heights of insight and declaration; he sinks to the lowest depths of denial and failure. He's "every man" wrapped into one person — the reflection of our secret ambitions fulfilled and the picture of our visible embarrassments revisited. But over whatever span or spectrum of his exploits or his flops, whether at a pinnacle or with a pratfall, Peter inevitably ends up at the right place, showing the right attitudes, aiming the right direction, and en route to the right goal.

He's the opposite of the person described by "The Peter Principle"; the person who finally rises to a point beyond his competence or effectiveness. And it's this quality about Peter that makes him a desirable point of reference for an earnest disciple of Jesus Christ, because Peter models a pattern of response that grows *through* and grows *up*.

In recent years, I've been inclined to think of him as the Bible's *Rocky;* not only because his name — Peter — means the same thing (*petras*, Greek = "rock"), but because there are some similarities between the real person of history and the fictional one in the movie series. Both are rough, unpolished men; both are products of a distinct ethnicity; both are laden with undeveloped potential — until trainers get hold of them, and both end up finding their possibilities maximized and rising to the level of champion. Peter is some kind of a person!

But so are you! And that's a proposition Peter himself asserted.

In Peter's first letter (call it either "1 Peter" or "Rocky 1"!), the Holy Spirit moved him to inscribe something about every one of us which Jesus specifically said of Peter. Jesus called him "A Stone" (John 1:42) and thereby prophesied of the strength and stability He would eventually build into the man. Similarly, Peter writes of us who believe in and follow the same Lord Jesus: "You also, as living stones, are being built up as a spiritual house" (1 Peter 2:5). They are words of promise and prophecy—pointing the way to the possibilities which Christ can bring about in the life of any one of His disciples. And it's not only Peter who says this, but Jesus as well. He makes a point of declaring His confidence in what He can do in you and me when He describes a rock-like strength and rising dimension of glory He will "make" of us:

> He who overcomes, I will make a pillar in the temple of My God and he shall go out no more.
>
> (REV. 3:12)

There are four ingredients here: *faith, creative power, formulated strength,* and *settled stability.*

Faith

The first ingredient is foundational, basic trust in Jesus—faith in who He is and what He's done as mankind's only Savior. It's the definition of "overcoming":

> For whatever is born of God overcomes the world. And this is the victory that has overcome the world—our faith. Who is he who overcomes the world, but he who believes that Jesus is the Son of God.
>
> (1 JOHN 5:4-5)

The question is settled as to "who" may be a candidate for a role as a "pillar" like Jesus described. It doesn't require achievements of magnificence, only a full-hearted acknowledgment of the Master. Soul-saving faith with life-transforming potential is found in trusting Him. The seed of eternal life which brings new birth holds within it the holy DNA to grow us up into Christ's likeness and unto pillar possibilities.

Creative Power

The reason such potential is present in every redeemed son and daughter of God is because of the awesome, creative power of the Living Lord. Jesus says, "I will *make* him a pillar." He speaks with precisely opposite terms to human programs and philosophies of self-help or self-cultivation-unto-achievement. He says, "I will make it happen."

Of course the full process requires a ready heart and an obedient response on our part, but the power and the process—the dynamic and the strategy—are His, and He won't withhold either. He's committed to "making" us into everything the Father originally intended.

Especially moving is the verb's meaning and form, "I will *make*." The verb is broad enough in meaning to encompass *both* the shaping of something already present, as well as the bringing into existence whatever is lacking. In other words, Jesus is saying, "I'm going to take the raw material of your life and shape it, but if you fear something's lacking which will hinder My finishing—don't be afraid. I can *create* things in you which are now nonexistent!" And of equal encouragement is the future tense of the Greek verb, *poieo;* literally, "I will keep on making, creating, shaping, and bringing into being, until the project is done!" It's His way of saying, "I've got the will and the power if you've got the willingness and the availability."

Formulated Strength

It's a *pillar* He's talking about making; a strong support to others, an architecturally strategic column upon which structures lean and find strength. It's the picture of my being made into a father my kids can lean on, a husband my wife can trust, a friend my associates know won't fail them. Whatever your gender or your circle of influence, it means the same to you in whatever terms apply: faithful church worker, dependable employee, loving spouse, wise parent, good pastor, considerate boss, helpful neighbor, etc. Jesus is in the business of making *pillars*—and in terms of the historic setting in which He spoke these words, the pillars were *beautiful* too!

Most architectural textbooks show pictures of pillars— drawings with dignity and grace that capture the imagination and influence styles to this day: Doric, Ionic, Corinthian columns—

pillars of beauty, carved and splendidly shaped, as well as strongly supportive. And if the analogy seems to stagger you momentarily, as you think of what shambles your life may be in and doubt the possibilities of "beauty" coming out of such rubble, remember the promise:

> The Spirit of the Lord is upon me . . . to comfort all who mourn . . . to give them beauty for ashes . . . [and] everlasting joy shall be theirs.
>
> (ISA. 61:1, 3, 7)

Settled Stability

"I will make him a pillar . . . and he shall go out no more" is a statement about settledness; about the end of vacillation and undependability; about the removal of the flim-flam ways of unpredictable behavior or the foot-dragging ways of stubbornness or stupid pride. Christ is saying, "They won't go in and out of the boundaries of My will or the room of My appointed purpose any longer." Home to serve, and home to stay—as the Lord's, and as His only. And remember, this is all wrapped in the prophetic words of no less than the Savior who died to save us, and who is alive to fulfill this high promise—unto our rich possibilities.

It's this truth and warm promise that met a man called Simon long ago. The truth was incarnate and the promise was being fulfilled even as He spoke. Jesus was there, looking into a big fisherman's eyes, saying, "Your name is Simon, but you will be called Peter—a Rock."

And it happened.

And since it did—through a process you and I can watch happening as we trace Jesus' dealings with Peter across the pages of God's Word—we can be encouraged to believe. Because Jesus Christ is still in the pillar-forming business. It's a principle of His— *The Pillar Principle.* It states, "I can and I will take those who put abiding faith in Me, and make them reliable (and beautiful) people, who are dependable and who are strategic in the ongoing building of My church!"

Those aren't invented words—they're *revealed* ones; rising to speak to you and me as the Holy Spirit takes the texts we've reviewed and says, "This is for right here, right now. Let's go!" So I'd like to invite you to do that with me for the next several pages.

Let's *go—into* the Word to see a pillar being processed (Peter), *forward* in faith as we receive the truth applied to us, and *unto* God's purpose and glory as "becoming" pillars of His formation. The prospect will bring a song to your lips if you open to it!

Something beautiful, something good,
All my confusion He understood.
All I had to offer Him was brokenness and strife,
But He made something beautiful out of my life.
                                        Bill & Gloria Gaither

Chapter Two

The Processing of a Pillar

The imagination is captivated.

What went on in Simon's mind that night? What thoughts ricocheted through his head as he mentally recast that moment, remembering how Jesus had looked him full in the face—just having met him, mind you—and said, "Your name is Simon, but someday you'll be called Peter."

He may have lain awake long that night, his head couched on his pillow as he reviewed the day's events.

The Day of Encounter

That morning he'd just put into dock at the Capernaum wharf to unload last night's catch, when Andrew came running across the stone quay, calling to him. His brother's first words had irritated him. "Hey, bro, you've gotta come with me today! We've gotta leave now if we're gonna make it!"

Simon had hardly acknowledged the words—simply grunted something, and pointed to the jumbled nets and the writhing fish in the hold—clearly indicating there was work to do before anything else could even be thought of. And Andrew, just like the great kid brother he was, pitched in full tilt—not only as a compensation for the fact he'd not been with the crew the night before as he usually was, but anxious to clear the task and get on with the plan he'd proposed.

And it was Andrew who had headed off the near-fight with the sales agent at the wharf. Anger nearly swelled again as Simon thought, "That crook would sell his own kids for dirt if he had a chance!" The price offered for the catch was disgustingly low, but the agent had insisted the day-before word from Rome was impacting the market—every way. Simon had sworn a blue streak—cursing the system and the agent as both born of hell—and had doubled his fist to challenge a fight, when Andrew stepped in.

Andrew—younger, but no weakling—prevailed upon the moment, and while Simon's temper cooled, his brother had settled the deal; in fact, coming out better than Simon had thought they might. And then the "C'mon, let's go!" was issued again. There's no way he could refuse now—Andrew's help, his intervention preventing a brawl, his sharp negotiation: "OK, brother. I'm with you. Let's go see this Jesus guy you've been talking about."

As they hiked toward Bethabara—a distant trek, but briskly traversed—the hours on the road allowed time for review. Everyone was aware of John's ministry and the sweeping call this prophet was issuing to repentance. Simon had heard him a couple of times and couldn't escape either the truth or the hope the man represented. First, Simon knew John was right—and, in fact, had been baptized, confessing his sins. That's one reason the morning marketplace episode was still heavy on his mind. Fistfights and profanity had been commonplace—until John. And now, the fisherman flinched inside as he strode forward on the dusty road. "I've done it again. Except for Andrew I'd have busted that guy's nose!"

But John's words had spoken of more than sin. He'd also spoken hope—of a Savior—of Messiah, "Who will take away your sins and baptize you with the Holy Spirit and fire!" The chords of thousands of hearts were being strummed by the prophet's promise, because everything about his way and his words resonated with the sound of heaven. Having been raised in the synagogue, Simon knew full well the words of Malachi, "I will send My messenger, and he shall prepare the way before Me. . . . He will turn the hearts of the fathers to the children, and the hearts of the children to their fathers" (Mal. 3:1; 4:6). Yessir! This man sounded like the prophet forecasting the Real Thing: Messiah.

And then Andrew had come.

"We've found Him. The One John talked about. Messiah! Some of us have met and talked with Him, and I want you to come! C'mon! His name is Jesus. He's Galilean too, from over in Nazareth. C'mon!"

And then the meeting.

He'd hardly walked into the room of the small house where a half dozen men were engaged with Him in conversation, when their eyes met. He stopped—kept looking Simon straight in the eyes—and said: "You're called Simon now, but not in the future. You'll be called Peter."

Now, remembering the moment, reflecting on it all as he rolled over in bed, pulling the sheets over his chest: "Another name?" he thought. "Tall order!"

Every Hebrew knew that names were more than convenient tags. To name was to do more than describe, it was to prophesy; to suggest life, purpose, and direction—in the case of a child, to forecast basic temperament and attributes.

"He called me 'Rock'!"

And he would have chuckled beneath his breath there on the bed, except for the fact that when Jesus had spoken to him it was different than anyone he'd ever heard speak before. Now, instead of a chuckle, he trembled.

He was glad it was dark; glad that Abigail couldn't see his eyes moistening with tears. His wife had already fallen asleep and hardly anything interrupted the night sounds around Lake Galilee. The quiet was compounded by the fact it was Shabbat, and the Sabbath meant no fishermen were at work tonight as they otherwise would be.

His trembling stopped, but the tears kept returning. "It's a frightening thing to have a Person like that say something so wonderful about you," Simon thought. "Peter? A Rock!" And his mind raced again to the quayside explosion of temper and speech that morning . . . early . . . before he met Jesus. Not very solid behavior there.

"It's almost too much to believe," Simon thought. But he couldn't escape the words—the *name*. And that's why, just before Simon of Bethsaida, in Galilee, turned over to surrender to sleep that Shabbat night so many centuries ago, he likely said,

"It's tough to believe I could be that. But if *that* Man says so. Well, who knows?"

Chapter Three

The Power and Blessing

Every thoughtful Christian has been there, almost "cornered" by the dual reality which doubtless bewildered Simon-to-become-Peter. The contrast between what we see ourselves to be, and what God's Spirit prods toward and promises we will become, is like blinding sunlight striking the eyes as the shades of a darkened room are suddenly raised.

> [That] the eyes of your understanding may be enlightened; that you may know . . . the hope of His calling!
>
> (EPH. 1:18)

Hear it! Believe it! The power and blessing of God are intended for you!

Simon of Galilee would awaken the next morning, not much different from the night before. But a process had been set in motion—a promise from the One who embodies promise. And in Peter's case the rest is history. We're to take heart as we see this reasonable "case in point"; the story of Jesus of Nazareth processing Simon of Bethsaida into a pillar.

That's *power*—the power of God both birthing and bringing about; God at work in human clay, shaping, molding, and fashioning until the earthdust of your humanity becomes a treasure chest invested with divine wealth.

That's *blessing*—for the joy of experiencing both the agony and the ecstasy of the unfolding purpose of God in your life is overwhelming; rising with praise when the high moments come, standing firm at other times, even though tears mark the path forward unto fullest realization of God's completed plan.

There's a name for this process. It's called *discipleship*. It's the term which describes the process of *learning to live,* even though some mistakenly think "to be discipled" only means "to learn." But there is a vast difference between learning, and then finding that truth applied and operational in your life. It's the difference between information and incarnation. The first is truth in *facts;* the second is truth in *flesh*.

And the Word became flesh and dwelt among us, and we beheld His glory, the glory as of the only begotten of the Father, full of grace and truth.

(JOHN 1:14)

Hear it? It's the *power* and the *blessing:* The *power,* which by the work of the Holy Spirit brings God's Word into an incarnate form; the *blessing,* which is the end result of a fullness of God's good grace and releasing truth. That's what *happened* in the coming of Jesus. And that's what the coming of Jesus has enabled to *happen now,* in each disciple of His—*Christ in you!*

So permit me to warn you. Our glimpse at the processing of a pillar, in the person of Simon Peter, will only enable us to witness Simon's metamorphosis in order to find how the Holy Spirit will work our own. We are not on a track to gain *information,* but *incarnation.* I'm not inviting you to step into a program of rules and regulations, as though the disciplines themselves are what makes a disciple. Rather, my invitation is to a new dimension of availability to the Holy Spirit.

It's the Holy Spirit who can make truth become flesh.

As surely as the miracle of the incarnation of Jesus Himself did not take place solely on the basis of inscribed prophecies, so it is with us. The prophecies then and the promises now are true, but it is still only by the power of the *Spirit* of that prophetic Word of promise that the reality of its potential is brought into human form. With Jesus, it involved the miracle of a sinless baby being born that a sinful world might be redeemed. For us, it involves the miracle first of a sinful soul being saved, *then* of a human body becoming a dwelling place of the Most High. By this investiture, it becomes possible for human flesh, slowly but relentlessly by grace, to become a habitation of the glory of the Lord:

> The glory of the Lord shall be revealed, and all flesh shall see it together.
>
> (ISA. 40:5)

See it in that promise! The power and the blessing: the "glory of the Lord" (unmatched excellence and *power*) being "revealed" *to* and *within* human beings (immeasurable privilege and *blessing*)!

The Entry Point of Glory

The starting place for this "glory" to enter humankind was preached by Peter himself, on a day long ago when the power and blessing first overflowed from heaven. For the first time, it spilled forth at a dimension that would enable all mankind to become recipients, to whatever degree each one would allow. It happened at Pentecost, after a dying Savior's redemptive work for sinners had been confirmed by His rising from the dead. Jesus, who had now ascended to heaven to take His worthy place at the right hand of God, His Father, poured the Holy Spirit out with profusion. Those in that first band of believers miraculously experienced the overflow of heaven's glory into vessels of flesh. The impact of the moment ignited supernatural worship.

> And suddenly there came a sound from heaven, as of a rushing, mighty wind, and it filled the whole house. . . . And they were all filled with the Holy Spirit and began to speak with other tongues. . . . Then they [those hearing them] were all amazed . . . saying . . . "We hear them speaking in our own tongues the wonderful works of God."
>
> (SEE ACTS 2:2, 4, 7, 11)

These amazed onlookers asked, "What does this mean?" and Peter—the once-Simon-but-now-rocklike-leader—rose to answer them. The man who dismally failed, denying his Lord seven weeks before, is now standing with a boldness beyond himself. And the answer Peter gave to his inquirers is still the key to each generation's finding their own experience of God pouring "glory into flesh" — of His transforming their humanity unto the possibilities of heaven's power and blessing.

Peter declared the pathway:

> Repent and let every one of you be baptized, in the name of Christ . . . and you shall receive the gift of the Holy Spirit.
>
> (ACTS 2:38)

There it is — "the promise"; *the Holy Spirit* given in response to human availability to God's terms. The Holy Spirit "given" here is the same one who brought about the incarnation of Jesus, *through* Mary in a spiritual sense; hers was the prototypical pathway to "glory" being "revealed" to "flesh." Just as the Holy Spirit performed that biological miracle in Mary, He is able to work a spiritual one in you and me; to bring Jesus alive *in* and *through* us. He's ready to *birth* divine life within us when we repent and believe in Jesus Christ, and He is able to *grow* the life of Jesus within us — His character and His traits. Then, His desire is to *flow* Christ's power and ministry through us! It's the *spiritual* experience of *incarnation* — of "Christ in you!"

But it's the *growth* that takes the longest: the real objective of real discipleship — growth in grace, in love, in giving, and in ministry — all through the *power* of Jesus' life within us! This growth process is one of *life* being incarnated in us by the Holy Spirit, not by *laws* being implanted in us by a program of human accomplishment. And that leads to the question: "Have you received the overflowing fullness of the Holy Spirit?"

Peter and Paul were both concerned with this crucial question. They asked it of early believers in the Lord Jesus, because they knew this: *salvation has always been intended to incorporate more than forgiveness for sin and going to heaven.*

Salvation is God's grand design for recovering His original plan: *God tabernacling with man!* Whether it was God-with-man in the Garden, or God-visits-man in the tabernacle or temple, the intent with the Father has always been, "That I may dwell among them" (Ex. 25:8). So it is that in Immanuel (God with us), that Jesus our Lord came to dwell among us, that by the *power of His salvation,* the *blessing of His incarnation,* He may multiply His life, person, and grace in each of us. According to the Word of God, the plan is working!

> The mystery which has been hidden from ages and from generations, but now has been revealed to His saints [that is, to us]. . . . To them God willed to make known what are the riches of the glory of this mystery among the Gentiles: which is Christ in you, the hope of glory.
>
> (COL. 1:26-27)

This "hope of glory" is yours and mine too!

The idea of "glory" mentioned here is synonymous with *both* (1) the *power* of God's transforming work in our lives by the Spirit's working, and (2) the *blessing* of our coming to experience the joy of Jesus' life and purpose occurring *through* us in our living and serving. And this "glory" is not mystical in its operation nor restricted in its availability. "Glory" is specifically defined in God's Word: first, as to *how* it works and, second, as to *what* it works. "Glory" is realized through a process which has a biblical/scientific name: *metamorphosis*.

In science, *metamorphosis* is the term used to describe the biological process by which an insect moves through successive changes that eventuate with its maturity in the created order. It is most dramatically seen, and most commonly illustrated, in the transformation of a caterpillar into a butterfly. In the Bible, metamorphosis is precisely the ancient New Testament term: *metamorphoomai*. It occurs several times, but most meaningfully for us in 2 Corinthians 3. Speaking of how Christ's way of transforming us exceeds the Old Testament system of laws and regulations for self-improvement, Paul describes the New Testament grace of *life* and *glory* (i.e., of power and blessing):

> Now the Lord is the Spirit; and where the Spirit of the Lord is, there is liberty. But we all, with unveiled face, beholding as in a mirror the glory of the Lord, are being transformed [*metamorphoumetha*] into the same image from glory to glory, just as by the Spirit of the Lord.
>
> (2 COR. 3:17-18)

Notice three things in these verses: the *promise* of the Word, the *process* of obedience, and the *power* of the Holy Spirit.

The Promise of the Word

The "mirror" mentioned in this text refers to the revelation of God's Son, Jesus Christ, as He is shown in the Word of God. That revelation entails *all* of the Bible, for Jesus is in more than the Gospels. You'll find Him in the whole of the Scriptures. As Jesus said, "Search the Scriptures, for . . . they . . . testify of Me," "and beginning at Moses and all the Prophets, He expounded to them in all the Scriptures the things concerning Himself" (John 5:39; Luke 24:27). This may help us see the reason why some people think of discipleship as being an *educational* process, that is, informational instead of incarnational. Because discipleship *is* so closely linked with the use of the Bible, it can seem to be an academic program. However, the text above speaks of more than our coming to a mound of information. Rather, we're called to a mirror of revelation, and that "mirror" is God's Word.

It is in that Word that we'll see two persons: Jesus and ourselves. The comparison we're shown isn't intended to embarrass us unto hopelessness or call us to attempt to imitate Him by our own efforts. Rather, the dual picture mirrored in the Bible shows *both* the power and promise of His person (the ways He's come to dwell *in* us!) and the present state of our growth-in-process (so we keep honest with ourselves and Him). This leads us to the second issue our text presents.

The Process of Obedience

The mention of our remaining "unveiled" before the Word addresses the fundamental issue of our willingness to remain "opened" toward the Holy Spirit's dealings. Just as surely as we "open our hearts" to welcome in Jesus Christ as our Savior (see Rev. 3:20), so we are called to a lifelong *process* of obediently *keeping* open: an open ear to hear the Word, and an open heart to obey the Spirit. The direct appeal in Ephesians 4:30, "Do not grieve the Holy Spirit," refers to our human tendency to "close up shop" when God's deeper dealings by the Spirit seek to apply His Word to practical or demanding matters in our lives. This isn't necessarily to suggest that you or I would dare to say to the Holy Spirit, "Shut up!" But the end result of *my* "shutting up," through indifference or disobedience, is every bit as drastic. Obedience, availability, teachability, shapability, a will to repent when corrected by Him — this open "unveiled-ness" is essential to the disciple's growth process.

The Power of the Holy Spirit

Finally, though my looking into God's Word-mirror is basic and my "unveiled" response is essential, the *power* which brings the *metamorphosis* — the change "from glory to glory," i.e., from one stage of my development in Christ to the next — is solely the Holy Spirit's. This is the reason we so frequently hear the term "renewal" in association with the Holy Spirit's work today. Where He is welcomed without restraint, individuals, families, groups, churches, and communities are *renewed!*

Earlier we noted how deeply concerned both Peter (with John) and Paul were when they discovered young believers who had not yet "received" the Holy Spirit. In Acts 8 and 19, respectively, these two leaders came to groups of believers who had (1) repented of sin, (2) been born again, and (3) been baptized in water. Yet somehow, there had not come a "breakthrough" in their experience of the supernatural inworking of the Holy Spirit. Accordingly, in each passage, we see that action is taken.

In Acts 8, Peter and John begin special ministry to those in Samaria because "[the Holy Spirit] had fallen upon none of them" (Acts 8:16). They neither demean Philip's effective evangelistic efforts nor denigrate the reality of the experience of the newborn saints there. They simply teach, pray, and minister, with an awareness that *nothing* more of salvation is needed, but that *something* more of the Holy Spirit is.

In Acts 19, we read of a similar situation occurring years later in Ephesus. The scenario is only slightly altered by reason of different personalities and geography, but the Bible seems to record these two events as an instructional device to us, saying: Be sure you not only believe salvation's power *for* and *unto* you, but see that you enter into salvation's power *in* and *through* you. The power of the Holy Spirit also needs to be "received" (Acts 8:18; 19:2), just as decisively as we receive God's gift of forgiveness in Christ when we first come to Him.

The evidence in God's Word, making this point so clear, presents us with an inescapable call to the same hunger and pursuit shown by early believers. As honest readers of Scripture, as earnest disciples, let's open fully to all of the Holy Spirit's workings. The only difficulties we face are that various theologies, however sincerely framed, tend to impose certain demands on all of us — restrictions, fears, or formulas. They all have their own effect and tend to breed a suspicion and a separatism among Christians.

But this need not be so with any of us. How can we avoid such deterents?

Let's simply come to Jesus!

God's Word says that Jesus, and He alone, is the One who administrates the Holy Spirit's ministry toward us! So, let's freely ask:

He [Jesus] poured out this which you now see and hear.

(ACTS 2:33)

This is He [Jesus] who baptizes with the Holy Spirit.

(JOHN 1:33)

For over thirty years of ministry, I have watched believers in our dear Lord Jesus move into the dimension of the Holy Spirit's power on these terms alone: *Seek the Lord Jesus and pray!*

Lord Jesus Christ,
I want to follow You as a disciple who knows
both the power of Your cross, and
the power of Your Holy Spirit.
I believe Your death and shed blood have
accomplished FULL SALVATION for me. I
thank You for eternal life through Calvary!
But I also want to grow in the FULL DIMENSIONS
You have for my life—
To *live* in the way You lived and served;
To *love* with the grace and mercy You showed,
and
To *move* in the power of the Spirit as You did.
And that's why I ask YOU—
You, who have saved and forgiven me,
You, whom I have turned to for life,
You, who have given me of Your Spirit,
I ask YOU to fill me to overflowing with the
power of the Holy Spirit.
Just as You instructed us, I want to receive Him in fullness.
So now, Lord, I humbly ask that You fill me with the
Holy Spirit.

And with that prayer, I now resolve to enter into the Spirit of praise—to expect You to begin to manifest Your overflowing grace now—in Your way . . . and by Your Holy Spirit. I praise You, Lord Jesus!

And Then . . . Forward

The power and blessing of being filled with the Holy Spirit is not for the sake of mere enjoyment. It is *rejoicing*, to be sure! But at the core of a life of growing discipleship with Jesus Christ, the Holy Spirit *working* is what's most important.

- *It is the Spirit* who keeps the Word alive, and progressively being "incarnated" in me, rather than it becoming a mere informational program of laws, regulations, and rituals;

- *It is the Spirit* who infuses prayer and praise with passion and begets vital faith for the supernatural;

- *It is the Spirit* who teaches and instructs me so that the "mirror" of the Word shines Jesus *in* and crowds sin *out;*

- *It is the Spirit* who brings gifts and giftedness for power-ministry to my life, and directs what He wants distributed as "a gift" when He wants one ministered through me; and

- *It is the Spirit* who will bring lovingness, graciousness, and a spirit of unity to my heart; so that I not only love the lost and want to see people brought to Christ, but I love all other Christians, and refuse to become an instrument of injury to Christ's body—the church.

So on the front end of our studying the "processing" of Simon into a "pillar" called Peter, be clear that such discipleship is a *spiritual* process far more than it is a religious or intellectual one. Yes, it will involve *discipline*, and in the sense of "vital, virile, loving commitment," and some might even call that "religious." And, since the *mind* is animated—in understanding, repentance, and learning—this process could be called "intellectual"—the intelligence being employed. But my point is, we're not to be either stultified by religious forms or satisfied merely with intellectual knowledge. Beyond all ritual or a sum of information, our objective is *to move into relationship with Jesus;* to an ever-growing, ever-life-shaping dimension of availability to the Holy Spirit's work in our hearts.

To use Jesus' own words, this is a lifetime call to a childlike pathway:

> Assuredly, I say to you, unless you are converted and become as little children, you will by no means enter the kingdom of heaven. Therefore whoever humbles himself as this little child is the greatest in the kingdom of heaven.
>
> (MATT. 18:3-4)

"The kingdom of heaven," as Jesus speaks of it here, is not a home in the sky when we die, but a place of living power under the rule of God on a day-to-day basis. Thus, we hear His call to a lifelong, childlike dependence on the Spirit and a continuing teachability and obedience to His "processing" in our lives.

It's foundational to The Pillar Principle.

Chapter Four

Seven Days in a Lifetime

The strength of a pillar is related to the compression of the elements constituting its rocky substance; a result, by most common measurements, of millennia of sifting, settling, and packing. The granite or marble carved into a column is made of the stuff only *time* can produce.

The same is true of the substance of a human soul. Holy strength in the soul is not the result of either instant actions or insistent determination. It's an amalgamate, as with stones. An "amalgamate" is the mixing of substances, blended together, until they become a unified whole. You've witnessed the beauty of polished rocks, with swirls of various colors gleaming in the light, revealing the stunning splendor of what can occur when a mixture comes under pressure, and it all comes together.

It's part of The Pillar Principle too.

To study what we find of Simon Peter in the Scriptures is to discover a striking variety of situations, none of which, alone, explains the man, but all of which together became compacted under the touch of God. And made a rock.

Scattered through the years following Peter's introduction to Jesus, seven days stand out as pivotal events. All were probably days which, at each one's beginning, seemed to be "just another." But by their end, each day had become another instance of a man's response to a "determinative moment"; an incident determining more of his future than he realized at the time. Together, such instances form "the days of a lifetime," for while thousands of other days come and go, it's the way we respond to life's pivotal moments that determine the content of life. Responses at such seasons or moments determine the future depth of a person's character, his stability in life, or the substance of his soul.

Look with me at seven days in Peter's lifetime.

In doing so, I'm not proposing we discount the continuing context of his *daily* walk with Jesus during this period. Nor do I think we should overlook the fact he came from a Hebrew *background* and not a pagan upbringing. Whatever Peter's weaknesses, it's worth noting that he probably had a headstart over most new believers who come to Christ at this end of the twentieth century. As a Jewish child, a boy, and a young man, he'd been exposed to synagogue life and the Scriptures since birth. It's worth our noting this advantage, such as it was, not as an excuse for any slowness of our growth which may be attributable to our own unresponsiveness. But it can encourage our patience if it takes us more than the three to three and a half years it took Simon to become "rocklike" as a disciple.

To look at the pivotal days, then, is to investigate "kinds of things" which happen to growing disciples; to see Simon's "moments of response," however inept he may have been at times. Stepping into these moments with him — to see ourselves in the picture of a person undergoing the discipling process with Jesus — can instruct us toward responses that may not expedite our growth so much as it will avoid delaying it. So we're not looking for "shortcuts" through study, but wanting to find some of the component principles which amalgamate to form The Pillar Principle.

We've already visited the "First Day" — Simon's day of encounter with the Messiah, and his meeting with the Man who said, "You're going to become something more than you ever dreamed — a Rock." Besides that day, let me list six other pivotal events in Simon's experience of Jesus Christ's "processing a pillar."

Day 1 — The Day of Encounter, John 1:40-42.
Day 2 — The Day of Commitment, Luke 5:1-11.
Day 3 — The Day of Submission, Luke 6:12-14.
Day 4 — The Day of Affirmation, Matthew 16:18-23.
Day 5 — Two Days of Repentance, Luke 22:31, 54-61.
Day 6 — The Day of Stretching, John 21:15-22.
Day 7 — The Day of Beginning, Acts 2:14-39.

Let's walk into these days with a man who came to be known as Peter, the rocklike apostle. But before we do, let me offer one word of explanation.

I want to anticipate a question that any Bible student might ask sooner or later on this subject, because already in our study we've made clear that the Holy Spirit is the fountainhead resource of the possibilities awaiting us. Understandably, then, someone may ask, "Since the Holy Spirit wasn't poured out upon believers until the 'Seventh Day' we're studying in Simon's life, how does he exemplify what can happen in *me*, as a disciple in whom the Holy Spirit is processing growth?"

The answer to this question is that the Holy Spirit was present in abounding fullness in Jesus Himself. Peter's—that is, *Simon's*—readiness to follow Jesus, allowed our Lord, by the Holy Spirit, to begin a shaping work which only God Himself could do.

Remember, please—there is no higher or lower status in the Godhead; therefore, Jesus was able to work with Simon, as well as the other disciples, in a unique way—fashioning depth, development, character, and a capacity for power-ministry in the Spirit—even before Pentecost. Why?

Because the Holy Spirit—indeed, *GOD*—was incarnate in complete and sufficient power in His Son Jesus Christ, to enable everything essential to the fulfillment of His mission. Listen: Jesus says, "The Spirit of the Lord is upon Me, because He has anointed Me to preach . . . the . . . year . . . of the Lord" (Luke 4:18-19).

And of Jesus we read, "For He whom God has sent speaks the words of God, for God does not give the Spirit by measure. The Father loves the Son, and has given all things into His hand" (John 3:34-35).

Such statements in the Word of God indicate that through the ministry of Jesus, *the Father* was being revealed and *the Holy Spirit* was fully at work. Even His climaxing work on the cross, capstoned by the glory of His resurrection, was achieved in the power of the Holy Spirit:

- "Christ, who through the eternal Spirit offered Himself without spot to God" (Heb. 9:14); and Jesus was

- "declared to be the Son of God with power, according to the Spirit of holiness, by the resurrection from the dead" (Rom. 1:4).

From the instant the Holy Spirit came upon Him at His baptism in Jordan (Matt. 3:16-17), Jesus not only ministered *in* the power of the Holy Spirit—preaching, healing, casting out demons—but He was also shaping a band of disciples *by* the same power.

There is only one difference in our case today.

It doesn't have anything to do with our experiencing less power or expecting less of God's grace and might than Jesus' first disciples.

It doesn't have anything to do with our being less "chosen" than any of His earliest disciples or appointed apostles.

It only has to do with one thing.

There will be a creative difference in what He does in you, in me, just as surely as the distinctive things we see in Simon or in any other of His disciples. God's detailed purpose and working with each of us will *always* carry His own unique creative stamp. Nothing works out precisely the same for any of us in the details, but everything progresses and processes according to the same principles.

So with these points of understanding and wisdom in view, let me repeat Andrew's invitation: "C'mon. You've gotta meet this Man."

Chapter Five

The Day of Commitment

I t had been weeks since the first day. The encounter which Simon had with Jesus, the day Andrew had goaded him to go, and the day which peaked in a moment of announcement, "You'll be called Peter!" was past now. But not forgotten.

During the weeks since, Simon had on more than one occasion hiked to neighboring villages where Jesus was ministering. His itinerary through Galilee was attracting increasingly larger crowds as the common people came to hear "the gospel of the kingdom"—that God was *here*, mightily in their midst, *right now!*

And the miracles proved it. So the crowds increased, and that's what set up this day.

Simon was there, close by among those who early began thronging the site, when Jesus turned to speak with someone—suggesting a possible plan for allowing Him to more clearly address the crowd. Then, they both turned toward Simon, and came over to him to make their request.

"I'd like to use your boat for a platform, Simon," Jesus said. "If you could push out, just a small way from the shore and anchor, I could sit in the stern facing the shore and preach from there. It would certainly help the people hear better. And as you can see, they're about to crowd Me into the water already." He smiled.

Simon was quick. "Absolutely, I'd be honored," he consented. But it isn't hard to imagine the thoughts that likely accompanied his willing response.

"Why'd He pick my boat? . . . There's another one here. I *am* honored, but why. . . ?" And as the fisherman's thoughts returned to that first meeting, a mild uneasiness began inside as he and

Andrew pushed their boat away from shore, after Jesus had waded to the side and had climbed in.

What follows became a day not only which Simon would always remember, but which in some way is essential to every disciple's experience: The Day of Commitment. It's the day when the Savior you've already encountered calls you to not only *hear* of His promised purpose for you, but to *act* on it. Luke's record tells us how it happened.

> Now so it was, as the multitude pressed about Him to hear the word of God, that He stood by the Lake of Gennesaret, and saw two boats standing by the lake; but the fishermen had gone from them and were washing their nets. Then He got into one of the boats, which was Simon's, and asked him to put out a little from the land. And He sat down and taught the multitudes from the boat.
>
> Now when He had stopped speaking, He said to Simon, "Launch out into the deep and let down your nets for a catch."
>
> But Simon answered and said to Him, "Master, we have toiled all night and caught nothing; nevertheless at Your word I will let down the net."
>
> And when they had done this, they caught a great number of fish, and their net was breaking. So they signaled to their partners in the other boat to come and help them. And they came and filled both the boats, so that they began to sink.
>
> When Simon Peter saw it, he fell down at Jesus' knees, saying, "Depart from me, for I am a sinful man, O Lord!"
>
> For he and all who were with him were astonished at the catch of fish which they had taken; and so also were James and John, the sons of Zebedee, who were partners with Simon.
>
> And Jesus said to Simon, "Do not be afraid. From now on you will catch men."
>
> So when they had brought their boats to land, they forsook all and followed Him.
>
> (LUKE 5:1-11)

This day takes its theme from the words which conclude the Gospel narrative: "They forsook all and followed Him." But what is so singular about the occasion is not the commitment alone. I think it's also in the climate in which the decision takes place. There are three noteworthy components to it all: the *choice,* the *surprise,* and the *exclamation.*

The Choice

Make no mistake about it—Jesus knew whose boat He had chosen to use: He was choosing to confront Simon. And there's something about this fact that points to a pattern God employs in dealing with us. He knows the *time* to make His move with us. As *He* sees it, it's always the best time.

We don't know all that transpired between the first day and this one, but both Jesus and Peter did. The evidence suggests that Jesus had been watching Simon for weeks—probably noticing him as he stood as one of the crowd during Galilee preaching occasions. Had He seen tears, brusquely wiped away as Simon fought against appearing less than manly? Had He noticed people's response to the big fisherman, even when he was simply part of the crowd? We can't answer those questions, but we can answer this one: "Did Jesus know what was going on inside Peter?" The answer:

> But Jesus . . . had no need that anyone should testify of man, for He knew what was in man.
>
> (JOHN 2:24-25)

Just like Jesus knew Nathanael's thoughts "while you were under the fig tree" (John 1:48), and knew the number of the Samaritan woman's lovers (John 4:16-18), He knew what was transpiring deep inside Peter. That's why He made a choice of *this* moment to indicate His choice of the man.

It's His way of dealing with you and me too.

Jesus Christ is very direct with disciples. He is never premature in issuing a call to something we're incapable of responding to, but His timing in calling us seems *always* to be too soon to our mind. We *always* think we need more—more time, more money, more preparation, more qualifications, *more.* . . . But the Savior is also a saver of time when it involves His purposes. He won't waste it either in calling us out and into His purpose *before* it's best, or in allowing us to linger *beyond* His timing.

Waiting for *our* time is always prompted by our human need for something we feel is necessary to *secure* us. Whereas, stepping forward at His call, and in His time, inevitably forces us to make Him our sole point of support and security. The disciple en route to becoming a pillar will early learn this song:

When He calls me, I will answer . . .
I'll be somewhere listening for my Lord.

Or,

I'll go where You want me to go, dear Lord,
Over mountain or plain or sea.
I'll say what You want me to say, dear Lord,
I'll be what You want me to be.

Settle it in your heart, dear one. You're *chosen:* "just as He [Father God] chose us in Him [Christ] before the foundation of the world" (Eph. 1:4). And seeing that is settled, it's wisest to answer to His call on His schedule. Always.

The Surprise

It's significant that Jesus chooses to make this confrontation in Simon's boat—right there in the place where Simon worked every day. The Lord has the most remarkable ways of calling us to commitment when we're right in the middle of the place where our life's daily grind occurs. Some of my most dramatic moments of God's dealing with me have taken place in the middle of my muddle, rather than at a holy moment of high spiritual exhilaration or retreat.

Further, there is a profound statement in both the words and the action Jesus expresses. "Deeper waters!" He commands—an expression which can translate any number of ways into our lives today, perhaps as a call to new dimensions of depth, or possibly calling us to walk a pathway of trial unto eventual triumph. In Simon's case it simply meant to steer his boat toward fishing waters. But there was one problem:

Daytime isn't fishing time in Galilee.

Simon knew Jesus was savvy enough to the area industry to know better, and he raised a mild protest. However (and wisely), he concluded, "Nevertheless, Lord—at Your command." It's a good principle to remember: Jesus knows more about my business than I do. *Besides, He's the LORD!* Do *what* He says, *when* He says. It works.

And suddenly the nets were breaking with fish!

The Exclamation

There's a touching pathos to Simon's personal response. After signaling for help from a second boat to help handle the catch which was now so large it was threatening to sink his ship, Simon falls on his knees before Jesus, who is seated. Listen to his words: *"Depart from me, for I am a sinful man, O Lord!"*

On the face of it, these words might sound to some like the confession of a sinner seeking salvation, or possibly the hopeless cry of a derelict telling God to get out of his face. But we need to gain a more penetrating insight into Simon's cry if we're to catch the significance of his "moment" on this important Day of Commitment.

The man later to be called Peter,

—Isn't really asking Jesus to leave (not really);

—Isn't confessing sin to find forgiveness (though we all need it); and he

—Isn't angry about what's happening, nor is he frustrated with what's going on in his about-to-sink working place.

No. He is *none* of these things. There's another reason for his saying, "Depart from me."

He's afraid.

Simon of Bethsaida, the brash, cursing, dock-fighter who bowed to no man, is now kneeling before *the* Man—trembling and pleading. And what his words are really saying is,

Jesus, You're getting too up-close-and-personal for me; and I know it's because You think there's something that can become of me—something rocklike, as You said. And I want to say, right here and right now, You've got the wrong guy! You may be able to miraculously load my boat with fish, but I'm too much of a sin-traditioned man to ever become what You think—what You'd want. Jesus, You'd better leave now while You're ahead. I'm a bad risk for the kind of things You want to do in a man.

Hear it, loved one. That's what Simon's saying, and it strikes home, doesn't it? Have you ever found yourself shrinking from God's call—His prompting to believe, to step forward in faith, to answer to a moment of commitment—and you felt, "I'd like to, but You've got the wrong person, Lord. I don't have that kind of stuff in me!"

And that's just the point.

Jesus Christ *never* calls us on the basis of what "stuff" we have in ourselves. It's always on the basis of what He can work in us by *His* power—by *His* Holy Spirit. He has "the right stuff" and He knows how to install it in each of us who will let Him have His way.

The Pillar Principle never fails. It contrasts with secular society's "Peter Principle," which emphasizes how easily people are placed in positions which exceed their potential. Jesus never calls you or me to something beyond what He will faithfully work in us. So *real* commitment is never a decision we make with fear's white knuckles or self-determination's grinding teeth, as though to say, "I'll try, God, but I don't know if I can make it!" Rather, a holy and healthy commitment is made with our empty hands uplifted, saying, "You know best, Lord. I surrender to the possibilities to which You're calling me to open. It's up to You!"

And there's no end to what the Savior-Creator can remake with a surrendered soul wise enough to say, "Yes, Lord."

From Day Two, Simon followed Jesus not only as a believer, but as a committed follower learning the way to see his life's purpose realized.

Chapter Six

Days of Submission and Affirmation

Two things every disciple needs are to *do* right and to *feel* right. And in that order! The first begets the second, not vice versa. It's worth seeing how this essential priority, and its extremely fulfilling reward, can become "processed" in us.

It happened to Peter on a pair of days: one when Jesus said, "I'm picking you for special service," and the other when He said, "You are — *already!* — exactly what I said you'd become!" Let's read the report of the first of these two days — Day Three.

The Day of Submission

> Now it came to pass in those days that He went out to the mountain to pray, and continued all night in prayer to God. And when it was day, He called His disciples to Him, and from them He chose twelve . . . Simon, whom He also named Peter, and Andrew his brother . . . that they might be with Him.
>
> (LUKE 6:12-16; MARK 3:14)

Perhaps few words have suffered at the hands of human misapplication more than "submission." The word is doubly abused, having been rendered the equivalent of "patsy" or "wimp" if a person chooses to be "submitted." And submission has also mistakenly been made synonymous with "subjugation." But "to submit" is neither to become somebody's doormat, nor is submission the enforced requirement of a conqueror or tyrant.

The Word of God has a great deal to say about a disciple's

learning "submission," but it never suggests that to do so is to resign human dignity, intelligence, or good sense. To the contrary, God is the author of *true* human dignity (which is the opposite of *pride*, fallen man's substitute), and the God-given human capacities of intelligence and good sense are never denigrated by Him (though faith will often overreach both, while denying the practical value of neither).

Submission has to do with our sensible acceptance of our appropriate place in God's order of things. It has everything to do with clear-headed thinking and nothing to do with empty-hearted self-centeredness.

To apply the text, Jesus was calling the Twelve — including Simon — to "submit" to the next step of His purpose by subordinating their own private programs to His. He was calling them to "be with Him" and to take a demanding place of future responsibility as servants under His authority.

To some, being named "one of the Twelve" would be anything but a humbling experience. Indeed, to them, at first, it hardly seemed anything less than highly distinguishing. And there would come days ahead when Jesus would be forced to aim brutally direct correction at the Twelve because of this, crowding them away from human presuppositions about position. It wouldn't be easy for them, but later they would come to learn, "He who would be the greatest among you must be the servant of all." Yet, on the day of their appointment as "one of the Twelve," we can be certain that none of them foresaw the day that each of them (minus Judas) would suffer as martyrs, serving as apostles of the gospel of Jesus Christ.

Being "designated special" isn't always as special as it seems in the eyes of outside observers. That's why "submission" to the purposes of Christ, as He beckons us another step higher in intensifying His program of shaping us for His purpose, is important for us to understand. It means: (1) to *align* with His purposes, (2) to *accept* His disciplines, and (3) to *advance* in becoming His servant.

One of the most difficult things about accepting Christ's call to "come out from among them and be separate" (2 Cor. 6:17) is that once answered we can never be the same again. Even Judas couldn't "go back," he could only "back out." The difference? To "go back" is to be the same way you were before Christ's call; while to "back out" is to remove yourself from what you might have become.

The day Simon accepted his designation as one of Jesus' closest disciples, he might have preened or gloated: "Hey—we're movin' on up!" But he probably didn't, because to have been around Jesus for even the relatively few months that would have preceded this would already have taught him that the Savior's system was vastly removed from the world's.

What he *did* have to acknowledge was one of the most difficult things for each of us once the Living God has named us His own son or daughter through the blood of Jesus Christ. That is to learn to acknowledge *the inevitability of our own extra-ordinariness.* That's not pride, asserting superiority. That's honesty, acknowledging our distinct call to destiny. It's Jesus' way, to use Charles Allen's words, to produce "extraordinary living for ordinary people."

This "Day of Submission" basically means for each of us that we have come to the place of accepting (1) God's will *in* our lives, (2) Christ's mission *for* our lives, and (3) the Holy Spirit's directives *over* our lives. We don't need to be called as "one of the Twelve" apostles to face this summons. We only need to open our Bibles:

> Or do you not know that your body is the temple of the Holy Spirit who is in you, whom you have from God, and you are not your own? For you were bought at a price; therefore glorify God in your body and in your spirit, which are God's.
>
> (1 COR. 6:19-20)

This, of course, is generally understood by most thoughtful Christians: "I am not my own!" But what is not always joined to that truth is the recognition that Jesus is not simply in the business of "getting us to submit." *Christ's highest purposes are not fulfilled in gaining mastery over our lives, but in releasing His glory through them.*

(Read that again, please.)

And, then, let us remember: The reward of submission is *always* in view with Jesus, while its price so often seems to preoccupy and challenge us.

In any case, Jesus designated Simon that day as destined for distinct responsibility, and when he responded, the way was opened for an ordinary man to enter into God's extraordinary possibilities for his life. It's the same call today. With the same potential. And you and I are called to hear, understand, and respond accordingly.

The Day of Affirmation

Once we enter the school of discipleship it's not uncommon to wonder, "How'm I doin', Lord?"

It's not the kind of thing one sidles up to the throne of heaven and asks.

It's more of a private thought. One that tempts us to compare ourselves with others (when we're commanded not to) and taunts us to think we're less than loved by Him because of our stumblings (which we never are).

> We dare not class ourselves or compare ourselves with those who commend themselves. But they, measuring themselves by themselves, and comparing themselves among themselves, are not wise.
>
> (2 COR. 10:12)

> What then shall we say to these things [with which we struggle]? If God is for us, who can be against us? He who did not spare His own Son, but delivered Him up for us all, how shall He not with Him also freely give us all things?
>
> (ROM. 8:31-32)

For Simon, the answer to what has to have been a recurring question, came on a day Jesus Himself asked one: "Who are people saying I am?" It's not difficult to suppose Peter had sometimes wondered, "What does Jesus think about me, now that He's seeing the 'real me' every day and then remembering He said I'd be a 'rock' someday?" But even though Simon didn't ask that, both Jesus' question and his were answered on that Day of Affirmation.

The first affirmation came from Simon.

After the disciples had given a variety of answers as to what society's opinions about Him were, He asked, "Who do *you* say I am?"

Among the most memorable words in the Bible are Simon's, who spoke first, and who probably expressed the joint feelings of most of the Twelve: *"You are the Christ, the Son of the Living God"* (Matt. 16:16). The words are rich with meaning, giving clear definition to what Simon had come to believe about Jesus. This is more than a catch-phrase. It's a complete and monumental declaration of faith. Add it up:

- *"You are the Christ"* — that is to say: *"Jesus,* You're the Messiah, the anticipated King of glory, the promised One from heaven in whom all our hopes and aspirations are found."

- *"The Son"* — that is to say: *"Jesus,* You are God-become-flesh, the Word from eternity incarnate in time; the offspring of David's kingly line without the taint of Adam's failed line."

- *"Of the Living God"* — that is to say: *"Jesus,* You are God! You are more than a superhuman, more than an exceedingly wonderful teacher, more than the sum of humanity's highest potential. You are the Ultimate Deity, the Creator of all things come to be the Redeemer of all mankind."

We know from the passage that follows that Simon didn't yet understand the pathway by which redemption would be purchased for man, but his confession of faith indicates he was on track with the full idea of who Jesus is. That's why Jesus responds with equally glorious words, including a full disclosure of His intentions to create a people (His church) who will overthrow the dark kingdom (the gates of hell).

Jesus answered and said to him, "Blessed are you, Simon Bar-Jonah, for flesh and blood has not revealed this to you, but My Father who is in heaven. And I also say to you that you are Peter, and on this rock I will build My church, and the gates of hades shall not prevail against it. And I will give you the keys of the kingdom of heaven, and whatever you bind on earth will be bound in heaven, and whatever you loose on earth will be loosed in heaven."

Then He commanded His disciples that they should tell no one that He was Jesus the Christ.

(MATT. 16:17-20)

Among the splendors of this passage, don't miss the affirmation Simon received: "I say to you, you are Peter." Read it again, but this time, "You ARE Peter!"

Can you imagine Simon's elation? Can you place yourself in his shoes that day (realizing his human fumblings and blunders are not only oft-apparent, but so very much like our own) and can you *not* sense Peter's inwardly shouting for joy? "Jesus said it's happened! I *have* become 'rock'!"

It couldn't have escaped Simon's notice. And the way Jesus said it—first stating Simon's given name in stark contrast—makes clear that He meant it to be a signal to Simon: *"It's happening, Simon! It's happening!"*

Seeing the reason for Jesus' words in this very encouraging facet of this event, look with me at exactly *what* occasioned Jesus' affirmation. Because it wasn't *achievement* on Simon's part, nor was it an acquired *infallibility*. Simon's vulnerability to stumbling and disappointing behavior—even as *Peter*—will be well-attested to over the days and years to come. But still, Jesus says, you ARE Peter! And His words teach us something central about what makes a rock a *rock*—what certifies the stuff a pillar is made of has become solid enough to assert that it *is* a pillar. What is it?

It's *living faith* begotten through *supernatural revelation!*

● *Living faith* is more than a creed. It's a life-controlling conviction. It is the settled stance of the total being on the solid ground of changeless truth undergirded by everlasting love.

● *Supernatural revelation* is more than a theological insight. It's being caught in the grip of the Holy Spirit, and seeing the tangible reality in invisible things and believing the here-and-now substance of eternal things.

Only God can work it in a person.

This kind of confession comes from something Almighty God does in the heart—indeed, penetrates through the whole being—of a person who has not only begun to believe and then follow Jesus Christ, but who has concluded rightly *who* He really is—and is given over to that!

If there is such a thing as "eternal security" (that theological football of debate over the "perseverance" of the saint—whether a person "once saved" can ever be lost again), this is the point at which it might be settled. Not that I would preclude the possibility of a believer's somehow recanting his faith and returning, as Peter would later say, as "a dog returns to his own vomit, and a sow, having washed, to her wallowing in the mire" (2 Peter 2:22). But, dear one, *there is a place*—a solid rock of settled faith and relationship with Christ in God—where *something so real and so inescapably changeless and durable occurs in the soul,* that the question is forever settled: "No going back! Never!" And not only does the substance of that kind of faith qualify as rocklike, but that's what will make people like you and me "pillars" upon which others may lean and find strength.

The "rock-likeness" has started to actually happen!

Chapter Seven

The Repentant Pillar

Years ago, a respected leader was asked what was the secret of his apparent spiritual growth beyond most of his peers. He looked puzzled, and without acknowledging the question as though he agreed with the proposition inherent in the inquiry, he simply smiled and with a twinkle in his eye said, "I guess I just repent more than others!"

There's an important insight in those words. It's in the fact that repentance has never been set forth in the Scriptures as merely an initiation rite. In other words, our personal need for "repenting" is not only at the time of our turning from our sin to the Savior. As important as that act is—reversing our mind-set from self to Christ and from sin to God—it is not the climax of our repentance. It is simply the commencement of a lifetime of the same "mind-changing" work of the Spirit in our thinking and practice.

Tracing the forward growth and shaping process of Simon Peter, as a means of seeing how Jesus shapes disciples and processes them into pillars, brings us to this practical truth: *lifelong repentance*. To begin, we need a clear and biblical definition of the meaning of repentance before we attempt an *ongoing, practical application* to our daily lives and thought. Along with a look in the lexicon to lay hold of the concept in this word, we'll also gain dramatic insights as we look at another "Day"—in fact, in this case, *two* days—in the life of Simon Peter.

Defining Repentance

First, to define repentance we need to separate it from ideas we may have of either *emotion* in repentance, or from presuppositions we might have that relate *condemnation* to repentance.

That emotions may well become involved when a genuine sense of repentance is realized is not uncommon. But the word "to repent" separates our *mind-set* from our *feelings. Metanoia,* the New Testament word for "repent" is derived from *nous* (the mind) and involves a reversal of the mind's perceptions and attitudes, bringing about a reversal of actions and behavior.

- To repent is to turn "with a different mind-set."

- To repent is to apologize for or acknowledge mistakenness, error, failure, or transgression, *as soon as it is seen for what it is.* (The prefix *meta* means "after" as well as "with," and *metanoia* not only focuses the *mind's* decisiveness — "with another mind-set" — but the immediacy of the decision — "*after* I realize my shortcoming.")

As to emotions, repentance may very well be accompanied by a godly grief, a sorrow for sinning (2 Cor. 7:9-10). But the essence of repenting is "to change one's mind," and to reverse one's thoughts and deeds until they align with righteousness. So, as Christ's disciple, I need to remember my lifelong call is to submit to repentance — to correction and change — *not* by reason of my feelings but by reason of the truth — no matter *how* my flesh craves to serve its own feelings.

Further, repentance must also be distinguished from condemnation. Jesus' disciples *are* to adopt repentance as a way of life, but we certainly *aren't* to adopt a life of guilt! By submitting to an ongoing availability to have my mind corrected and my pathway adjusted as I advance in Christ, I'm not required to nurture guilt feelings, as though "feeling condemned all the time" is what life-long repentance calls for. Where any condemnation or guilt hovers over or lingers in my soul, it is due either (1) to ignorance of how completely uncondemned I am, having been justified through the blood of Christ (Rom. 5:1; 8:1); or (2) to unconfessed sin that I need to deal with in prayer — then, to receive the promise of full forgiveness (1 John 1:7-9).

Settle it.

The place of repentance in our ongoing program of discipleship with Jesus doesn't intend for us a lifetime of "walking on eggs"; of feeling as though God sees us as an intruding cockroach

creeping into His presence and which He's about to squash!
Never!

Instead, let's see how Simon Peter illustrates Jesus' discipling program which includes that order of availability to "repent" which requires my constant correctability, my continued teachability, and my lifelong shapability:

- Correctable, because I heed the Spirit's admonishing;

- Teachable, because I choose never to presume I know anything so well that there isn't something new I might understand or perceive more clearly; and

- Shapable, because I refuse to suppose I have "arrived" — or for that matter, that I ever will!

It's always wise to remember that, however much we learn, advance, or progress, our finite and fleshly being is well-served by a mind-set which keeps us available to renewal. A spirit of lifelong repentance will contribute to that.

Two Days of Repentance

Jesus had now called Simon "a rock": "You are Peter," He'd said that day. It's significant to be reminded of that, because the fact of Simon's beginning to manifest "rocklike" traits didn't remove either (a) his capacity for miscalculation or failure, or (b) his need for that style of repentance — i.e., mind-reset/renewal — which continues the advancing of the "pillar process."

In this respect, there are two notable examples of Peter's schooling which reveal basic categories of yours and my ongoing need for "repentance" as we've described it here. The first relates to our propensity for presumption, and the second involves our capacity for drastic failure.

There is no conclusive time indicator to confirm exactly how long after Jesus said, "You are Peter," that He looked him in the eyes and said, "Get behind me, Satan!" In Matthew and Mark it appears it may have been a few hours at least, if not days later, while Luke's report seems to show the confrontation as almost immediately following that glorious moment of affirmation. In either case, the astounding fact is there: Simon, who has just been affirmed for his coming into at least the beginnings of strength and stability, is now confronted as being a virtual personification of the prince of darkness.

It's bone-jarring!

This event ought to forever eclipse any notions of self-sufficiency to which the most mature of us might be tempted. The subtlety of the serpent is clearly warned against in the Scriptures, and his tireless, individual pursuit of each of us is never to be overlooked:

> Be sober, be vigilant; because your adversary the devil walks about like a roaring lion, seeking whom he may devour. Resist him, steadfast in the faith, knowing that the same sufferings are experienced by your brotherhood in the world.
>
> (1 PETER 5:8-9)

Notice that Peter wrote that! And it seems more than likely that as he did, it probably brought to mind his own sin of presumption on that day we're looking at. Read what happened:

> From that time Jesus began to show to His disciples that He must go to Jerusalem, and suffer many things from the elders and chief priests and scribes, and be killed, and be raised again the third day. Then Peter took Him aside and began to rebuke Him, saying, "Far be it from You, Lord; this shall not happen to You!"
>
> But He turned and said to Peter, "Get behind Me, Satan! You are an offense to Me, for you are not mindful of the things of God, but the things of men." Then Jesus said to His disciples, "If anyone desires to come after Me, let him deny himself, and take up his cross, and follow Me."
>
> (MATT. 16:21-24)

The time frame for this scene is almost exactly six months prior to Jesus' crucifixion. Not one of these disciples can begin to imagine what's ahead. Even though Jesus now starts to regularly reference His forthcoming suffering, death, and resurrection, the whole idea goes straight over their heads. Like their whole society, they have become so enchanted with popularized notions of what Messiah will do and how He will do it, that they are oblivious to the clearest statements about what redemption will really cost.

It's that presumption which trapped Peter: the idea that his theological information, based on current viewpoints among his people, was right. It blindsided him so thoroughly that—think of it—he ended up "speaking for the devil," if you please.

"You're wrong, Jesus! Such a thing will never happen!"

Peter's presumptuous notions do not allow for a cross, so he takes it upon himself to advise the Son of God that *He's* the one who's confused! Don't miss the fundamental issue here. It's the *cross* which is being denied. Not a refused call to love, serve, give, or "be busy for God," but refusal to give place to *the cross!* That, dear one, opens broader issues than simply the awesome horror of suggesting an optional way for mankind's salvation. It goes beyond that, and strikes through the heart of God's way for *all* our life as Jesus' followers.

The cross is not only the *place* where salvation was accomplished for us, but it's a *path* as well. It's a walk with Christ that involves our dealing with our recurrent carnal tendencies. Hear it again: "If anyone desires to come after Me, let him deny himself, and take up his cross, and follow Me."

The irony of so many believers' lives is seen in their capacity to *rejoice* in the cross as an instrument of redemption and to *refuse* the cross as a call to identification. By "identification" I mean to use Paul's words:

> Knowing this, that our old man [i.e., yours and my carnal nature] was crucified with Him. . . . [therefore] Reckon yourselves to be dead indeed to sin, but alive to God in Christ Jesus our Lord.
>
> (ROM. 6:6, 11)

This passage is a direct application of exactly what Jesus was saying in the words, "Take up your cross and follow." We need to understand what this does and doesn't mean.

He didn't mean us to struggle through annual reenactments of the Via Dolorosa, stabbing our bodies or flailing our backs with ropes or chains. You've seen such pageantry, and however sincerely pursued, it's sadly shaped by superstition, not truth. Christ's call to you and me to take up His cross is *not* to *repetition* but to *identification*. It's to say, "Jesus, I *identify* with—*I take my place with You in Your cross*" (not *on* His cross). Only He can die *on* His cross. But you

45

and I can so join in the spirit of surrender to the Father's will for our lives that we are one with Him *in* His cross:

> I have been crucified with Christ; it is no longer I who live, but Christ lives in me; and the life which I now live in the flesh I live by faith in the Son of God, who loved me and gave Himself for me.
>
> (GAL. 2:20)

Listen carefully, please. For this path of the cross is not to be mistaken or misunderstood.

> It *isn't* intended as a habit of commiserating over life's tough stuff, while muttering, "I guess it's just my cross."
>
> It *isn't* a life of religious self-denial, pretending a prudish, bookish, self-styled piety is what He calls for.
>
> It *isn't* a call down a dour pathway of supposed faith that touts suffering and defeat as the ultimate expression of true holiness! Never!

The cross *is* a pathway of surrender and of refusal to be dominated by selfishness or carnality. But beyond it all, at the bottom line, the cross is a pathway of *triumph!*

> Now thanks be to God who always leads us in triumph in Christ.
>
> (2 COR. 2:14)

And,

> We are more than conquerors through Him who loved us.
>
> (ROM. 8:37)

Can you see why Jesus was so explicit and discerning? When Peter argued against the cross, he was arguing against more than the pivotal event providing mankind's salvation and eternal life. He was also resisting the power-event that models the pathway to each person's release *for all* of life—through trial, past carnality, and unto victory—here, now, every day!

So that's the reason Jesus' words of confrontation called Peter to repentance. And you can be sure, Peter "shaped up"—fast! Similarly, as with him, The Pillar Principle calls us to lifelong learning, and a great deal of the time it will require us to admit it when we discover how easily we've been more controlled by our own ideas than by Christ's.

The "Other" Day

I'll not keep you long on this point, but using Simon Peter as a study guide for processing growth as a disciple does entail one other classic episode of needed repentance. But in this case the failure is so obvious, and the repentance so necessary, that it would seem redundant to elaborate. The narrative is long, and should be read in Mark 14:27-72, and you probably know the story well—

— an Upper Room supper, including a warning to Peter that he will deny Him before morning . . .

— an invasion of Gethsemane, with Peter starting to fight in Jesus' defense, then being told by Him to stop . . .

— a following at a distance, ending up in the high priest's courtyard, seeking to "stay faithful and nearby" the Lord who is now captive . . .

— a scattered series of inquiries by people there, saying, "You're with Him, aren't you?" . . .

— a self-surprising denial—confirmed with cursing and swearing, then . . . the crowing of the rooster; the very signal Jesus prophesied would follow Peter's denial.

It's a painful story to read, not only because of the sympathy we can't help but feel for Peter in the midst of his failure, but painful because in one way or another we've all lived it out.

Disciples do. Yes, they do. Sin.

That's no argument for sin's acceptability; nor is it even to declare its inevitability. Sin doesn't *have* to happen! But it does to most of us, and the saddest part is that however zealous our intent to do otherwise, we too often end up as willing participants in compromise, in veiled deceptions, in dishonesty, in lovelessness, in unforgivingness, in hardheartedness, in bigotry or sectarian small-ness, in bitterness or resentment, in the selfish fear of sacrifice . . . et cetera, et cetera, et cetera!

Still, Simon Peter becomes a poignant point of encourage-ment. His recorded failure—and his full-hearted repentance—*shout* to you and me: "YOU CAN BE RESTORED!" However deep the pit, however dark the stain,

> There is a fountain filled with Blood,
> drawn from Emmanuel's veins,
> And sinners plunged beneath that flood,
> lose all their guilty stains!

And that goes for sinners who, having been saved—having begun to grow in Christ as "pillars in process"—have sadly, dismal-ly fallen prey to the siftings of Satan.

Jesus had said only a few days before: "Simon . . . Satan has asked for you, that he might sift you as wheat." (Literally, in our day, to "put you through the wringer"!) "But," the Savior contin-ued, "I have prayed for you that your faith should not fail" (Luke 22:31-32).

It didn't.

And neither need yours or mine when failure topples us. For,

> Seeing then that we have a great High Priest who has passed
> through the heavens, Jesus the Son of God, let us hold fast
> our confession. . . . Let us therefore come boldly to the throne
> of grace, that we may obtain mercy and find grace to help in
> time of need. . . . Therefore He is also able to save to the
> uttermost those who come to God through Him, since He
> ever lives to make intercession for them.
>
> (HEB. 4:14, 16; 7:25)

There it is, loved one! See it?

Jesus is *right now* present with the Father, alive and well, *and praying for you and me!* We have exactly the same attention being given to us that Jesus gave to Peter: "I'm praying for you . . . and your *faith* won't fail."

That's the kind of Savior we all need.

Even *after* we've become pillars.

Chapter Eight

The Stretching of a Pillar

"After these things Jesus showed Himself again to the disciples at the Sea of Tiberias, and in this way He showed Himself: Simon Peter, Thomas called Didymus, Nathanael of Cana in Galilee, the sons of Zebedee, and two others of His disciples were together. Simon Peter said to them, 'I am going fishing.'

"They said to him, 'We are going with you also.' They went out and immediately got into the boat, and that night they caught nothing. But when the morning had now come, Jesus stood on the shore; yet the disciples did not know that it was Jesus.

"Then Jesus said to them. 'Children, have you any food?'

"They answered Him, 'No.'

"And He said to them, 'Cast the net on the right side of the boat, and you will find some.' So they cast, and now they were not able to draw it in because of the multitude of fish.

"Therefore that disciple whom Jesus loved said to Peter, 'It is the Lord!' Now when Simon Peter heard that it was the Lord, he put on his outer garment (for he had removed it), and plunged into the sea. But the other disciples came in the little boat (for they were not far from land, but about two hundred cubits), dragging the net with fish. Then, as soon as they had come to land, they saw a fire of coals there, and fish laid on it, and bread.

"Jesus said to them, 'Bring some of the fish which you have just caught.' Simon Peter went up and dragged the net to land, full of large fish, one hundred and fifty-three; and although there were so many, the net was not broken. Jesus said to them, 'Come and eat breakfast.' Yet none of the disciples dared ask Him, 'Who are You?'—knowing that it was the Lord. Jesus then came and took the bread and gave it to them, and likewise the fish. This is now the third time Jesus showed Himself to His disciples after He was raised from the dead. So when they had eaten breakfast, Jesus said to Simon Peter, 'Simon, son of Jonah, do you love Me more than these?'

"He said to Him, 'Yes, Lord; You know that I love You.'

"He said to him, 'Feed My lambs.' He said to him again a second time, 'Simon, son of Jonah, do you love Me?'

"He said to Him, 'Yes, Lord; You know that I love You.'

"He said to him, 'Tend My sheep.' He said to him the third time, 'Simon, son of Jonah, do you love Me?' Peter was grieved because He said to him the third time, 'Do you love Me?'

"And he said to Him, 'Lord, You know all things; You know that I love You.'

"Jesus said to him, 'Feed My sheep. Most assuredly, I say to you, when you were younger, you girded yourself and walked where you wished; but when you are old, you will stretch out your hands, and another will gird you and carry you where you do not wish.' This He spoke, signifying by what death he would glorify God. And when He had spoken this, He said to him, 'Follow Me.' "

(JOHN 21:1-19)

I n Peter's first general epistle, he speaks of "living stones," to describe believers in Christ who are learning to fill their place in His will. *"Living"* rocks is an appropriate term, because that's the kind of stone it takes to allow for the s-t-r-e-t-c-h-i-n-g which a growing disciple experiences.

When I set forth the "seven days" of Simon's lifetime, we had already discussed the day which climaxes the series: Pentecost. That's the day of the church's beginning, and the day Peter stepped into his larger role of leadership in the first stages of the church at Jerusalem. We had also taken an early look at his first meeting with Jesus—the "First Day," when the promise of Simon's potential was announced to him by our Lord.

So we've traced Simon's path through a number of pivotal days and it would be possible to elaborate many more, if we wished. Think of—

— The night Jesus came to the disciples as they labored against adverse winds, toiling to reach the other side of Galilee, and suddenly—amazingly!—they see Him walking on the water.

Peter walked on the water that day too!

And think of—

— The three days the crowd gathered to hear Jesus, and now becoming weak for want of food, He answers their need by means of the miracle we call "The Feeding of the 5,000."

Peter was one of the men through whose hands Jesus multiplied and distributed the bread!

And think of—

— The day that Peter, James, and John were invited to join Jesus, just the four of them, on the high mountain where the supernatural visitation called the Transfiguration took place.

Peter was involved in a moment when heaven's glory spilled around Jesus and would later say, "We were eyewitnesses of His Majesty!"

And think of—

— The day Peter watched Jesus heal his own mother-in-law!

— The day Peter cut the ear off an assailant trying to capture Jesus, and then saw Jesus return the ear—whole—to the man's head!

— The night he spent with the others in the Upper Room, where Jesus washed their feet—an action Peter at first protested—and then introduced the Lord's Supper to them!

The "think of" events could go on much longer, and each one holds a lesson for us. Even in these few unelaborated events, there is a parallel application—a potential, similar experience for you and me:

• Jesus *still* invites those He's discipling to "Walk into a miracle and watch Me sustain it." It may not be "on water." Sometimes it's even more wonderful than that!

51

- Jesus *still* multiplies blessing through the hands of those who serve others. It may not be bread and it might not be a crowd. But people are "fed"—buoyed up by a power that transcends human resource or explanation.

- Jesus *still* invites people like you and me into intimate times alone with Him; and it is so often true that it's there the Holy Spirit reveals something more glorious than ever before about the Savior we serve. It may not be on "Transfiguration Mount," but you still know you've touched the invisible in a new way.

- Jesus *still* heals loved ones, showing us how truly dear to Him are those dear to us;

- He *still* takes situations in which our zeal has cut and injured another—however well-meaning our action; and He heals.

- And He also *still* comes to teach us of His servant-like spirit, and then calls us to dine with Him and know more of His love.

These things don't change. And they become the distinct and special portion of every disciple who is willing to walk with Jesus in an ever-moving, forward-striding commitment to *be* His and *do* His will.

The Day of Beginning

But to conclude, I invite you to look with me at John's last episode regarding Peter. It isn't the end for Peter—indeed, it was very near what becomes the Pentecost beginning. But there is something so conclusive about this encounter between Jesus and Peter, that it seems the place to finalize our study.

As I've said, it wasn't the end at all, but the lesson Jesus taught that day might well have been "the finishing touch" that finally qualified Peter to move toward Pentecost and the incredible years of ministry beyond. What I've called his Day of Beginning was a day of stretching.

In John 21 the story unfolds with an apparently calculated

objective at underscoring the priority of *loving Jesus—above all*. It starts with a peculiar fact: Peter's gone back to work at the docks!

Nothing is explained. The text simply reports Peter saying, "I'm going fishing!" Please note: This isn't a man suggesting a recreational night of sport, but a man who's trying to feel his way into his future.

He's bewildered.

He's still embarrassed by his having denied Jesus, even though he knows he's been forgiven. On Resurrection Day, Jesus had made special mention of Peter to some: "Tell My disciples— and Peter!" This expression wasn't a disclaimer, but an inclusion. Jesus wasn't separating Peter from His "team," removing him by separate reference. Rather, here was a special reminder that, in Jesus' view, Peter had never been *off* the team—and *he needed to know it!*

Now, weeks later, the night waters of Galilee are offering nothing of success to Peter and his crew of close friends. His ineffectiveness had to be haunting him. It's not hard to imagine this experienced fisherman-turned-traveling-preacher musing, thinking to himself:

> I came out here because I thought—Here's something I *do* understand! Because I *don't* understand what's been going on these past few days. His resurrection was *real*, I know *that*. But I haven't seen Jesus since . . . well . . . since He said He'd meet us here in Galilee. Now I'm here and He hasn't shown up, and I can't help but think it's my fault. So, I thought I could at least go back to fishing. At least I know *that* business—I understand *it!*
>
> But then he looks at the sagging nets in the water with nothing—absolutely nothing: "Well, at least I *thought* I still understood that."

It's the destiny of a disciple experiencing the last "stretch" before he or she is ready for breakthrough into God's next phase in His high purpose for them. It involves the same things for us all:

- Wondering if nothing's happening because you *think* it's your fault.

- Trying your hand at something you *think* you know, because you don't understand what's going on.

- Discovering that even what you *think* you know is not something you know as well as you thought.

It's the stretching process of self-doubt, of wondering if you're out of commission, of still believing Jesus is real but deciding you're not—at least not real enough for Him to be able to use you as you had hoped.

But Simon Peter is about to find out that all of this is a holy "setup." The moment rebounds with a miracle visitation of nets filled with fish again—like it was that day years before! And suddenly, Peter is sitting across the small seaside fire on which breakfast has just been cooked, and Jesus is looking into his eyes again:

"Simon, son of Jonah, do you love Me more than these?"
Peter winces, thinking, "Why *'Simon'*? Have I lost my rock role?"
He answers, "Yes, Lord, You know I love You."
Jesus replies: "Feed My lambs."

There's an interesting use of words here which our English language doesn't reveal. Jesus has asked if Peter "loves" Him— *agape*, that is, "with a divine quality of love." Peter doesn't match terms with Jesus, doubtless being reticent to make any high claims about his capacities, since he failed miserably after his last high-sounding promise—"Lord, if everyone forsakes You, I won't." Peter's not about to overstate himself again.

He replies, "Lord, I love You"—*phileo*, that is, "with the love of a good friend."

That's what the verbs contrast: Divine love compared with human friendship. Peter's nervous about suggesting he's capable of any more. I don't think it's because he loves Jesus any less, but rather it's because he so drastically doubts his own readiness to rise to become what he would hope to be.

Yet Jesus has answered: "Feed My lambs."

What is He saying?

Whatever else may be intended by His words, an assignment is being given. The continuing figure of speech—"Feed My *lambs*

... Feed My *sheep*"—will indicate one inescapable fact: Jesus is saying, "Your fishing days are over, Simon Peter. From now on, you're to be a *shepherd*—for Me!"

It's another part of the stretching process in fashioning a pillar. Christ has this way not only of calling us to *serve* His purposes, but of calling us often to an unfamiliar environment that requires new dependency and the stretching to new points of character.

Shepherds and fishermen are nothing alike.

- A fisherman can *talk* about "the one that got away," while a shepherd has to go out and *find* that one.

- A fisherman is esteemed as a *clever* sportsman or professional, while a shepherd is unsung, *thought ignorant* and beneath recognition.

- A fisherman can do his job and not even get his feet *wet*, while a shepherd who's doing his job can't keep his feet *clean*.

"Feed My lambs . . . and My sheep, Simon. I've trained you for My purposes, so let's make today the day you come to the end of your own."

The final stretching settled down to one word: *Love*.

The question Jesus asked wasn't, "How great a job can you do? How many successes will you garner? What mighty achievement do you want to accomplish for Me?"

And neither was it, "Say, Simon, how about standing firm when everyone else forsakes Me? You sure blew that one, didn't you, man!"

No.

Never.

Nothing of the sort, because the Lord Jesus Christ never measures the size of His potential pillars by the failures of their past. Only by the love exchanged in the present.

And Peter—that is, Simon, the son of Jonah—said, "I love You, Lord."

There's a great deal more to be said—about this text, about Peter's words, about Jesus' final point, and about all that would be forthcoming. But I want to leave this here—noting that in the final analysis, the primary thing Jesus wants to know about you and me is simply this: "Do you love Me?" Because if that love is in place, however fragile our sense of our own capabilities or capacities to follow through, *He can take us from there!*

And moreover, He can take us farther than we ever dreamed. Consider Peter beyond this day:

He became the first to identify with the supernatural demonstration at Pentecost (Acts 2:14);

He became the first to proclaim the crucified, resurrected Christ to a crowd (Acts 2:14-39);

He became the first to see multitudes won to Christ — numbering in the thousands (Acts 2:41);

He became the first to touch-with-a-miracle, "in the name of Jesus" (Acts 3:6);

He became the first to be persecuted, and to bear stripes for the name of the Lord (Acts 5:40);

He became the first disciple of Jesus to function with discernment against demonic intrusion into the body (Acts 5:1-11);

He became the first disciple of Jesus to raise someone from the dead! (Acts 9:36-43)

It's a pretty good track-record for a stumbling saint. But even there, "being first" isn't really the goal Jesus has for any of us. He only wants us to be stretched enough to allow Him to work in us in all the "firsts" awaiting each of us who walk with Him; to believe He's able to bring us through them with effectiveness.

But as we walk, remember that in serving Him, everything flows out of "first love": loving Jesus *first*, and following Jesus ever.

It's the ultimate discipline. And it always bears the fullest fruit . . . unto the highest fulfillment of the one He's taken and made "a pillar, in the temple of my God."

Go ahead. Accept the possibility.

II

FUNDAMENTAL
DISCIPLINES

"Continuing with the Fundamentals..."

There's something almost nasty that's distilled around the word "fundamental." It's too bad that's happened.

It's the result of a collective of things, any one of which would probably not be enough to have accomplished the semi-demise of the acceptability of a word but, joined together, have all but killed it.

"Fundamentals" are unpopular in education. For example, supposedly new, creative approaches may have sounded bright and snappy when they were proposed. But we've produced a generation peppered through with a near-fifty-percent being limited in or virtually devoid of practical literacy. The same observation could be made in any number of fields of labor or study, where "the fundamentals" have been decried as "too stodgy," as too disinteresting to a person wanting to enter a field of work but undesirous of "digging in" deep enough to find the roots of what grows there.

Further, the word "Fundamentalists" has become virtually a public media epithet—a cuss word for Christians who believe in such things as God the Creator, Jesus the Savior, the Bible as God's Word, and the Holy Spirit, heaven, hell, and other "invisibles" as being real. Of course, some of this "cussing" from some quarters might have been self-invoked by people on the flip side of that criticism; Christians who retaliate in kind when the world slings its arrows, rather than living in the discipline Jesus taught us to employ when we're attacked: "But I say to you, love your enemies, bless those who curse you, do good to those who hate you, and pray for those who spitefully use you and persecute you" (Matt. 5:44).

But whatever negative notions have been conjured up around the idea of "fundamentals," there is no way life can be lived successfully without finding and applying them, whatever your field of interest. Like the pop song of another generation says, "The fundamental things apply as time goes by."

That's what this section of the book presents: "fundamental things" that have proven "The Power and Blessing" found through their careful application *as time goes by.*

There are three important things to know as you continue this portion of our study as disciples: (1) the *reason* for the disciplines discussed, (2) the *spirit* of our approach, and (3) the *background* to their presentation.

The *reason* for selecting the ten specific disciplines has to do with my perspective, and mine alone. They are matters that have come to matter most to me, and while they might be broadened or deepened in either number or content, I've focused these few "basics" because I think they determine the *climate* of a soul. If these things are pursued, everything else will *grow.*

The *spirit* of my approach is nontechnical, insistently practical, and what I like to call "incarnational." By that, I refer to my conviction that God is not so interested in educating us as He is in transforming us. As I've said during our look at Peter's life, the call to being a disciple is ultimately a matter of "Christ in you, the hope of glory." The ten disciplines here will, I think, help us toward the experience of ongoing transformation into the image of Jesus.

Finally, a word to help you navigate the form of these pages requires your knowing the *background* of their presentation. These talks were originally produced in a series of audiocassette studies I did for the Christian

Broadcasting Network. This section's content is a modification of the original transcripts of those studies. Intentionally limited editing has been exercised—enough to assist readability, but at times not as polished in literary terms as would otherwise be the case. I hope this neither distracts nor inconveniences you, if you notice it at all.

One last comment: I don't know how anyone could make a final determination on what order of priority these disciplines should be listed in. Perhaps it's immaterial: they aren't *observed* in a sequence, but we live and make progress in all of them at the same time. So I've simply dealt with the ten here and you can prioritize them as you wish, but please, don't allow that to reduce the importance of any in your lifestyle.

So let's proceed, now that we've taken a *fundamental* look at our *fundamental* need for a *fundamentally* disciplined walk with Christ!

Chapter Nine

Committing to "Hear" God's Voice

The disciplines of Christian, Spirit-filled living are not a deadening removal of joy, but the keys to opening a ceaseless resource of that grace in our lives. Joy is completely unrelated to the glib or the giddy, yet it is linked to genuine happiness and confident contentment. It flows with assurance of God's abiding purpose being realized in us, but always on God's terms.

God's Word is the primary instrument revealing His "terms" for life, and to live with the discipline of the Spirit requires our being "in the Word." To do this means to make use of the Bible in a way that builds your life, as opposed to simply reading it for the accumulation of information. Obvious approaches to God's Word might be considered:

- Reading the Bible on a daily basis;

- Studying the Bible to learn its content and practical meaning;

- Memorizing the Scriptures for personal refreshing and strength;

- Quoting the promises of God to affirm a conviction or expectation; and

- Preparing through study to present the truth to others.

These are among the most common ways God's Word is approached, and each is valid. Further, most of these have been thoroughly discussed in other writings which are abundantly available to any Christian. Thus, I have chosen not to elaborate what has already been provided in profusion by a multiplicity of teachers and writers. Instead, I want to deal with what I believe is the most essential attitude of the disciple when coming to God's Word.

Open your Bible to Mark 4. Lay it side by side with this book and let us study together what I believe is the most important truth in God's Word concerning its use: Jesus' *"Lesson on Listening."*

To begin, let me state the principal truth we will witness in this passage. It is the absolute importance of *"hearing"* the words of the Bible. But this order of "hearing" has much more to do with an attitude a Christian disciple must have than it does one's ability to hear the sounds and understand the meanings of words. Before elaborating Mark 4, read these two passages:

> Therefore lay aside all filthiness and overflow of wickedness, and receive with meekness the implanted word, which is able to save your souls. But be doers of the word, and not hearers only, deceiving yourselves. For if anyone is a hearer of the word and not a doer, he is like a man observing his natural face in a mirror; for he observes himself, goes away, and immediately forgets what kind of man he was. But he who looks into the perfect law of liberty and continues in it, and is not a forgetful hearer but a doer of the work, this one will be blessed in what he does.
>
> (JAMES 1:21-25)

> So then faith comes by hearing, and hearing by the word of God.
>
> (ROM. 10:17)

These texts make it clear that "hearing" has to do with (1) a person's willingness to be *changed* by what he or she hears, and (2) that living faith—not merely *belief* but the power to *see things changed*—comes from this kind of hearing. In short, our willingness to *be* changed by the Word of God's truth determines our ability to *see things changed* around us by the power of applying the Word's promises. With that preamble, let's examine Jesus' teaching about truly "hearing" the Word—the foremost expression of the "voice" of God.

A Strategic Encounter

Nothing has become more of a strategic point in my own spiritual journey than an encounter I had with the Holy Spirit while opening the Bible for study one day. I had been progressing through the Book of Mark, outlining each chapter for a teaching assignment I had, when I came to the fourth chapter.

My outline had progressed nicely:
1. The setting, vv. 1-2
2. The "sower" parable, vv. 3-9
3. The disciples' question, vv. 10-12
4. The Lord's explanation, vv. 13-20

At that point I came to the words of Mark 4:21-25:

21 And He said to them, "Is a lamp brought to be put under a basket or under a bed? Is it not to be set on a lampstand?
22 For there is nothing hidden which will not be revealed, nor has anything been kept secret but that it should come to light.
23 If anyone has ears to hear, let him hear."
24 And He said to them, "Take heed what you hear. With the same measure you use, it will be measured to you; and to you who hear, more will be given.
25 For whoever has, to him more will be given; but whoever does not have, even what he has will be taken away from him."

As I paused to determine how to describe these five verses in my outline, I was stymied. The five verses seemed to have little continuity with the rest of the chapter. They appeared to me to be unrelated to each other, as though they were a series of proverbs, meaning something like:

v. 21 — Let your light shine for God.

v. 22 — Better be good. Somebody's going to know how you *really* lived when God shows the video of your secret life for all to see when you stand before Him someday.

v. 23 — This seemed a kind of "Amen," that might fit in anywhere.

v. 24 — Look out what you do to others, because you're gonna get the same right back!

v. 25 — Life's tough. The rich get richer and the poor get poorer.

I'll make no defense of my candid commentary, for to my eyes the passage was simply a collection of sayings with an "Amen!" in the middle. But knowing that God's Word is more coherent than my superficial view on these words was revealing, I stopped.

I prayed.

Kneeling beside the place where I was sitting, I said, "Holy Spirit, I know there must be a reason for these words in verses 21-25. Will You help me understand it?"

Instantly, these words flashed on my mind: *"The candle is the parable."* I had been answered so quickly I could hardly contain it.

I went back and read verse 21, and the light dawned. I suddenly realized that verse 21 was a direct follow-up by Jesus, after He had explained the parable to His disciples as a response to their asking what it meant (v. 10). In short, having explained the parable in detail, Jesus goes on to say: "After all, isn't a lamp to shed light?" He's explaining, "I'm using these parable 'story-pictures' to be sure no one misses the point. So if you don't get the point, *ask*." Verse 22 elaborates His desire that His disciples listen and learn, and understand with clarity. Jesus essentially says, "There isn't anything that's been secret until now but that I'm going to be sure it's revealed to you! I want you to *know*."

The Central Point

Then comes the stinger. The point. "He who has ears to hear, let him hear." And it's right *there* that the Master's words issue timeless terms for knowing God's Word — *really* knowing it: YOU HAVE TO BE A GENUINE LISTENER!

That's what "having ears to hear" means. The verb *akouo* refers to more than hearing sounds, but to a person's *receiving* and *responding* to what they have heard. Thereby we see how Jesus' next words become so dramatically decisive.

"Take heed what you hear," the Savior warns; then adds: "Only to the degree you *hear* [*receive* and *respond*] will you be able to experience what God has for you." The issue is that you and I must respond to truth, not simply learn it.

Now the Lord's demanding provisos summarize to say: "Whoever *has* [that is, ears to hear, or a will to receive and respond to the truth the Holy Spirit reveals to him or her] shall receive *more*." Then, He adds a frightening consequence of unresponsiveness to God's Word: "Whoever does not have [who evidences a capability to hear the sounds but not respond to the truth of the

Word] will eventually lose what they originally had!"

Can you see why I was so moved to find the key to this series of verses?

What a towering truth! What powerfully poignant observations Jesus makes on the dangers of being *around* the Living Word and our still not responding; of having it fall on our ears only as optional pieces of information rather than as required "hearing" for personal *change*.

In this light, look at the whole passage. Beginning at verse 3, note Jesus' call, "Listen!" It's not merely to gain the crowd's attention. It is a command to discipline our souls toward a constantly receptive, responsive stance when the Living Word speaks. This parable is far more than a simplistic description of the process of evangelistic preaching. It's a personal message to *all* of us for *all* our lives.

- *Every time* God's Word is heard or read, we are accountable to Him for that privilege. Don't let the seed of Truth fall on a barren heart, on stony attitudes, or weeded terrain of a mind so preoccupied with temporal things it's lost sight of eternal things.

- *Every time* we hear a sermon or open the Scriptures, our assignment is to tune our souls to a readiness to be shaped, taught, corrected, or advised. If I come with a closed agenda, presuming "I know this stuff already," I'm on the brink of a distinct order of eventual spiritual bankruptcy: "It shall be taken from him what he already has."

Understanding this text also clarifies the seemingly peculiar words of Jesus in verse 11:

And He said to them, "To you it has been given to know the mystery of the kingdom of God; but to those who are outside, all things come in parables."

A casual reading of this verse almost sounds as though Jesus were intentionally trying to make it difficult for some to understand. But clarity comes when we remember the broader context of His ministry at this point.

You see, Jesus had been ministering for many months in the regions around Galilee. He had made a complete circuit of towns and villages, with the crowds gathering to witness the miracles—the power ministry of the kingdom of God.

Now, "He began to teach by the sea" (v. 1), as He is about to start another preaching circuit of the area. But on this round, He's going to require more *response*—more willingness to be *changed*, not just watch.

There's a lesson on human nature here, and Jesus' way of dealing with it. He chooses this time to begin using these story-lessons—the parables—to emphasize His teaching. Until now, crowds have gathered to revel in the wonder of miracles and to rejoice in the gospel of forgiveness. Now, though Jesus will not reduce either the power manifest or the love offered, He is going to increase the requirement of a responsible response among hearers of His message.

So, when the disciples asked, Jesus precedes His exposition with an explanation: "I'll show you the parable's meaning. These things are for your understanding." Then, He sets a contrast. He notes the difference between those who are willing to be discipled and those who are "only along for the ride." He says, "But to those who are *outside*" (that is, "outside" the circle of a will to accept the call to discipleship—to *following* Him, not just gathering for the miracles and the introductory things of the gospel), "these things are in parables." So we learn: Jesus' use of parables wasn't to puzzle people, but *to make the message so clear that nobody ever need misunderstand!* (Or, if they did, their asking would find a willing and ready answer.)

Often, some have thought the words in verse 12 to be a statement of some divine intent to *make* people misunderstand. But instead, a closer look shows it's a quotation of Isaiah's prophecy (6:9-10) that Jesus was applying to His ministry as well. He was essentially acknowledging what we have already. The crowds were eager for excitement but not for *change:* "These *see* the truth, but they won't let it penetrate their vision; they *hear* it, but they won't grant an understanding response." Jesus quotes the prophet in explaining why people don't *really* "listen." He said it was "Lest they should *turn*"; that is, turn to God's ways and be changed through the transforming power of "their sins being forgiven them." He was noting how much human nature doesn't want to submit to change. We prefer *not* being "untangled" (forgiven) from sins we would rather embrace!

Listening unto Fruitfulness

Can you see, dear one, why this foundational lesson on how God's Word is to be approached becomes so very, very important? Here is a most sobering warning against passivity, presumption, indifference, or a stolid predisposition that suggests, "I already understand this." Or "I have this down 'pat.' " Or, "I'm *right* and *I know it* and there's *nothing* or *no one* going to change my mind!"

But there is a glorious promise here.

In contrast to a human disposition toward self-will or stubborn pride, Jesus describes the certainty of a holy fruitfulness where a person responds to the Word of God with an openhearted, receptive spirit of availability to be taught—for a whole lifetime!

> But these are the ones sown on good ground, those who hear the word, accept it, and bear fruit: some thirtyfold, some sixty, and some a hundred.
>
> (MARK 4:20)

Listen to His assuring promise: "Thirtyfold . . . sixty, and some a hundred." They're all great measures of return, but they're more than a crop gathered in the autumn.

This is our Lord Jesus Himself talking about His truth manifesting in fruit in the issues of our human experience. It is God saying, "If you keep an openness to My Word, there will *always* be a fruitful harvest of that Word's promise and power in your life and circumstance!"

And, let no one make the mistake of thinking that 30–60–100 is a figure predestining some of us to a small measure and others to a greater one. The truth is, Jesus is pointing toward a promising increase! Read it this way, and you've caught the spirit of Jesus' words:

> This time you may only have a thirtyfold return, because your understanding and response is limited. But if you keep an openness to My Word and My Spirit, you'll find a constant increasing as seed-sowing-cycles continue. Dear child, you're headed for an eventual hundredfold increase of grace, purpose, and blessing in your life!

The primary message is this: God's Word has been given to increase growth, fruitfulness, and blessing, both in and through your life. And it is only as you and I keep open to it—keep teachable, shapable, and responsive, *listening* with a ready heart to be taught and to obey—that fruit will appear and increase.

A Final Note

Finally, it's worth noting that every time the words, "He who has ears to hear, let him hear" occur in the New Testament, Jesus is the One who is speaking. This is no casual expression, merely filling space as a human "Amen." Rather, it is the divine Son of God saying, "Don't ever close your ears or your heart to your need to be taught. It's the key to growth, to fruitfulness, and to the joy of a multiplied harvest of God's blessing in your life."

His is the power.

Ours may be the blessing.

How we listen will determine it all.

Chapter Ten

The Spirit of Forgiveness

This one discipline is the Key to Everything.* If any single truth has become dominative in my understanding of Christian living, it's in the *breadth* of the implications Jesus teaches regarding forgiveness. Before reading the story *He* told to make His point, let me tell one which describes how He helped *me* understand *His.*

Shortly after Anna and I were married, we went to the Nebraska plains where she had been raised as the near youngest of nine children. It was an initiating trip for me, for I hadn't met most of her family or relatives before. That's when I met Joe.

I was so warmly received by most everyone, it was a little surprising when Joe responded differently. I sensed a low-grade rejection, but I took it in stride, for I understood Joe's aloofness. I recognized it was related to his spiritual condition.

Joe was away from God.

Even though he had been raised in the things of the Lord, Joe now had a way of distancing himself from anyone whom he felt might possibly crowd his lifestyle. Of course, understanding this, I did nothing to make him feel as though I were on a crusade for his soul. The last thing I was about to do was to come onto him with "hot gospel." So, as a matter of fact, I went out of my way to be friendly—to treat him as a brother; one I would accept and trust, no matter what he chose to do.

I didn't try to "slip in" spiritual messages or push agendas when we were together, but just tried to be a friend. Naturally, I obviously wanted to see him return to a walk with Christ, but I

---

* Dr. Hayford has related the story in this chapter in his book by this name, *The Key to Everything,* a broader study of the concept of forgiveness as it relates to giving.

wasn't about to try to push it on him. So there was no reason for Joe to be less than brotherly to me. Even though I was his "relative-in-training-for-the-ministry," I didn't do any offensive "religious things" but just worked at winning his friendship.

But it didn't work.

Though I tried to be sensitive and winsome over the years, Joe wouldn't crack—not even slightly. I thought his coolness would wear away with time, but it didn't. He always retained a distinct relational distance. Notwithstanding my warmest of overtures, he withdrew—clamming up, and eventually I lost patience with his cool distancing.

The turning point came fifteen years into my acquaintance with Joe. It wasn't good.

Tired of Trying

Anna, the kids, and I had made a trip back to Nebraska to celebrate her folks' fiftieth wedding anniversary. It was a marvelously heartwarming time, with friends and family gathered from all points of the compass—and that's the mood and setting which turned out so bad; at least "bad" for me.

I was out in the backyard talking to Joe one day, and as we conversed, his studied reserve started to rankle me; and though I didn't recognize it, I was on a headlong path to hardheartedness. We'd now been relatives for years and talked together many times, but on this day my frustration with his chilling treatment reached its breaking point. Something unobservable to the eye yet very real in the soul "snapped" inside me. It was the closing of a door; a private, unspoken decision resulting from years of becoming tired and impatient with Joe's attitude—that almost snobbish air of rejection. I was through, and I decided to "shut him out."

I'd never felt this way toward anyone, but neither had I ever felt this "shut out" *by* anyone. I knew it wasn't paranoia on my part, because I felt this rejection from no one else. But now as he had shown personal resistance to common decency, I was about to silently retaliate in kind. I remember the decisive moment well: I simply but angrily thought to myself: *"I'm through!"*

That was it. I was simply tired of trying.

I didn't turn my back and walk away from him at that moment's setting, but in my heart and attitude toward Joe I had. I was washing my hands of him; through trying to be his friend. I thought: I've tried long and hard enough. I don't need to put up with this drippy unresponsiveness anymore! The words weren't spoken, but my heart slammed a door. I wouldn't realize it until later, but with that "fed up" action, Joe was being made a victim of my unforgiveness.

Summer and autumn passed that year, and now it was Valentine's Day. I'll never forget that overcast morning at home in California when God stabbed me with the truth. Until this day I had been entirely oblivious to my true failures for I had felt entirely justified for determining to be as indifferent to our relationship as he obviously was. Joe was far from my mind and heart. Very far. I hadn't thought about that summertime decision since the moment it occurred, but it was all about to come crashing around my head with dynamic spiritual understanding.

As I strolled into the kitchen that morning, my eye was caught by a Valentine card lying on the table. I flipped it open, having read the front, which was a setup—a humorous preview to what I knew would be a funny punchline. But the joke turned out to be on me.

Stabbed to Awareness

While I'll never remember the punchline printed in the card, I'll never forget the handwritten words at the bottom. They were from Joe's teenage daughter, who had sent the card to our daughter. The two teen girls had struck a nice friendship, even though their "growing up together" was a half-continent apart, and this card was simply a part of their continuing correspondence. But this card was about to become an ice pick in God's hands to shatter my frozen heart. The note below read: "Dear Becki, I just wanted to add a note to thank you for mentioning in your last letter that you are regularly praying for my dad to come back to Jesus."

That's the moment the Holy Spirit employed to jab me awake to two things. *First*, He exposed the unworthiness of my counter-rejection attitude toward Joe. He had used my daughter to jar me to an awareness that two teenagers were exchanging mutual concern and sharing prayer for a man I had the unholy, blinded audacity to "give up on." Worse, I awakened to a *second* humbling fact.

Don't ask me to try and explain the "why" of this, because I *did* care about Joe's soul, and I *was* pursuing faithful ministry during all the intervening years. But the awful truth is that in the fifteen years I had known him, I could not remember even *once* specifically praying for Joe!

Go ahead, fire the questions: *"Why,* Jack?" *"What?* Never prayed for him *once* — you mean *even before that summer 'decision'?"* And the only answer I can give is, "Yes." I *cared,* but apparently my attitude was so hardened by his rejective ways, it had blinded me, blocking my recognition of my own neglect. Still, there was another dynamic at work this Valentine morning. In mercy, the Spirit of God was birthing a repentance in my heart — and a love.

I literally fell to my knees there alone in the kitchen, and began to weep. I repented for my blindness, for my hardheartedness, for my impatience, for my "signing off" — and I asked God's forgiveness for the prayerlessness which the mix of unperceived and known attitudes had begotten in me.

Then I prayed for Joe. I prayed with an entirely new sense of love — for the *man,* for his *soul,* for Joe "no-matter-how-he-is, I *care,* Lord!" And I truly did.

That experience was one of my life's greatest lessons for it introduced me to a path which resulted in understanding the power of a "spirit of forgiving-ness." That "spirit" involves learning to remember how much *more* God's mercy has been shown to *me* than I'll *ever* need to show someone else. It's a fundamental requirement to every disciples' learning and living, and Jesus gave a lengthy story to illustrate it; showing both (1) the need of our learning this spirit, and (2) the dangers if we don't. So before I tell you the rest of my story about Joe, take a look with me at Jesus' story. It's a long passage, and possibly so well known you might think you know it better than you do. So read it slowly, please; perhaps even penciling in an underscoring of key points you notice.

Jesus' Lesson on Forgiveness

Then Peter came to Him and said, "Lord, how often shall my brother sin against me, and I forgive him? Up to seven times?"

Jesus said to him, "I do not say to you, up to seven times, but up to seventy times seven. Therefore the kingdom of heaven is like a certain king who wanted to settle accounts with his servants. And when he had begun to settle accounts, one was brought to him who owed him ten thousand talents. But as he was not able to pay, his master commanded that he be sold, with his wife and children and all that he had, and that payment be made.

The servant therefore fell down before him, saying,

"Master, have patience with me, and I will pay you all." Then the master of that servant was moved with compassion, released him, and forgave him the debt.

But that servant went out and found one of his fellow servants who owed him a hundred denarii; and he laid hands on him and took him by the throat, saying, "Pay me what you owe!"

So his fellow servant fell down at his feet and begged him, saying, "Have patience with me, and I will pay you all." And he would not, but went and threw him into prison till he should pay the debt. So when his fellow servants saw what had been done, they were very grieved, and came and told their master all that had been done.

Then his master, after he had called him, said to him, "You wicked servant! I forgave you all that debt because you begged me. Should you not also have had compassion on your fellow servant, just as I had pity on you?" And his master was angry, and delivered him to the torturers until he should pay all that was due to him.

So My Heavenly Father also will do to you if each of you, from his heart, does not forgive his brother his trespasses.

(MATT. 18:21-35)

For closer examination, let me divide this text into four segments to help us see the potent truths revealing the importance of a disciple's spirit of forgiving-ness.

Nice Try, Pete! (vv. 21-22)

The setting for this lesson is a follow-up question Peter asked Jesus immediately after the Master had talked about forgiving people who violate you or have a fault that offends you (vv. 15-20). Peter, feeling generous in the wake of Jesus' call to graciousness, asks, "Then, Lord, shall I forgive *seven* times?"

Don't make the mistake of thinking that wasn't a quantum leap. To Peter's understanding, "seven times" was more than twice anything he'd ever been taught.

You see, the rabbis of that day literally taught that God Himself didn't forgive more than *three* times! On the basis of their interpretation of Amos' prophecy, where God says He would judge nations "for three transgressions and for four" (Amos 1–2), the ancient teachers concluded: "If God Himself comes down heavy on the fourth violation, we have no obligation to be any more patient than that." So Peter's *two*-times-three-*plus*-one = *SEVEN!* seemed more than generous.

But Jesus comes back with a stunning statement that essentially says, "Stop counting, Peter." His 70 x 7 obviously isn't a recommendation to set up a tote board, notching every grievance until we can justify retaliation or rejection. He's calling us to *forgiveness* as a way of life; to "the spirit of *forgiving-ness*." His story provides the grounds for this call to this discipline.

The 100-Million Dollar Man (vv. 23-27)

Jesus calls His disciples to a lifestyle of forgiveness as a principle of discipleship. He roots it in the lesson that we have all been so *greatly* forgiven, we are logically obligated to *be* forgiving. By saying, "The kingdom of heaven is like this," He is invoking this principle upon all of us who have been born again into that domain — His kingdom of love (John 3:3, 5).

His parable shows the amount of money owed by the first servant to, in actuality, be an unpayable debt. The man is a mere daily wage earner. The debt — calculated by today's economic conversion rates — would be at least $100 million if the talents mentioned were gold. The picture's clear: Jesus means to project an absolutely impossible debt. The man could never pay it off. It's the story equivalent of our absolute lostness in sin apart from God's forgiveness through Jesus' cross.

The story-picture of "selling" the man, his family, and his holdings, causing slaves and servitude, are not intended to be seen as God's style. Jesus is using the contemporary custom to illustrate the binding, destructive potential of human helplessness outside God's grace.

And then the grace flows!

The total and complete wiping away of all indebtedness, the freeing of the man in response to his cry and by reason of his master's compassion, is as dramatic a statement as we'll ever find illustrating God's forgiveness to us in Christ.

Here is a "mega-million dollar man" — multiplied times more miraculous in his restoration than the fabled technological recovery of TV's "Six Million Dollar Man." The servant is *freed* — a masterpiece story-painting of God's divine level of forgiveness. Like our freedom in Christ, His freedom is complete, undeserved, and restoring.

The 99¢ Store Frame-up (vv. 28-30)

Jesus intends the stark contrast which follows to shock us. The man forgiven a fortune virtually races to claim a pittance from a fellow servant. He drives the man to his knees, choking him as he demands payment. The actual sum was probably about $50, converted to today's currency. At most, by any estimate, it couldn't be more than three months' salary. In other words, it was an amount that *could* be paid, IF. . . .

But there are no "ifs" in the unforgiving servant's system. He not only shows himself small in soul, but stupid in style. He throws his fellow servant into the debtors prison "until you pay it up"; a place where the jailed man can do nothing to change the financial facts of his circumstance. Here Jesus pictures the way our unforgiving-ness "freezes" the relational possibilities between us and those we don't forgive. By *casting into iron* any present problem or stress between me and another, nothing can change. It's lived out every time I react to an attitude or deed which hurts me and I "bind" the person to it; that is, when I decide, "If that's the way *they're* going to be, then that's the way *it's* going to be!"

The cheapness of the forgiven servant, wholly forgetting the enormity of the forgiveness which has been shown him, ends in a 99¢ Store "frame-up." He jails another servant who ought to have been given the same wealth of forgiveness he had received. He might have seen himself as "freed to free others," but he didn't.

The Double Disaster Ending (vv. 31-35)

Jesus concludes the story with a two-edged truth rarely noted to its full implications.

First, he uses the action taken by the lord of the servants to indicate both what unforgiveness does and doesn't do. Just as the unforgiving servant's master *didn't* revert to the original status of the man (when he would have sold the man, his family, and his holdings into slavery and endless poverty), so Jesus shows that being unforgiving *doesn't* reverse our salvation and return us on a course to eternal judgment. However, what He *does* say is powerfully impacting as it relates to psychological/physiological facts we know about human beings.

As surely as Jesus notes that "torturers" (literally, bill collectors, v. 24) will regularly be exacting payment from the man from now on, so the spirit of unforgiveness takes a sure and tortuous toll on our bodies and souls. Doctors, psychologists, and psychiatrists all have noted that the vast majority of human ills are related to repressed attitudes of bitterness, resentment, unforgiveness, hate, anger and self-pity, self-justification, and self-centeredness. All these converge in the picture of unforgiving-ness Jesus draws, and the price is clearly taught: unforgiveness exacts its toll on our lives, bodies, relationships, for as long as you or I carry that wearisome spirit. God says so (v. 35).

But there's a second, seldom noted fact. As the story ends, the second servant is still in debtor's prison.

"Why?" you ask.

Because his situation had nothing to do with his relationship with the landlord. His imprisonment was strictly between him and the unforgiving servant.

While we may speculate that the unforgiving servant may have seen his folly and repented of this action, Jesus leaves the story at this point. And it's for a reason.

You see, dear fellow disciple, you and I need to apply the lesson ourselves. Whenever we have left a relationship on the shelf—like I did with Joe—we need to let the Holy Spirit bring our blinded folly into the light. Where are the "fellow servants" of our own relationship being placed?

Are they allowed within the circle of forgiveness to the dimension we've received, or are they left outside? Do we ignorantly reserve our "rights," administrating our own private counter-judgments? Do we insist on returning something of unforgiveness as a payment-in-kind for the injustice, unkindness, rejection, or disfavor we've been shown?

The principle applies deeply; right on through to attitudes we hold toward people simply because we don't like their difference of style, of manner, of expression, of doctrine or worship, of ethnicity or culture, etc. That they are "fellow servants" ends up making little difference, because the capacity of an unforgiving servant to forget the grandeur of the grace he or she has been shown is virtually incalculable.

But that attitude isn't unbreakable.

And the lesson isn't unlearnable.

That's why Jesus *taught* His disciples the need of this discipline, and He can also *break* any bonds of unforgiveness we invite Him to shatter. The freedom is joyous, and the *healing* power—the releasing triumph in it—is absolutely glorious!

And so it was with me . . . and Joe.

The Rest of the Story

It was the next August, the summertime following the "Valentine Day massacre" of the spirit of my unforgiving-ness.

That Sunday night Anna and I had come home from church — the kids had gone to prepare for bed, Anna to the kitchen for a snack, and I to the bedroom to change into something more relaxing. And the phone rang.

It was Joe. "Hi, guys!" he greeted brightly, as Anna and I had both picked up extensions simultaneously. He didn't take long to get to the point.

"Jack, Anna — I just wanted to call you both tonight, because I felt you'd want to be among the first to know." He paused, then he almost shouted: "I came back to the Lord today!" He was jubilant. He was free.

And I was weeping, laughing, and praising God at the same time!

We visited for some time, and before concluding the call had a holy reunion around the throne of God. But when I put the phone down, I lay back on the pillow in our bedroom. I thought pensively, and heart-searchingly: "Lord, could it be that my unrecognized attitude of judging Joe because he was rejective of me had somehow 'bound' him away from a spiritual breakthrough — until I became forgiving, and lovingly prayerful?"

I didn't receive an answer, until I later discovered this text — and the servant left in the debtors prison.

I realize that each person is responsible for his own relationship to God. And I realize that it isn't my call or mission to impose guilt on you if you have failed somehow and succumbed to unforgiveness in anything of the same way I had. But I couldn't escape a parallel. You and I both realize that we are mutually responsible to take the gospel to nations and peoples who will never know Christ unless someone accepts the responsibility to reach them. Sure! If we *do*, they'll be saved. If we don't . . . ? And if that question remains in the mission of world evangelism, perhaps it's equally true that forgiveness only flows where God can find forgiven people to dispense it. That seems to be exactly what Jesus says:

> If you forgive the sins of any, they are forgiven them; if you retain the sins of any, they are retained.
>
> (JOHN 20:23)

The message—no, the *mandate* to becoming *forgivers* as we've been *forgiven* is absolute for us as disciples of Jesus. You and I are called to *never* withhold a largeness of attitude or forgiveness of spirit toward *anyone* else. Jesus wouldn't want it.

And the "Joes" of this world can't live without it.

Chapter Eleven

Living in the Power
of Baptism

S pirit-filled" is not a mystical, unattainable life that God keeps just out of our reach. It is a life of "process"—a life of "becoming" under the leadership of the Holy Spirit.

We have dealt with the essence of discipleship; i.e., remaining shapable, teachable, and flexible under our Lord Jesus Christ, who by His Spirit is processing pillars. So, let me lead you into a second aspect of Spirit-filled living.

I want to deal with elements that are foundational or fundamental to our life in Christ and growth in Him. To do that, let's give time to a consideration of the "sacraments."

The idea behind what we call "the sacraments" is a striking one in the history of the church. To begin, "sacrament" is derived from a Latin word which refers to an oath of allegiance. In church terminology, it refers to the practice of a sacrament (for example, the Lord's Table) as a declaration that *trust* is being placed in the potential power of that exercise, that faith is being manifest by the action taken.

Prior to church usage, the idea of a sacrament involved a deposit which was made by two parties to a lawsuit. It was an action they were establishing together in order to secure justice in a court of law; an attempt to receive a right or a claim. Similarly, then, the concept of "sacrament" proposes two parties; *God* has made a provision and as certain actions or specific deeds are exercised, *we* are responding to the provision. We become the "second party" to the "sacrament," God being the "first" or the initiating party. As with the original idea of sacrament, from His side, God *has made* a deposit— gracious provisions; from our side, we *are making* a deposit—our faith to believe and our willing obedience to participate.

The two sacraments most common in the life of the church are the sacraments of water baptism and the Lord's Table (also called Communion, Eucharist, or Mass). Catholic church tradition has observed as many as seven sacraments: baptism, confirmation, eucharist, penance, holy orders, matrimony, anointing the sick. But in Protestant church tradition, these are not all observed. For our study, I am only dealing with those two sacraments we see as *biblically foundational* to our walk with Christ; specifically, water baptism and the Lord's Table.

Water Baptism

Even if you have already been baptized in water, there are three reasons meriting your attention anyway. Whether you've "already been" or not, a solid grasp of water baptism is essential as a part of cultivating the inner life.

First, our own growth and the depth of life as disciples of Christ, depends on our moving beyond initiating experiences. It requires our seeing those truths and practices we've already obeyed (like water baptism) as intended to be *more* than "done," but for all their implications, literally to be incarnated. In other words, a disciple never simply "experiences" a truth or "performs" a sacrament or act of faith, but he or she goes forward *living in* that truth.

Therefore, the wisdom of rethinking the power and blessing inherent in the truths surrounding our having begun in Christ (here, rethinking baptism) is clearly perceived. Because its power was not simply for the moment it occurred, but also in its potential to be "lived out" ongoingly. So we'll review the ongoing validity of water baptism (and later, the Lord's Table) as a power principle at work in us *still* today, if we abide in it.

Second, we need to rethink the discipline of water baptism so we can sensibly and sensitively relay the truth to others. As disciples, we have opportunity to teach or influence new believers and deepening our insightfulness is thereby obviously desirable.

Third, it's also possible that you, dear reader, *haven't* yet been baptized. Over the years of my walk in Christ and as a leader, I have been surprised to discover the large number of believers—by no means a majority, but a substantial number—who have walked with Christ for *years,* and for some reason or another have never been baptized in water. Because that's sometimes so, let me talk about it a bit. Whether it helps *you* or helps you help others, it's worth the time.

The primary reason I've found believers simply disregard baptism is they've somehow come by the idea that to be baptized "is just a church tradition," and so maybe it's only "man's idea." In these cases, water baptism has never been taught to these people either in the depth of its meaning or in the clarity of its biblical mandate by our Lord Jesus.

We all need to *know* water baptism is a distinct, biblically commanded, *personal responsibility*, not simply a religious idea. And I don't mean "personal" as though it is "ours to choose," but *personal* in that Jesus has commanded it of *each one of us!*

And He said to them, "Go into all the world and preach the gospel to every creature. He who believes and is baptized will be saved; but he who does not believe will be condemned."

(MARK 16:15-16)

Fourth, some people don't take steps to be baptized in water because they have experienced the baptism in the Holy Spirit *first,* and suppose somehow that *now* baptism in water isn't necessary. But the Bible shows quite the opposite. Look at Acts 10:44-48:

While Peter was still speaking these words, the Holy Spirit fell upon all those who heard the word. And those of the circumcision who believed were astonished, as many as came with Peter, because the gift of the Holy Spirit had been poured out on the Gentiles also. For they heard them speak with tongues and magnify God. Then Peter answered, "Can anyone forbid water, that these should not be baptized who have received the Holy Spirit just as we have?" And he commanded them to be baptized in the name of the Lord. Then they asked him to stay a few days.

Though the group at the house of Cornelius had received the infilling of the Holy Spirit, Peter still directed that they be baptized in water. There's no way around it. *No* experience, however grand and glorious, substitutes for water baptism.

Fifth, some believe in baptism, but don't accept the discipline for themselves. They have reasons. For example, I've encountered a surprising number of dear believers who haven't been baptized because the thought of being immersed beneath the water is

THE POWER AND BLESSING

tormentingly frightening to them. Someone may think this exaggerated or ridiculous, but such fears are real. However sympathetic and understanding we should be, this reluctance still must be confronted. And I'm thrilled to report many cases where we have dealt with such people in the Holy Spirit's love, when we have together bound and overruled the spirit of fear, in Jesus' name and with biblical authority, we have seen great deliverances occur as the individuals obeyed and were baptized: Obedience followed by deliverance! Hallelujah!

Another problem hindering baptismal candidates I've known is a few who avoid baptism because of fear of embarrassment—of "looking funny all wet." But this obviously must be graciously confronted as well. While the Bible doesn't mandate that observers be present at baptism, there usually are—and it's *desirable*.

Baptism is one of life's greatest opportunities to be a witness! Let's capitalize on it. Invite friends to this occasion, and let's make this triumphant moment *count!* And if there is still a lurking concern that perhaps he or she may not appear "all that neat" when he or she comes up out of the water ("my hair streaming in every direction!"), it's good to obey *simply to overcome pride!* It's *always* wise for a disciple to challenge *any* preoccupation with "how good I look." Obedience to Jesus our Savior and Master is the ultimate issue for all our lives, and all others must bow to Him.

As a disciple, such thoughtfulness can enhance your ability to assist others. Strange or simple as the above concerns may seem, they are issues I've needed to address with individuals in order to assure their personal obedience to baptism.

Depth of Meaning

Now, let's examine water baptism for more of the depth in the meaning of this fundamental discipline. Though we *have* been baptized, fully acknowledging its importance, we're still called to *live* in principles of baptism; *abiding* in the truths baptism expresses, through an ongoing evidence in our lives. So, let's deepen our perspective to assist our own understanding as well as to more ready ourselves to *minister* the truth and principles of baptism to others, by both precept and example. How can we more fully live in the *power* of those principles applied to our living as Jesus' disciples?

Turn with me to the Gospel of Luke. I want us to examine this passage of Scripture for a combination of reasons, to note the significance of God's purposes in our being baptized.

Now when all the people were baptized, it came to pass that Jesus also was baptized; and while He prayed, the heaven was opened. And the Holy Spirit descended in bodily form like a dove upon Him, and a voice came from heaven which said, "You are My beloved Son; in You I am well pleased."

(LUKE 3:21-22)

Of course, when we come to the subject of baptism, there are various Christian traditions, both in the *form* of baptism as well as the *time* of baptism. Perhaps someone reading these words was baptized as an infant at the wish and direction of his or her parents. There may be another who was baptized earlier in his or her Christian life who, in the intervening time, has wandered from a close walk with God.

Now, having returned to the Lord, he or she may wonder, "Should I be baptized again?" Still others were baptized in their youth or adult years, *after* receiving Christ. The central issue, dear friend, is *that* you be baptized!

When I'm asked the question, "Since I was baptized as a child or an infant and I didn't really know what I was doing, would it be irreverent for me to be baptized again?" I hasten to reply, "Never!" How could it *possibly* be irreverent to *now* confirm, by your own decision, what was volunteered for you by parents or loving influences on your life who earlier desired you to make a commitment to the Lord? That's how I have answered that question for years, without *demanding* a rebaptism.

But I've found that the reason people ask this question is usually because the Holy Spirit is dealing with their hearts. And if He does, they ought *never* to feel hesitant or guilty. Listen: You are *not* violating the love and the care that was shown by parents or other authorities in your life, who requested and directed that you be baptized when you were younger. Rebaptism *isn't* rejection of that parental love!

Further, if you were baptized earlier in your walk with Christ, and for a season distanced yourself from Him through disobedience, but now having returned, feel prompted to be rebaptized, you are *not* negating the reality of your earlier walk. Thus, the act of baptism in water is to be monitored by your *heart's* obedience to the Holy Spirit, not by undue fear *or* reverence for the past. The issue is, *"Obey the Lord of your life! Be baptized!"*

First, in Matthew 28:19-20, Jesus commanded His disciples to baptize:

"Go therefore and make disciples of all the nations, baptizing them in the name of the Father and of the Son and of the Holy Spirit, teaching them to observe all things that I have commanded you; and lo, I am with you always, even to the end of the age." Amen.

Hear it? Baptism is as important as the Great Commission. Jesus told His disciples to go to the world, preach the gospel, *and* "*Baptize them in the name of the Father and of the Son and of the Holy Spirit.*" It's His commission: it is a straight-on matter of obedience to Christ.

So, let's come to the waters of baptism, influence others in that direction, and then "*live the baptized life.*" What does this mean?

To live "the baptized life" is to live in an abiding recollection of my baptism with this mind-set: "I have submitted myself in obedience to Jesus' lordship, and this is my lifetime commitment: *My will is to do His will.*" That's the fundamental issue in water baptism (see Jesus' words in Matt. 3:14-15).

Second, be baptized because of the promise waiting you there. Look at Acts 2:37-38, where the Apostle Peter answers the questions of those now cut to the heart with conviction: "What shall we do now?" He's very direct: "Repent, and let every one of you be baptized," then he adds glorious words of promise, "and you shall receive the gift of the Holy Spirit."

Hear these words — *now!*

Just as *Jesus* calls us to baptism, to obey His lordship, Peter calls us to baptism as a moment for our receiving the fullness of the Holy Spirit. I know this is true when it's taught and believed.

There is hardly a week goes by in my pastorate that we don't witness people who, *as they come up from the waters of baptism,* are at the same time filled — right there — with the Holy Spirit. They begin to worship the Lord supernaturally by the power of the Holy Spirit! And Peter's words in the above text are a pointer toward that possibility, noting that when you and I come to the waters of baptism we are not only obeying Jesus, we are also opening to the fullness of the Holy Spirit.

Third, Romans 6:3-4 reveals another aspect of baptismal truth.

Or do you not know that as many of us as were baptized into Christ Jesus were baptized into His death? Therefore we were buried with Him through baptism into death, that just as Christ was raised from the dead by the glory of the Father, even so we also should walk in newness of life.

Notice how the truth of baptism's significance continues to expand. Paul's words show baptism not only as (1) an act of obedience and (2) an opening of Holy Spirit fullness, as we have seen, but shows water baptism as (3) an action of commitment to *burial*. He converts the baptismal site to a graveyard, where we "bury" our *old* ways in the waters where Jesus has called us to meet Him. It's a real "commitment" if you will. We use the word "committal" at funerals as the casket is put into the ground. Similarly, my commitment to Jesus Christ is manifest in my willingness to say, "My life—all the remaining years of it—I shall be dead to my past and my own carnal ways."

But that's not all, for while I'm "dying" to myself, I am also making another Bible-taught announcement. Just as I am "buried," immersed into the water, I am also *rising again!* As I come up, I am saying, "From now on I will draw on the power of the resurrection life of my Lord Jesus!" Just as He was buried, so we have been buried with Him: just as He arose, so we have risen in the newness of His life and the power of His Spirit.

But if the Spirit of Him who raised Jesus from the dead dwells in you, He who raised Christ from the dead will also give life to your mortal bodies through His Spirit who dwells in you.

(ROM. 8:11)

That word is both *truth* and *power,* and where we'll find the life-giving enablement of the Spirit on a daily basis, "resurrecting"—*lifting you* above the past's dead habits and into today's and tomorrow's newness of life.

Fourth, in Colossians 2:11-12 there is yet another figure linked to the idea of our water baptism:

In Him you were also circumcised with the circumcision made without hands, by putting off the body of the sins of the flesh, by the circumcision of Christ, buried with Him in baptism, in which you also were raised with Him through faith in the working of God, who raised Him from the dead.

Linked to the picture of our death, burial, and resurrection unto the newness of life in Christ, God's Word presents the figure of the Old Testament rite of circumcision. Of course, most know that ancient rite involved the removal of the foreskin of the male sex organ. The physical nature of the practice could distract from the dynamic symbolism applicable today. We need to capture this, because a brief moment of insight into the implications of "baptism as circumcision" can reveal a very practical truth. In the delicacy of the literal physiology of circumcision, a powerful picture is present for us to understand. In the *physical* aspect of that most private part of the body, there are figurative, *spiritual* lessons:

A. In baptism, God wants to "cut away flesh," that is, remove carnality from our lives—things that are surplus to the needs for which He has created us. Understand it: Just as the removal of that small portion of excessive flesh from the physical organ of the body does not reduce or inhibit the capacity of that part of the body, there is "surplus," excessive aspects of our behavior which God may want to remove from any one of our lives. This removal will not inhibit our capacity for good things in His *order*, but will remove unnecessary things outside His purposes and design.

B. By way of illustration, notice that it was not until *after* Abraham was circumcised that the miracle of Isaac's conception and birth came about! I have often wondered, "How many people are there who never experience the release or fulfillment of promises because they have not been baptized in submission to the Lord—i.e., fully obedient and open to the "Spirit of promise," and to possibilities yet to be born in their lives. For Abraham, reproductivity in God's realm of promise didn't happen until after his circumcision. Similarly, there may be realms of fruit-bearing capacity in many lives that are only waiting their obedience to Jesus—to "circumcision" in the waters of baptism.

Thus, baptism is not a ritual to be performed but a dynamic to be experienced! The figure of circumcision links baptism to a time when God (1) cuts away "flesh" as we come under His order, and (2) releases power to bring about His promised life and purpose through us. And just as circumcision dealt with a private part, so these things happen in the privacy of our hearts as our Lord works His will and power in us.

To this add one last figure regarding baptism further showing us its dynamism.

> Moreover, brethren, I do not want you to be unaware that all our fathers were under the cloud, all passed through the sea, all were baptized into Moses in the cloud and in the sea.
>
> (1 COR. 10:1-2)

Here's a marvelous picture—Israel's coming out of Egypt, which brings to mind history's most dramatic deliverance *from* slavery *unto* destiny! God's Word says: See how Israel, coming out of Egypt, "*all were baptized* into Moses in the cloud and in the sea"! In adopting the figure of baptism, the Bible shows the miraculous moment of the sea's opening as a dynamic insight into the kind of thing God is ready to do at *our* water baptism.

See the picture: Moments before, the Israelites had their backs to the wall, but now they have "come through" a pathway of deliverance. Can you imagine their joy? Their oppressor, Pharaoh and his troops, who had enslaved them for centuries, were vanquished as the waters swallowed them. The very ones who had been their masters are now drowned in the waters of the sea by God's great deliverance.

Listen, loved one. Water baptism is intended to be a moment of deliverance for us too:

- When things to which we've been enslaved;

- When bonds by which we've been entangled through actions of our Adversary;

- When deliverance is needed from hellish oppression; *all are broken!*

Absolutely! Let's joy in the multiple truths! Water baptism is *not* just a church tradition, it is a miracle moment. In it I obey the lordship of Jesus. In it I welcome the Holy Spirit. In it I bury my past. In it my heart is circumcised so new life power and God's fullest promise for my life might be realized. In it every bondage and yoke are broken and my future is opened to fullest freedom in Christ so I may arise in the life-giving power of my living Savior.

These are the reasons for and the dynamism in water baptism, and each is a present reality awaiting the disciple's obedience. So, come—whether you've been baptized or not—come and possess the promise.

Be baptized. *Live* baptized.

Say, "Jesus, today I want the power potential for a baptized person to be mine; walking in openness to Your Spirit, dead to my past, circumcised from unproductivity so fruitfulness might abound, and freed from every bond and yoke of the Adversary."

And to put a cap on all this, remember what happened at the waters of baptism when Jesus experienced it. When the sinless Son of God volunteered to submit to be baptized, *the heavens opened* to Him, *the Spirit descended* upon Him, and *the Father spoke* from heaven. And these blessings *also* await the believer who will follow Jesus in baptism. Read of it:

> Then Jesus, when He had been baptized, came up immediately from the water; and behold, the heavens were opened to Him, and He saw the Spirit of God descending like a dove and alighting upon Him. And suddenly a voice came from heaven, saying, "This is My beloved Son, in whom I am well pleased."
>
> (MATT. 3:16-17)

"The heavens were opened" doesn't mean there was a "crack" in the sky and He saw something of the eternal city in the distance. Rather, it means that the realm of invisible reality became perceptible; the spiritual realm became a functional, perceived arena of impending action.

The Lord wants the same for us; an entrance into a realm of relationship with Him where the invisible is not mysterious, but is perceived as an arena in which we function with confidence. God makes us disciples who, "seeing the invisible" (not as bizarre, but as a real dimension of life), are as comfortable in relating to it as we do in the physical realm.

Just as Jesus entered this dimension, from that time warfaring against the devil, casting out demons, insightfully looking into human need, so He invites us to the same way of life. The Lord wants us to be baptized into a practical relationship of insight and perspective in the spiritual issues of life.

The record also reads, "The Holy Spirit came upon Him," and we have already observed the Holy Spirit fullness is to be expected at water baptism. But let us remember, *living* in the power of water baptism's dynamic means *abiding* in that fullness.

Concluding, remember the Father's approval: *"This is My Son, in whom I am well pleased."*

Was this important to Jesus? Imagine with me. Why would the Father have spoken those words if they were not expressing something that would be confirming and affirming to His own Son? I suppose someone might object, "There is *no way* Jesus needed to be affirmed!" But wait, dear friend, don't overlook the reality of His humanness. He came, taking on the same *feelings* that we have, and even though He lived in absolute sinlessness, He also knows what it means to desire a Father's approval.

You and I do too.

And as you and I accept the discipline of baptism—both by *being* baptized and *living* as one baptized—the same joyous realization will be ours as well. It's the portion of obedient sons and daughters, and you'll sense it, as His words resound in your soul: *"I'm pleased with you."*

Chapter Twelve

The Resources of the Lord's Table

Turning from the sacrament of baptism, let's think together about the sacrament of the Lord's Table, which is often called the "Eucharist," "Mass," or "Communion"—different terms being used in different traditions. As with water baptism, this is a practice the Lord Jesus established, directing us to do it in remembrance of Him.

> For I received from the Lord that which I also delivered to you: that the Lord Jesus on the same night in which He was betrayed took bread; and when He had given thanks, He broke it and said, "Take, eat; this is My body which is broken for you; do this in remembrance of Me." In the same manner He also took the cup after supper, saying "This cup is the New Covenant in My blood. This do, as often as you drink it, in remembrance of Me." For as often as you eat this bread and drink this cup, you proclaim the Lord's death till He comes.
>
> (1 COR. 11:23-26)

He established no calendar for this practice. He simply said, "As often as you do it, remember Me." I have friends who partake of the Lord's Table daily as a part of their private devotions. Other traditions only observe it once a year—usually on Good Friday or on the occasion of the Hebrew Passover. And some Christians observe the Lord's Table every week. Our church partakes the first Sunday of every month and adds a few special seasonal occasions throughout the year.

While Jesus did not give specific direction as to frequency, He did say that He wanted His people to *regularly* return to the fountainhead of life—to His cross and His victory there. Why?

Remembering to "Remember"

One well-known entertainer, who happens to be a member of the congregation I serve, seemed to learn at least one reason "Why?" It happened this way.

By reason of his many travels and irregular schedule, he is often away on Sunday. But when he is home during the week, I might say to his credit, he'll be present at the midweek service. He is committed to assembling with other believers, as well as ministering to those with whom he fellowships.

One Sunday he commented, "I was so glad to be here for the Lord's Table." He said, "You know, Jack, I recently went through a time of real affliction, when suddenly, I realized it had been five months since I had been present at church on the first Sunday when we observe the Lord's Table."

That morning he received nourishment and strength, both spiritually and physically. He went on to testify of his sense of dynamic spiritual renewal centering on the refreshing which came to his whole being as a result of celebrating Communion, in "remembering to 'remember.' " There were very few calories in the small portion which was served. But the power and benefit available "at the Table" is not something that comes from human nutrients but comes from divine sustenance promised to us in the Word of God and linked to Communion.

When Jesus said, "Do this in remembrance of Me," He was not calling us to commiserate over either His suffering or our sin. He was calling us to commemorate His announcement: "It is finished!" And in His triumph over all sin, death, and hell, He's bringing us to the reminder, "This is for you and it's for you today." Never forget it! Regularly come back to the cross, to rejoice in and to freshly receive Christ's victory!

It's a good way to begin new seasons of your life. Have periodic participation of the Lord's Table in your home, with members of your family. You could lead it, or invite others to participate in its presentation. Of course, this is not to suggest nonattendance at church, or the superimposing of a layman's role of ministering Communion as rendering unnecessary the pastoral-elder ministry of the church. But let home celebrations of "the Table" *complement* the regular practice in our churches; doing this *not* as a substitute for body-life, but as a means to apply the power of the sacrament in our homes.

With what understanding ought we to approach the Lord's Table? Jesus shows us on the occasion of the Last Supper, when He gave this instruction, Matthew 26:26-29:

> And as they were eating, Jesus took bread, blessed it and broke it, and gave it to the disciples and said, "Take, eat; this is My body." Then He took the cup, and gave thanks, and gave it to them, saying "Drink from it, all of you. For this is My blood of the New Covenant, which is shed for many for the remission of sins. But I say to you, I will not drink of this fruit of the vine from now on until that day when I drink it new with you in My Father's kingdom." (See parallel passages in Mark 14 and Luke 22.)

Having taken the bread and the cup and partaken together, there was from that point a movement toward Calvary. He then enacted in His death what He was prophesying at the Last Supper.

The remembrance being summoned by the Apostle Paul to the Corinthians is in the light of Jesus' commandment, "Do this in remembrance of Me."

> For I have received from the Lord that which I also delivered to you: that the Lord Jesus on the same night in which He was betrayed took bread; and when He had given thanks, He broke it and said, "Take, eat; this is My body which is broken for you; do this in remembrance of Me." In the same manner He also took the cup after supper, saying, "This cup is the New Covenant in My blood. This do, as often as you drink it, in remembrance of Me." For as often as you eat this bread and drink this cup, you proclaim the Lord's death till He comes.
>
> (1 COR. 11:23-26)

This passage is the most elaborate in the New Testament in showing how to apply the practice of the Lord's Supper. Focusing this text, I'd like for us to consider this sacrament and its beauty as well as dynamic in our living. There are five points which unfold certain realities related to our observation of the Lord's Table.

First, It's a Celebration of Victory

Revelation 12:11 says,

> They overcame him by the blood of the Lamb and by the word of their testimony, and they did not love their lives to the death.

This proclamation notes a dominion that is assured to the church. We will triumph over the powers of darkness in the last days' struggle, and victory is related to the abiding testimony of the blood of Jesus. Every time I take the cup of the Lord's Table in my hands, I am reminded it is intended to be the celebration of not only the victory *won,* but a victory *now* available. The victory that was accomplished in Jesus' words, *"It is finished!"*—that our salvation is complete, our sins are forgiven, we're justified by His death. It's a declaration Jesus wants us to never forget and that victory applies to every confrontation with flesh or devil we may face today. Knowing we *have* and we *can* overcome by the blood of the Lamb, carry that understanding when you give *thanks* at the Lord's Table.

The meaning of the word *eucharisteo* (the Greek verb from which Eucharist is derived) is "I thank." It's the central focus of our response, to be praiseful in a tone of victory. As we gather in celebration at the Lord's Table, the quality of your praise and thanks should be proportionate to Calvary's victory. Remembrance at the Lord's Table is to be one of feasting and celebrating. That's the reverent and praiseful style appropriate in the light of "It is finished!"

Second, It's a Proclamation of Redemption

> For as often as you eat this bread and drink this cup, you proclaim the Lord's death till He comes. . . . "I will not drink of this fruit of the vine from now on until that day when I drink it new with you in My Father's kingdom."
>
> (1 COR. 11:26; MATT. 26:29)

The Lord's Table proclaims not only the redemption that's been *accomplished,* but the redemption we *anticipate* at His return! It was Jesus' command that when we begin to see certain things coming to pass in our world, very much as they are now, that we lift up our heads, because our redemption draws near (Luke 21:28).

In this spirit, the Bible says that every time you and I partake of the Lord's cup, we're making a *preachment* (the word "proclaim" literally could be translated that way). Ours is a message of a Savior who not only is coming again, but who *right now* is available to save all who will receive the Good News of His death, resurrection, and salvation.

When we make the proclamation of redemption around the Table today, we are *sharing* the redemption He's given. "Communion" is from the word, *koinonia,* which emphasizes that in celebrating "Communion," we are mutually sharing in a *quality* of redemptive life which was secured at the cross. In 1 Corinthians 10:16, Paul said,

> The cup of blessing which we bless, is it not the communion of the blood of Christ? The bread which we break, is it not the communion of the body of Christ?

Our present victory over the powers of darkness—our anticipation of the joy of His coming—should bring high praise for such redemptive *glory!* Forgive me, please . . . and I hope it doesn't seem irreverent to anyone; but when I think about all of this— redemption past, present, and to come—I want to take the cup of the Lord's Table and say, *"Jesus, I'll drink to that! Hallelujah!"* This is the spirit of faith, celebration, and proclamation He wants us to experience together with Him at His Table—regularly.

Third, It's a Declaration of Dependence

Matthew, Mark, and Luke connect their teaching on the Lord's Table to the Last Supper, the night before Jesus was crucified. John 6 is a parallel teaching in the New Testament Gospels and is connected to an earlier season of Jesus' ministry in Galilee, after He fed the 5,000, and then met inquiries at another location. As the people congregated, recognizing Him, and hoping for another feast, He said, "You're not coming because you want what I have to minister. You're coming because you saw a miracle that filled your stomachs" (see John 6:26).

He challenged them with the issue of discipleship, beginning with a parallel—an analogy which became so vivid that it puzzled many onlookers and listeners. Many of the crowd left. Here's what He said: "You have to eat My body, and you have to drink My blood or you'll have no life in you" (John 6:53). It sounded to them as though He were introducing some bizarre form of cannibalism.

Jesus didn't bother to correct those who simply wanted "miracle loaves," but His words sought to comb the crowd to find those willing to learn a real relationship with Him.

When so many of the people left, some of His disciples said, "Lord, this is a very hard thing You've said" (v. 60). He answered, "Listen, the words that I'm speaking, they are spirit, and they are life" (see John 6:63). Listen again. Do you hear Him? He's saying, "I'm speaking of a *spiritual* truth. You *do* need to drink My blood in its *spiritual* power; you *do* need to eat My body for its *spiritual* nourishment!" To illustrate, consider how a person who is seriously anemic may need periodic blood transfusions to retain strength and health. Similarly, by partaking of the Lord's Table, we receive transfusions of His holy power through the pure dynamic of the blood of Jesus Christ—power to conquer sin in any way it seeks to dominate our lives.

The Israelites' deliverance from Egypt is another illustration of the Lord's Table. They took the blood of a lamb and put it on the doorway, but *then* they ate the flesh of the sacrifice in order to gain strength for the coming journey. So when Jesus, the Lamb of God, says, "Come and remember Me, and take of My body—this bread," He's saying, "be nourished and be strengthened for the journey ahead." As people who, like Israel, *are being* delivered (2 Cor. 1:10), we need strength for the road. Thus, we come to the Lord's Table in acknowledged dependence, to draw on God-ordained resources in Christ.

Fourth, It's a Time for Self-examination

In 1 Corinthians 11:27-34, the Apostle Paul underscores this need.

> Therefore whoever eats this bread or drinks this cup of the Lord in an unworthy manner will be guilty of the body and blood of the Lord. But let a man examine himself, and so let him eat of that bread and drink of that cup. For he who eats

and drinks in an unworthy manner eats and drinks judgment to himself, not discerning the Lord's body. For this reason many are weak and sick among you, and many sleep. For if we would judge ourselves, we would not be judged. But when we are judged, we are chastened by the Lord, that we may not be condemned with the world. Therefore, my brethren, when you come together to eat, wait for one another. But if anyone is hungry, let him eat at home, lest you come together for judgment. And the rest I will set in order when I come.

Dokimazo is the Greek verb used (v. 28, examine), a word descriptive of "running a test." In other words, the Word says, "At 'the Table,' " *test* your own heart toward the Lord and toward one another. What are your attitudes?

Remember earlier in this same book, how Paul was troubled over people within the congregation who had great stress between one another? He was concerned about people who were living with a reckless or indifferent attitude toward the sin of division and of lovelessness. In the words above, the truth resounds in such a way, we might apply the appeal this way:

When you come to the Table, take that occasion to examine yourself to see if there's division between you and members of the congregation. You can't take of the *Lord's* body, when your heart is divided toward others *in* your local "body," for whom Jesus allowed Himself to be broken! Don't come to the Table with such division or passive attitudes toward this or any other sin. It's *this very exercise* that commemorates Jesus' death for your sins, so receive His enablement to be *free* from them.

Hear it, loved one. Communion — the sacrament of the Lord's Supper — is a time to examine our relationship with God and our relationship with one another.

- We're coming to the Table of forgiveness, so we cannot be unforgiving.

- We're coming to the Table of cleansing, so we confess uncleanness in ourselves.

The significance of this heart preparation at the Lord's Table is distinctly important, but here's a reverse side of the "examine yourselves" truth that has been sorely distorted.

Have you ever heard it suggested that you ought not come to the Lord's Table because you've stumbled or sinned during the past week or month? In other words: "If you've failed the Lord of recent date, you'd perhaps better consider whether or not it's safe for you to come to the Lord's Table."

This "warning" is usually argued on the basis of verses 29-30: "[They partook] in an unworthy manner. . . . For this reason many are weak and sick among you, and many sleep." Through misinterpretation, the suggestion has often been made that God struck them dead; that "unworthy partaking" was the action of believers who came to the Lord's Table, even though they had recently sinned in some way. The idea conveyed is that thereby they invoked God's curse on them. And when such "teaching" prevails, fear and intimidation follow.

Worse, there are circles of Christian communion where the Lord's Table is used as a disciplinary device. For example: "Because you have failed, we won't let you observe Communion for three months (or six months, or a year) until you verify your holiness."

Now, it's not my business to administrate other peoples' tradition, but it is my business to handle the Word of God; and I want to challenge such abuse of the truth regarding, "Let a man examine himself."

The Word of God nowhere gives the directive that denied access to the Communion Table is a means for applying corrective discipline. To say to the person, "You can't come to the Lord's Table because you've sinned," is equivalent to saying to a starving man: "You can't eat any food until you get over your malnutrition." It's a ridiculous and counterproductive proposition.

We are called to come to *His* Table — *not man's* — to receive forgiveness for our failures. We are called to come to *this* Table to receive forgiveness, nourishment, and power for the practical living in Christ! And since it's *His* Table, His Word should govern who is allowed and who isn't, and Jesus says:

All that the Father gives Me will come to Me, and the one who comes to Me I will by no means cast out.

(JOHN 6:37)

Come to Me, all you who labor and are heavy laden, and I will give you rest.

(MATT. 11:28)

Fifth, It's a Provision of Healing

Now, if "to partake unworthily" *doesn't* mean we are to reflect on our unworthiness, what *do* these words in 1 Corinthians 11:29 mean?

First, let's settle an essential fact. If the question has to do with your or my "worthiness," then, there *isn't* any question! We *are* unworthy. Always.

None of us has ever been worthy of anything God has *ever* done for us! So, since this is true, what *is* Paul saying in exhorting us to "come to the Table in a *worthy* manner not an unworthy one"?

The answer is in seeing the meaning of "worthy" as it occurs here. The word translated "worthy" (*axios*, Greek) draws on the concept of *worthiness* as it had to do with *"weight"* not *"perfection."* For example, in ancient times, coins were made of substances the actual *weight* of the coin being what gave them their "worth." However, through frequent usage the coins lost small amounts of their weight or worth, and became reduced in value or "buying power."

Now, in this light, we can see that in this passage, the Apostle Paul is saying, "When you come to the Lord's Table, partake worthily"; that is bring *the full weight of your understanding and faith* to the Lord's Table.

Come to this moment recognizing the *full* weight and *full* worth of what Christ has done for you at Calvary. Come and partake of full forgiveness, full deliverance, and full healing!

For example, the Word not only tells us Jesus' blood was shed for our sins, but that His body was broken for our suffering and our afflictions. The Bible says, "He Himself took our infirmities and bore our sicknesses" (Matt. 8:17); so we're shown how healing is available to us, bequeathed among the many resources available to us through His cross. Thus, it becomes clear why Paul reflects on those who had come to the Table "unworthily" (i.e., without drawing on the full weight of resources available) and says, "For

99

this reason, many are weak and sick." He is *not* noting their lack of *perfection*, but their need for *participation;* for fully partaking in faith, receiving *all* Jesus has for them at His Table.

So as we round out our approach to the wealth and worth available to us at the Lord's Table, let's summarize these truths. And as His disciples, let's regularly enter into the

- Celebration of victory,
- Proclamation of redemption,
- Declaration of dependence,
- Examination of ourselves, and
- Provision of healing.

Invite the Holy Spirit to anoint your time of participation in this holy sacrament, so you may benefit *fully*. His Table is the central focus of our worship and the central resource for our walk in faith. The growing disciple will not only find he or she needs the spiritual nutrition afforded here, but the health, correction, and release from affliction which the sacrament of Communion intends us to receive.

Chapter Thirteen

Feeding on the Word of God

To begin, we all know and agree: The Word of God is absolutely essential to our personal lives, and it will only find its place there on the basis of our making a choice to read it daily and exercising that duty.

No argument.

But let me invite you to a brief tongue-in-cheek digression—a confession of sorts. It's a humorously registered complaint of a kind; a real look at the human frustration I've experienced (and I dare say I've *lots* of company) when trying to keep up with those "Through the Bible in a Year" reading plans. (Smile with me!) I recently "confessed" this problem to my congregation—like this.

I think I've read the first thirty chapters of Genesis 100 times! How many times have you "restarted"?

Of course, we all need a really good Bible reading program. Absolutely. But that "three chapters a day and five on Sunday" plan? I doubt it was even developed by a Christian! (Remember, "tongue-in-cheek.")

Anyone who's an *active* churchgoing Christian would *never* suggest you read *more* on a Sunday than other days. My heavens! You're already so busy with church and everything else for God that by the time you get home Sunday night, you're glad to get *anything* read before you collapse! The whole day's been "shot to heaven"! (Stay with me, please.)

"Well, I'm going to read through the Bible this year," I say with New Year's dedication, and I *did!* That is "did" manage to complete my three chapters on January 1; a monument to spiritual discipline, seeing I was bleary-eyed from football games by the time I got ready for pre-bedtime reading. (Not to mention I was *doubly exhausted* due to my short-night's rest after faithful participation in my congregation's New Year's Eve midnight Communion service!)

But I stuck with it, and I chalked up three more chapters the next day. Only 363 days to go (including fifty-two Sundays of five per day) and I'm *home!* However, things *vary* from day to day—at least with me. How about you?

Day three, I wake up late. My body's starting to reel from the accumulated impact of two weeks of holiday eating up one side of the table and down the other. So I only read two chapters that day: "I'll catch up tomorrow," I promise myself. But what really happens? Four chapters the next day? Nope, this turns out to be *another* two-chapter day by reason of a late wake-up, but I still feel reasonably successful: Only two chapters behind, but that's OK, "I'll do five tomorrow." Except, then I remember—tomorrow is Sunday! Now, it'll take seven to catch up.

Now it's Sunday night. What a great day with God and His people! Loaded with the Word and fellowship. Tired. "Well, Lord, forgive me, please. I was so busy today, could I just read three chapters? That's as many as most days, God. OK?"

It's wild, brother! You *should* be feeling pretty good about life. You've read the Bible *every* day, read no less than *two* chapters any day, but here you are starting the second new week of the year and feeling semi-condemned because you're already four chapters behind!

You know how it goes, don't you? C'mon! It's happened to you sometime!

By the time you arrive at January 20th, you look at your reading chart—*"I'm seventeen chapters behind!"* Guilt territory. Even though you've read the Bible *every day,* "the plan" still has you feeling like a failure. So you decide, "OK, this Saturday I'll catch up. I'll read the seventeen chapters." But, of course, you have to make it *twenty,* because there are three chapters for *that* day too.

You start early and give it your best. But while reading, you become fascinated with a side study—*using* your concordance, *searching* the Word, enjoying its wealth! And time runs out, so it turns out you *only* read fifteen chapters.

Well, fifteen chapters in one day should be one of the "triumph" days of your life, right! "But I'm still five chapters behind . . ." and *the next day's Sunday!* ("Let's see, five plus five chapters equals ten, and I'll be home late from a day of worship and" . . . and so it goes.)

Well, forgive my amusement with my own frustrating efforts at "Through the Bible in a Year." I don't know if I've made a recitation of your experience or not, but I've related this to people enough times to find it's something of a "syndrome of the sincere."

Please be sure you understand that my humorous elaboration of personal frustration certainly isn't to discourage regular Bible reading. *Never!* But I do want to *en*courage the *dis*couraged.

I certainly *do* believe that it's a marvelous and worthy goal to read through the Bible every year, and I move close to, if not completely fulfilling that goal most every year. But I want to lift up your heart to be assured: we *all* have difficulty keeping a perfect pace, and I don't think *guilt* should ever become added baggage to the already demanding (and appropriate) goal of daily reading of God's Word.

As we look into the place of the Word in our private devotional life, may I share with you a simple, personal guideline that I have found? It's worked for decades in my Christian walk, and I've recommended it to thousands. How I keep from failing to read God's Word every day: I simply *don't turn out the light.* That's right. I've connected that last action of the day to becoming "impossible" without reading the Word. It's as though I'm saying, "This light doesn't *go out* until This Light goes *in!*"

Of course, you may employ other means, patterns, reminders, and times. Many read the Word first thing in the morning, and I'm often there with them too. But at a personal dimension, I found that in the morning I often was too tempted to substitute devotional *reading* of the Word for devotional *time* in prayer with the Lord. So I usually read my Bible in the evening.

Nonetheless, the issue is that we establish the *habit.* The time and the coverage is yours to establish. And whatever difficulty you may have in becoming a *faithful* Bible reader, press forward. It's a *most essential* discipline to master, and we need to establish *at least* the habit of reading chapters (plural) almost every day.

Values in Bible Reading Habit

Look very seriously with me, will you, at *why* we need the Word of
God in our lives. You may want to jot down these key principles in
the blank front or back page of your Bible, as a reference point
and reminder that God's Word is essential to *everything* in our
lives—every *issue* of life is covered by truth and wisdom contained
in this precious Book.

1. *God's Word Ensures Certainty about Your Path.*
Psalm 119:6—*"Then I would not be ashamed, when I look into all Your
commandments."*

The word "ashamed" as used here literally means, I won't be
"embarrassed." In short, I'm *not* going to *come up short* when "I
have respect unto all Your Word, Lord." His Word will help
me avoid confusion and embarrassing stumbling around with my
life.

2. *God's Word Gives Direction about Your Path.*
Psalm 119:105—*"Your Word is a lamp to my feet and a light to my
path."*

Of course, simply giving place to the Word of God every day
is taking an oath of allegiance. "Lord, Your Word is foundational
and prior in all matters of my life." This acknowledgment brings
certain direction.

Proverbs 3:6—*"In all your ways acknowledge Him, and He shall
direct your paths."*

Notice too that the direction which comes from God's Word is
both immediately *at hand* as well as revealing that which is distant.
When the Bible says, "Your Word is a *lamp* and a *light*," the Hebrew words are the equivalent in today's technology to saying,
"You'll have a flashlight in one hand and a giant spotlight in the
other." Both aspects of my pathway come into view: *details* for
today and *discernment* for tomorrow.

3. *God's Word Gives Wisdom about Your Path.*
Psalm 19:7—*"The law of the Lord is perfect, converting the soul; the
testimony of the Lord is sure, making wise the simple."*

The word "simple" makes an honest reference to an "inexpe-
rienced" person, not a condescending slur as though the person
were being stupid or ignorant. Just as the Bible points the way to
wisdom, both for today's immediate situation and for the long-
range path we're to pursue, here the Word is promised as a resource to assure wisdom for things we face in which we have no
experience. This *doesn't* mean that every question we face finds an

immediate answer. It means *as I feed* on the Word, daily, the wisdom I need for living my life *will* distill in my soul. Let me elaborate.

I've learned that regular reading seldom gives me a "shot" of *perceived* wisdom each day. But I've found, nonetheless, the Holy Spirit has a way of causing me to *receive* wisdom as a *deposit;* not so much in phrases or words, but in the *elements* of wisdom, the *nutrients* of God's truth, flowing into my spirit. Then, when I need it, though I may not remember chapters and verses, the strength and wisdom needed will be available by reason of the spiritual resources *inside;* that which has accumulated through faithfulness to this spiritual habit.

Sometime back a friend of my mother's said to her: "Dolores, I feel so stupid when I study the Word of God. I just don't seem to remember anything at all."

Quite wisely, my mother said: "Lou, do you remember what you ate for breakfast on Tuesday, three weeks ago?"

She looked at her rather stunned and replied: "Well, no, I don't."

Mama explained: "It still supported and nourished you, didn't it?"

Get the point? Just keep reading the Bible. You may not remember everything, but *the Word is flowing into your spirit,* and as it does it's giving abiding strength to sustain as you simply obey—and read.

Jesus said, "Man shall not live by bread alone, but by every word that proceeds from the mouth of God" (Matt. 4:4). *There* is your daily bread! We can expect strength today, not only because of today's reading, but there's also a component of strength by reason of what we "ate" Tuesday, three weeks ago, when we fed on the Word of God!

4. *God's Word Ensures Our Victory in Our Pathway.*
Joshua 1:8— *"This Book of the Law shall not depart from your mouth, but you shall meditate in it day and night, that you may observe to do according to all that is written in it. For then you will make your way prosperous, and then you will have good success."*

Praise the Lord!

Listen, there's something about giving place to the Word of God that ensures not only today's nourishment but our *success!*

Joshua had just taken over the leadership reins of responsibility from Moses, following the latter's death. Can you imagine the impossible challenge this was to his viewpoint? But God gave Joshua a promise of His *presence* and His *purpose*—linking them to His *precepts*.

The promise of *success*, through God's promised presence and unfolding purpose being realized in our life, is offered today on the same terms as to Joshua. Keep the Word in your mind, in your heart, and on your lips! The Word *works*—richly and mightily:

- Let the word of Christ dwell in you richly in all wisdom. . . . according to His working which works in me mightily.

(COL. 3:16; 1:29)

- So the word of the Lord grew mightily and prevailed.

(ACTS 19:20)

5. *God's Word Keeps Us Pure in Our Path.*

Psalm 119:9—*"How can a young man cleanse his way? By taking heed according to Your Word."*

Psalm 119:11—*"Your Word I have hidden in my heart, that I might not sin against You."*

Another value of reading the Bible is the power of the Word to keep us pure. It's not just a spotlight which shines outward and gives direction, it's a searchlight which shines inward—prompting, correcting, adjusting, and instructing me. Jesus prayed, "Father, sanctify them by Your truth, *Your Word is truth*" (John 17:17). He also declared, "And you shall know the truth, and the truth shall make you free" (John 8:32). God's Word not only purifies *from* sin, it is a preventative *against* sin!

In every instance when Jesus faced temptation in the wilderness, as Satan came not only to taunt but to seek to destroy Him, Jesus responded to every thrust of the Adversary's lies with a counterthrust of the sword of the Spirit, the truth of the Word of God.

D.L. Moody said of God's Word, "This Book will keep you from sin, or sin will keep you from this Book." So, today, we have the Bible not only as a *"Resource Book"* to give certainty, direction, wisdom, and victory, but we have it as a *"Resistance Book"* for keeping us pure.

6. *God's Word Keeps Us Alert to the Times.*

First John 3:3—*"And everyone who has this hope in Him purifies himself, just as He is pure."*

The Scriptures sometime glare with flashing warning signs

showing the nature of our times, and signaling us to stay readied for Jesus Christ's return. With our eyes on the Lord—"loving His appearing"—the Word is key to keeping us sensitive; keeping us from falling asleep as the darkening hour and spirit of our age could lull us into carnal sleepiness or sensual indulgence. The Word will keep us walking a pure path and maintaining an alert stance; strong and ready to do battle in the name of the Lord.

The promise of Jesus' soon return is real! And steadfast, daily, heartwarming, self-examining, faith-building, soul-purifying *reading* is a key to "keeping ready." Luke 21:32-36,

> Assuredly, I say to you, this generation will by no means pass away till all things are fulfilled. Heaven and earth will pass away, but My words will by no means pass away. But take heed to yourselves, lest your hearts be weighed down with carousing, drunkenness, and cares of this life, and that Day come on you unexpectedly. For it will come as a snare on all those who dwell on the face of the whole earth. Watch therefore, and pray always that you may be counted worthy to escape all these things that will come to pass, and to stand before the Son of Man.

7. *God's Word Is Our Shield of Faith.*
Romans 10:17—"*So then faith comes by hearing, and hearing by the Word of God.*"

Our faith is our fundamental means to resist the devil; the shield we use to withstand him. Faith defends against attack as an implement which is forged and fashioned in one way: by our "hearing" the Word of God.

But remember, fellow-learner. "Hearing" is not a passive, sit-in-church-once-weekly-and-you're-done proposition. Rather, to "hear" the Word is (1) to *feed* on it as a steadfast practice, and (2) to *heed* it as a sensitive "hearer."

Earlier, in chapter 9, we elaborated this kind of "hearing" as a foundational practice to *all* disciplines—hearing the "voice" of God. But the starting place for life-growing faith is in the *heeding to reading;* obeying His *leading unto feeding* as one of Jesus' sheep. That's what will bring fullness of faith and build us as victors— from a sheep to a soldier!

Feed and heed! That's our call to "this Resource above all resources," "the Standard by which everything is gauged, the

Foundational Footing for everywhere you may walk in life" — *the living, eternal, holy Word of God.*

Live *in* it.

Live *by* it.

Live *through* it.

Daily.

Chapter Fourteen

Maintaining Integrity of Heart

E very year at my birthday, I receive hundreds of cards, not only because I pastor a large congregation, but because of a tradition that's accidentally evolved. About twenty years ago, on the Sunday following my birthday, I read a couple of humorous cards I'd received. It was so enjoyed, I did the same thing next year, and without realizing it a tradition was born. And so it is that today, a host of people in our congregation watch the racks all year looking for the funniest card they can find, hoping their card might be read! Each birthday is loaded with laughter for me, and the Sunday following for the congregation.

One card I recently received read,

> Hear you're telling your *real* age.
> What honesty,
> What humility,
> What integrity . . .
> (turning to the inside)
> *What a memory!*

There was a virtual explosion of laughter when I read that one. But let me turn from that "lighter" mention of "integrity" as a point of beginning, and take you to a weightier mention of one subject for study.

I would like to deal with "integrity of heart" and the maintenance of such a heart as a basic discipline of Christian living. The Bible says that it is out of our hearts that *all* the issues of life are distilled and resolved (Prov. 4:23). In its essence, that truth opens a promise of great significance and hope to a disciple. It says, if I can learn to be absolutely, totally, completely, and unreservedly *honest to God* — up front with every dealing of His Spirit in my heart, and respondent to His promptings and submitting to His corrections — there is immeasurable joy to be found and immeasurable sorrow I'll be spared.

Further, immeasurable blessings will be released to others through the channel of a heart that keeps unpolluted and available to the Holy Spirit's pure grace-workings! So this study deals with the matter of our openness and transparency before God and we start by looking at this idea — Integrity. It first appears in Genesis 20:1-6, in an incident in Abraham's life.

> And Abraham journeyed from there to the South, and dwelt between Kadesh and Shur, and sojourned in Gerar. Now Abraham said of Sarah his wife, "She is my sister." And Abimelech king of Gerar sent and took Sarah.
>
> But God came to Abimelech in a dream by night, and said to him, "Indeed you are a dead man because of the woman whom you have taken, for she is a man's wife."
>
> But Abimelech had not come near her; and he said, "Lord, will You slay a righteous nation also? Did he not say to me, 'She is my sister'? And she, even she herself said, 'He is my brother.' In the integrity of my heart and innocence of my hands I have done this."
>
> And God said to him in a dream, "Yes, I know that you did this in the integrity of your heart. For I also withheld you from sinning against Me; therefore I did not let you touch her."
>
> (GEN. 20:1-6)

The background to this episode centers on an agreement Sarah and Abraham had made years before. By reason of her beauty, he had asked that if, in their nomadic travels, they were ever to come to the place where his life would be jeopardized because a regional king might think to kill Abraham in order to take Sarah to add to his harem, in such circumstances, they would claim *not* to be husband and wife. It certainly sounds peculiar today, but their agreement, while less than faith-filled, was somewhat more understandable given the context of that ancient culture.

In any case, such a confrontation had happened, and Abraham had said, "She is my sister." Now, since Sarah agreed, Abimelech, king of Gerar, was about to take her for himself.

But *God* steps in!

In this gracious action of divine intervention to protect Sarah and Abraham from their foolishness and lack of faith, the Lord comes to Abimelech in a midnight visitation.

Notice how quickly God gets his attention!

"You're a dead man!"

Immediately, Abimelech protests the charge, appealing to his innocence of intent to take another man's wife, and he appeals to God with these words: *"I did this in the integrity of my heart."*

Look at that exchange again:

God says, "You're a dead man . . . because!" Then, in response, Abimelech replies, "But I was acting in *integrity*." (In other words, "I didn't get in this situation by means of a calculated plan for evil.") This brings us to the point, as God says, (and listen closely now), *"I know. That's why I'm here to correct you."*

An Introduction to Integrity

It's important for us to recognize this text as more than a story. We're being introduced to the principle of *integrity of heart,* a truth being dramatized for us in a way that establishes the concept in the Word of God.

There's a simple principle of Bible study, usually called, "the law of first usage": It's impressively consistent, in that it simply notes that the *first* time you encounter an idea or principle in the Bible, you will generally find "first usage" sets the pace for the idea in God's Word; and that the concept will be consistent throughout the Scriptures as it is found in its first occurrence.

This is the first time the word, "integrity," actually occurs in the Bible, and the incident is freighted with insight. It begins with an illustration of how all of us are vulnerable to confusion, to mistakes, to being misled, or to being subjected to the possible victimization of someone else's manipulations. Like Abimelech, without our awareness and completely outside our intent or cooperation, we become trapped.

But here, the Bible discloses a life principle: God is prepared to guard and deliver an honest heart—a heart of integrity; to defend that heart against the possibility of its own delusion. This powerful truth holds the promise for each of us keeping our life "on-line" amid the swirling seas of surrounding confusion everywhere present in our world. Through the simple but demanding discipline of my constantly living "honest to God"—walking in "integrity of heart"—God reveals He will protect and defend me from devices of evil or detours of self-confusion.

Integrity of heart is further understood as we look at other uses of this word in the Scriptures, as well as by examining this word's meaning.

First, with the Genesis passage, look at Psalm 25:21: *"Let integrity and uprightness preserve me, for I wait for You."*

At this time in his life, David's kingdom had realized broadened boundaries to such a degree that he had no way to adequately defend the entirety of its perimeter. In these words, he shows he's made a choice, as though saying, "Lord, there aren't enough troops to guard every border, so I'm asking, *'Let my integrity of heart before You become my defense.'* " The implication of this request would create an agreement something like this:

> *David:*
> Lord, I'm going to walk before You in absolute obedience; to *do* what I perceive to be Your will, and to *respond* to Your dealings with my heart. And then, in exchange, Lord, I ask You to so lead me, in the context of my honesty of heart before You, that I will be guided by Your providence, wisdom, and protection that I will remain wise in administrating my borders; kept by *Your* counsels as my defense against my enemies.

The Lord did that during David's lifetime—at every point. As long as David walked in "integrity of heart," he was preserved. When he violated it, he not only stumbled but his kingdom boundaries were penetrated.

In contrast, and furthering our study, look at Solomon, David's son. There is a severe lesson here for our learning.

In 1 Kings, 9:3-5, we are told how Solomon prayed at the time the temple was dedicated. He humbly opened himself to the Lord in a beautiful way, revealing the same spirit and attitude of his father David. He asked for God to perpetuate his kingdom, much the same as David had. In response to his prayer, the Lord establishes the terms; the same terms David had made: "If you walk . . . in integrity of heart [in the way your father David did] . . . then I will establish the throne of your kingdom over Israel forever."

With that promise of possible "perpetuation," we see integrity now keyed to three ideas: *prevention, preservation, perpetuation.*

- Abimelech was *prevented* from becoming "entangled" because he walked in integrity of heart.

- David's boundaries were *preserved* as long as he retained integrity of heart.

- Solomon was promised the *perpetuation* of a kingdom, if he maintained integrity of heart.

Even though Solomon's violations eventually lost the power and the blessing in God's promise, God *will preserve* us—you and me! He *will prevent* us from evil involvements which could cause us to stumble. He *will perpetuate* the good blessings He intends for us. But the clear condition for all this is that we maintain "integrity of heart."

What do we mean by this word . . . this phrase?

"Whole" of Understanding

In our language, "integrity" is a word related to a number of other familiar ones, terms which help us see the fuller dimension of its implications. "Integrity" is built from the root idea in our English word, *integer.* Now, as most of us learned in early math, an "integer," is a *whole number,* as in 1, 2, 3, 4—that is, *whole* numbers as opposed to fractions; that's *whole,* as in the idea of completeness or entirety of a thing or a number.

Similarly we find the idea of such "whole-ness" in such words as *integration* (fitting together ideas or units, as opposed to fragmentation) or in *dis*integration (the opposite, the fragmenting of what was once complete or together). Both *integer* (whole numbers) and *integration* (parts being made a whole) illustrate the concept inherent in "integrity."

In relating this word to a human being, it describes uncompromised character, an unjaded soul, an unsullied heart, an undivided mind. It requires the maintenance of one's heart in *entirety* before the Lord, as David said: "Unite my heart to fear Your name" (Ps. 86:11). Those words say, "God, draw the strands of my heart so firmly and in such reverence before Your throne, that I will be kept *wholly* and *entirely aligned* with You."

Wholeness or integrity of heart is also expressed in Psalm 119:10: "With my whole heart I have sought You; oh, let me not wander from Your commandments!" Here again, the psalmist is crying out, "Lord, don't let me come apart at the seams through my parceling out segments of my heart, through letting portions become 'sliced off' when I'm tempted to allow myself to yield to circumstances which conspire to segment my attitude. I want my *heart,* my *all,* to be kept *whole* and thereby kept *holy* before You, O Lord." Can you hear the spirit of this word, loved one? Wholeness of the heart: entirety!

What we've seen in the English is precisely the concept in the Hebrew word, *tom,* and in the New Testament counterpart, *eirene,* the word for "peace."

Colossians 3:15 says, "And let the peace of God rule in your hearts." The words apply the same spirit as found in the summons of Ephesians 4:30: "And do not grieve the Holy Spirit of God, by whom you were sealed for the day of redemption." These texts combine to show how the Holy Spirit will signal us at any time we "grieve" Him, by starting to fragment or segment parts of our heart rather than keeping it *all entirely* under God's rule.

Similarly, the mind or thoughts can be divided through doubt or self-justifying rationalizations when we're tempted to compromise or sin. But being honest to God when He deals with your *heart* observes a fundamental discipline that will *prevent* us from confusion, *preserve* us against the enemy's encroachment, and *perpetuate* us in God's blessing.

Diplomacy or Dependence?

A summary evidence of what happens when integrity is gradually eroded is seen in what happened to Solomon. Remember how the Lord had promised, "Solomon, if you will walk in integrity of heart as your father David did, I will perpetuate your kingdom." Did he? Could God keep His promise—a promise contingent upon the maintenance of integrity of heart? Look what happened.

Before his son's rule, during his office as king, David had said, "Lord, I don't have enough troops to guard all our borders. I will walk in integrity of heart and trust You to be my Defender." But in contrast, see what Solomon did.

Solomon began negotiating treaties with neighboring nations. Rather than his dependency being the Lord, as he walked in humility before Him, Solomon began to find his defense by means of political gamesmanship, his own skill at manipulating people. He began negotiating treaties, and every time he struck a treaty with a nearby nation—trying to "cover his borders"—he married a princess from that nation. Then, with each new princess, a new pagan god came to Jerusalem and was enshrined in honor of the treaty. With time, such shrines filled Jerusalem, eventually compromising the integrity of the worship of the one true God, and bringing decay to the kingdom.

The same thing can happen to you or me today.

Once you or I begin trying to manipulate *our* situations, once we begin trying to negotiate with human wisdom or reasoning, rather than depending on the Lord being our defender, our leader, our guide, we will inevitably end with our heart splintered in fragments as integrity of heart has been sacrificed on the altar of human expediency. How can we guard against that loss?

One day, as I was studying this word "integrity" in the Hebrew text, not long after this concept struck my heart as a mandated priority for a disciple's walk with God, I was astounded by a discovery while looking up the occurrences of the word *tom* (integrity) in a Hebrew concordance, I encountered the plural of the word is *Thummim*. Interestingly enough, this word is retained in its Hebrew form in most English translations.

For example, in Exodus 28:15-30, reading about the high priest's breastplate, verse 30 notes,

> And you shall put in the breastplate of judgment the Urim and the Thummim, and they shall be over Aaron's heart when he goes in before the Lord. So Aaron shall bear the judgment of the children of Israel over his heart before the Lord continually.

Notice, the "Urim and Thummim" were to be "over his heart before the Lord continually." How striking a picture! What can it depict?

To this day, no one knows what the "Urim and the Thummim" actually were. Rabbinical literature doesn't specify it, but what we do know is that *Urim* means *"lights"* and *Thummim* means *"completenesses, perfections, or wholenesses."*

We also have been given an idea as to how they were used. Keil and Delitzsch explain in their commentary on Exodus (pp. 198–99), exactly what was being done:

> What the *Urim* and *Thummim* really were, cannot be determined with certainty, either from the names themselves, or from any other circumstances connected with them. . . . This expresses with tolerable accuracy. . . . Illumination and completion. . . . Now, if we refer to Num. 27:21, where Joshua as the commander of the nation is instructed to go to the high priest Eleazar, that the latter may inquire before Jehovah, through the right of Urim, how the whole congregation should walk and act, we can draw no other conclusion, than that the Urim and Thummim are to be regarded as a certain medium, given by the Lord to His people, through which, whenever the congregation required divine illumination to guide its actions, that illumination was guaranteed. . . . Consequently the Urim and Thummim did not represent the illumination and right of Israel, but were . . . a pledge that the Lord would maintain the rights of His people, and give them through the high priest the illumination requisite for their protection. Aaron was to bear the children of Israel upon his heart, in the precious stones to be worn upon his breast with the names of the twelve tribes. The heart, according to the biblical view, is the centre of the spiritual life, — not merely of the willing, desiring, thinking life, but of the emotional life, as the seat of the feelings and affections (see *Delitzsch bibl. Psychologie*, pp. 203 sqq.). Hence to bear upon the heart does not merely mean to bear in mind, but denotes "personal intertwining with the life of another. . . . "

Thus we see the Urim and Thummim were consulted whenever the high priest needed to go before the Lord and ask, "What is Israel to do in this situation?" And we're taught the inescapable relationship between this guidance and the *heart* of the priest.

How was the Urim and Thummim consulted?

It is said that in doing this, the priest would go into the holy place and stand before (but outside) the curtain of the Holy of Holies, which only could be entered once a year. And there, the high priest would humbly inquire of the Lord God of Israel, "What should we do, Lord? What is Your will for us?"

See it, please. The high priest had gone past the brazen altar in the outer court, past the laver into the holy place, past the table of showbread, past the lampstand, and had worshiped at the altar of incense. Now standing in worship before the Holy of Holies, by the Urim and the Thummim, an answer was given.

What was it—light? Did a holy glow appear on the chest of the priest? What was the "completeness—the *Thummim*"?

While we don't know precisely, apparently the Lord was giving a "seal" by the radiant warmth of His presence and by a sense of "peace"—complete or *wholehearted* assurance—as to what was acceptable and what wasn't. If this kind of guidance was available to priests under the Old Covenant, what can this mean for us today?

Our understanding is enriched when we remember that under the New Covenant, God has made every one of us "priests" (Rev. 1:6). As such, we have been assigned prayer and worship ministries, but none of our responsibilities exceeds the stewardship we've been given in monitoring our own hearts before God. That's why Colossians 3:15 commands, "Let the peace of God rule in your hearts." Let His *peace*—the warm inner *glow* born of an uncompromised, unsegmented *wholeness*—be the arbiter, the umpire of our decisions, our situations, or our life's issues.

We aren't to negotiate by or with the flesh.

We aren't to try to work things out by our own wisdom.

Don't contrive or compromise.

The Holy Spirit will signal our hearts at needed times, with a very quiet inner sense—of either confirmation or correction. In *correcting*, a kind of "ping" may be sensed in your soul, and you'll know the Lord is "checking you."

I learned that phrase as a boy: "If the Lord *checks* you. . . ." I came to understand it to mean somewhat the same thing as when a person "checks" another in a chess match, *blocking* forward progress. So the Lord will "check" us when He knows we are moving or progressing forward in a direction He knows is wrong or unwise for us. We may not know why He deals as He does at times, and often we'll be tempted to push ahead anyway. But a wise, responsive heart of integrity will sensitively welcome His correction.

- You're engaged in conversation and suddenly realize you have turned a conversational corner which is about to compromise your honesty or purity. Let Him stop you when your heart signals that "ping" of correction.

- You're laying plans, and you sense the inner "stoplight" of the Holy Spirit. Immediately cease that direction in your planning, and trust that the Lord has a better plan for you.

- Perhaps you finished the plans. You *did* "sense" a signal but felt embarrassed to go back and say, "I really wasn't using wisdom. I need to change what I was going to do." But it's still not too late. Don't be unwilling to be honest with yourself and others. To fail to respond to God's "checking" or "blocking" of the situation will eventually cause frustration for everyone involved, so learn to respond quickly; in every situation say, "Lord, I want to be corrected and taught by You."

In sharing how integrity of heart was impressed upon me as a child, and has continued, I related the following incident in my book, *A Man's Integrity*, a study of how men can develop in godly character.

I Was about Eleven Years Old

When I was a boy, I was early introduced to a means my mother would use in dealing with each of us children—my brother, my sister, and me. Whenever Mama thought any of us might be tempted to be less than truthful because of the pressure of a situation where possible correction may follow an honest confession, she would take a precautionary step.

Instead of simply asking, "Did you do (such and such). . . ?" she would precede the question with a statement. This statement had a very sobering effect on me, because it so vividly evidenced the reality of my accountability to be truthful in the eyes of God. Mama would say, "I'm going to ask you a difficult question, Jack. But before I do, I want to say, I'm asking it 'in front of Jesus.' "

She wasn't playing games.

She wasn't threatening.

She wasn't using a religious ploy.

Rather, in our house we took the Lord seriously. Our home was a happy place to live, but we really believed in the genuine things about God's love, His kindness, His blessing, His salvation in Christ, and the beautiful truth of His Word. And when Mama would say, "In front of Jesus," a powerful image would come to my mind.

We all knew God is everywhere, all the time. But there was a unique sense of the immediacy of the Living Lord when those words were spoken. I could imagine Jesus seated on a throne immediately to my left as I stood face-to-face with my mother and prepared to hear whatever question she had.

A Visit to Dicky's House

I had come home from a friend's house one afternoon, having been most of the morning at Dicky's—a kid a few months older than I who lived across the street. We played together a great deal of the time, so there was no reason for anything unusual to be thought when I, an eleven-year-old boy, came home that day.

But I discovered the next morning as I was about to leave for school, that my mother had "felt" something about my return home that day.

I had just finished my breakfast and was about to leave the kitchen and get my school things so I could head out. But I was stopped before I left the room, when my mother turned from the kitchen sink, and while drying her hands said, "Jack—I want you to wait a minute. I need to talk with you."

Her voice had that tone which children recognize of their parents when the issue is sobering and the consequences might be undesirable. I stood there, nervously waiting for what she was going to say.

"Son, when you came home from Dicky's yesterday, I had a very strange feeling go through me." She paused, thoughtfully. "At first, I didn't know what to do about it; then, I prayed last night, and I believe the Lord showed me simply to do what I'm doing right now.

"Jack, I want to ask you what happened at Dicky's house yesterday. And I'm asking this—*in front of Jesus.*"

I was frozen to the floor. The moment was one of those crystalline ones which seems as though it could be shattered by a whisper. On the one hand, I *knew* what happened at Dicky's house and knew I didn't want anyone else to know. And on the other hand—there to my left—the throne of my Living Savior, Jesus Christ, was as real to me as though I were in heaven itself.

I began slowly . . . awkwardly . . . guiltily.

"Well, Mama," I said rather quietly and with hesitation. "When I was at Dicky's, after we'd been playing in the living room for a long time, he said to me, 'C'mon into my room a minute.'

"When he said that, he kinda laughed, and looked around to see if his mom or dad were anywhere they could hear. Right then I felt something bad was about to happen, but I went with him anyway.

"When we got to his room, he closed the door and then opened one of the drawers in the chest there. He reached way back and brought out a little tiny telescope."

I hesitated all the more, feeling the embarrassment of the confession I was about to make.

"But, Mama, it wasn't a telescope." I paused again. Waiting. Not wanting to go on. "Instead, Mama, when you looked into it, there was . . . a naked woman." My eyes were moist. I looked into the face of my mother, feeling ashamed.

"What did you do, Son?" she inquired.

"We laughed," I admitted.

"How did you feel then?"

"Mama," I said with sincerity, "I felt bad."

"Then, Son, What do you want to do now?"

I walked toward my mother, whose arms opened to me as I did, as I said, "I want to pray, Mama."

And we did.

And although that event took place over four decades ago, at its root is a truth that has always continued to be just as alive and present today as it was then. *I am living my life in front of Jesus.*

I'll never know how many things that morning's confrontation and confession may have saved me from in my yet-to-be-realized future as a teenager and young man. Just as surely as I don't really know "how many" of anything I do or have done may have contributed to some degree of fruitfulness in my life and ministry, as others have asked me to quantify human efforts.

But I do know this.

I know that there are no limits to what God can do *in* your life, what He can do *through* a life, and what He can grow *around* and *within* a life, when it's lived —*in front of Jesus.*

That's the place where integrity of heart will always be sustained. For our consciousness will be on Him, not on things. And with Jesus in view, all life, fruitfulness, and fulfillment are certain to be realized with time —however tempting or trying the path.

Let's live our lives out that way. In front of Jesus.

Chapter Fifteen

Abiding in the Fullness of the Spirit

I had just been seated on the platform, having introduced the guest speaker addressing our congregation. Before the guest had even said one word, the Lord had preached a sermon to me. The phrase whispered into my soul puzzled me, but also profoundly impressed me: *"Open to the spirit of enthusiasm."*

I knew it was prompting from the Lord, and I didn't argue with Him. But I must confess that I was surprised He would say *that* to me. Why? Because I think of "enthusiasm" as being superficial exuberance; people merely "whooping it up" into some kind of frenzy, akin to standing on the bleachers and screaming.

Now, I'm capable of that too, because I *am* quite a sports enthusiast. But I also knew something much deeper about the word, "enthusiasm," and it was that knowledge which sobered my response and stirred my expectancy.

"Enthusiasm" is derived from the Greek, *entheos*—that is, "God is in them." Thus, the idea of *enthusiasm,* historically and etymologically, has to do with a person being so full of God (or, in the pagan world, "the gods," or "the muses") that behavior is dominated by *Him* in a holy sense, or by *them* in a pagan or demonic sense. In short, *entheos* ("enthusiasm") makes a person dynamically or vibrantly alive with a resource from another realm than the natural.

As I thought through the "word" the Lord had whispered to my soul—"Open to the spirit of enthusiasm"—I knew He was seeking to address something of my own inclination toward reserve. I sensed that He was wanting me not to become so sedate in a "cool" response to Holy Spirit fullness that I overlooked the place, purpose, and desirability of the vibrant and the vital—the *expressive,* if you will. He wasn't issuing a call to *superficial* exuberance, but neither was He preempting the *expressively* exuberant.

Are you tempted to keep "being full of God" under a "cool control"? I'm inclined to believe that temptation to "maintain respectability" may be more dangerous than we might think. We are so surrounded by sophistication in our culture, that in our religious traditions and observances it becomes too easy a thing to somehow suppose that God equates our reserve with reverence—as though we were trying to impress Him—or worse, *others*—with our style.

But of course, God isn't impressed by either intellectual or emotional sophistry. And as for the society around us, it's all a matter of degree: how far will you go to "please the world mind"? We may feel we must pamper worldmindedness by, for example, "cooling" our praise in church. But inevitably, the flesh would have us cool our message, our convictions, our lifestyle as Christ's—completely. So before we too quickly dampen praise or forthright worshiping or witnessing, decide "how far toward cool" you think will ultimately satisfy the world.

Of course God is neither impressed by the raucous nor the reserved. And a call to "enthusiasm" might well be thoughtfully heeded, because it isn't a call to "stylized" fanaticism, as though there were some special merit in being rowdy or noisy for its own sake. If neither the fanatical nor the opposite (the sophisticate's mild-mannered, near-snobbishness of religious reticence) is impressive to God, what might I need to "open to"?

My sense of God's answer to my asking that question pointed to my need to learn a readiness to make myself fully open to the "spirit of enthusiasm"—in readily *allowing*, indeed *welcoming* the overflow, the vibrancy, the warmth and expressiveness of Holy Spirit fullness to find release in and through me.

As a result of that evening's platform encounter, I was drawn to John 7:37-39:

> On the last day, that great day of the feast, Jesus stood and cried out, saying, "If anyone thirsts, let him come to Me and drink. He who believes in Me, as the Scripture has said, out of his heart will flow rivers of living water." But this He spoke concerning the Spirit, whom those believing in Him would receive; for the Holy Spirit was not yet given, because Jesus was not yet glorified.

John explains the context in which the incident occurs, showing that Jesus is referring to something which would happen a considerable time later. This event—the celebration of the Feast of Tabernacles—took place about six months before the crucifixion of Jesus.

In ancient Israel this feast was the annual commemoration of the Israelites' forty-year journey through the wilderness. The last day climaxed a week of celebration—a week of high feasting. Can you imagine how it was in those days? Tents and little shelters built from branches housed the families which came from all around Israel. They didn't erect the tents and shelters simply as a traditional ceremony, but in this early autumn season they would need them for nighttime rest as well. And the tents, giving the feast its name, were holy reminders too; serving to commemorate the Lord's leading them through the wilderness those forty years.

Among other traditions, the feast included the great "Water Pouring Ceremony," reminding Israel of God's supernatural provision of water as they traveled through the desert wastelands. Rabbinical writings state that the priests had huge urns from which they poured water from the top of the temple steps, and it was a very dramatic moment as the water splashed and cascaded down as the Israelites lifted up high praise to God and rejoiced.

So it was, on the last day, in the above setting, that Jesus rose to shout aloud, *"He who believes in Me, as the Scripture has said, out of his heart will flow rivers of living water."* His loud proclamation was a call to Holy Spirit fullness, and as Jesus says, "rivers of living water." Please notice His use of the plural—*rivers.*

John's explanation that Jesus was making a prophetic forecast about *our* time, and the Spirit's work within us, gives immediate and practical significance to this pluralization of "rivers." Jesus is describing a way of life for us *today.* He points beyond an *initial* experience, in the Spirit—beyond only being baptized in the Holy Spirit, to a lifestyle *bathed* in an ongoing resource of Holy Spirit fullness, overflowing the life from day to day. All these thoughts converged as I had come back to that passage, drawn by the Lord's "word" to me: "Open to the spirit of enthusiasm."

When this occurred I certainly wasn't "deadbeat" in my walk with the Lord. I'd determined years ago to seek to *abide* in the fullness of the Holy Spirit, and I was reasonably current in the sense of His blessing and presence. But it seemed as though the Lord were showing me something; that the intensity of today's times required my expanding in His fullness all the more: "Let the *entheos,* the Spirit-fullness already in you, increase and abound!"

As a result of this encounter, and my sense of the Holy Spirit's desire to pour out a special refreshing on me—on *us!*—I began to think, what might these "rivers" be which the Lord wants to release in us? I took time to examine that thought in God's Word, and concluded with these *"rivers"*; streams of refreshing and mightiness the Holy Spirit waits to break forth in any of us who will allow Him to do so.

Rivers of Worship and Praise

> Peter said, "And they were all filled with the Holy Spirit and began to speak with other tongues, as the Spirit gave them utterance."
>
> (ACTS 2:4)

Peter explained this Holy Spirit begotten language after the praises to God they manifested brought the acknowledgment from onlookers, *"These all do exalt the name of the Lord God"* (Acts 2:11). In this regard, it merits noticing the relationship of spirit of praise and worship to the exercise of speaking with tongues. It's often debated as to whether this is or isn't a sign of being filled with the Holy Spirit. It *is* clear that people filled with the Holy Spirit certainly have access to this privilege of such a prayer and praise potential. But perhaps it's best not to press this as a doctrinaire requirement, but note this language of praise more as a dynamic *privilege.*

Rivers of Witnessing

> Jesus said, "But you shall receive power when the Holy Spirit has come upon you; and you shall be witnesses to Me in Jerusalem, and in all Judea and Samaria, and to the end of the earth."
>
> (ACTS 1:8)

> But when the Helper comes, whom I shall send to you from the Father, the Spirit of truth who proceeds from the Father, He will testify of Me. And you also will bear witness, because you have been with Me from the beginning.
>
> (JOHN 15:26-27)

He will glorify Me, for He will take of what is Mine and declare it to you.

(JOHN 16:14)

Fresh *entheos* fullness will bring a vibrant readiness in an experienced believer to start all over, joyously telling others about Jesus.

Rivers of Ministry

Jesus said, "And these signs will follow those who believe: In My name they will cast out demons; they will speak with new tongues . . . they will lay hands on the sick, and they will recover."

(MARK 16:17-18)

Here are sign-gift ministries waiting to flow from the Spirit-filled believer to people in torment, pain, and need of divine grace.

Rivers of Gifts (by the Spirit)

Now there are diversities of gifts, but the same Spirit.

(1 COR. 12:4)

Speaks of the Holy Spirit within, manifesting His presence by the distribution of gifts according to His will.

(1 COR. 12:7-11)

The Holy Spirit wants to "give away" *through* us — to give more and more of the Father's goodnesses and blessings. Freshness and renewal in the Spirit rekindles our availability to His gifts, that we might function as His delivery personnel, according to His will, becoming avenues through whom *rivers of gifts* may flow to others.

Rivers of Intercession and Prayer

Likewise the Spirit also helps in our weaknesses. For we do not know what we should pray for as we ought, but the Spirit

Himself makes intercession for us with groanings which cannot be uttered. Now He who searches the hearts knows what the mind of the Spirit is, because He makes intercession for the saints according to the will of God.

(ROM. 8:26-27)

The Holy Spirit wants to advance power-praying and prayer's warfare. As He helps our inability, there are many situations about which we may not know *how* to pray, but His fresh flowings will assist us.

Rivers of Fruitfulness

But the fruit of the Spirit is love, joy, peace, long-suffering, kindness, goodness, faithfulness, gentleness, self-control. Against such there is no law.

(GAL. 5:22-23)

There will never be any divine legislation against the fruit of the Spirit, and there will never be any human law against the beauty of God's grace in people. "Rivers" have always increased fruit-bearing in the agricultural realm, so we are wise to open new floodgates of the Holy Spirit's flowing in our lives to increased fruit in our character and conduct.

Rivers of Peace and Strength within Us

He who speaks in a tongue edifies himself, but he who prophesies edifies the church.

(1 COR. 14:4)

The Bible points to the distinct flow of Holy Spirit enabled prayer as a means of edification. No apology is needed, for this isn't a self-serving exercise — it's necessary.

God's Word says we are being edified by the Holy Spirit language as we worship supernaturally before God's throne in our times of private devotion, and such sensitive employment of this resource deserves to be commended. As God knows, we *all* need *all* the edification we can get.

Rivers of Revelation Are Promised

> The eyes of your understanding being enlightened; that you may know what is the hope of His calling, what are the riches of the glory of His inheritance in the saints.
>
> (EPH. 1:18)

The Apostle Paul said, *"I'm praying for this*—that God will give you the Spirit of wisdom and revelation." Why? Because Holy Spirit spawned refreshing and renewal *always* brings fresh vision and insight as to God's purpose in our lives.

There are *eight* different *flowings* of the Spirit. So, summarize it all and see the rivers of *entheos*—of holy enthusiasm—which the Lord can course through any of us who will open.

Open to the Spirit of Enthusiasm!

Here is a solid scriptural reminder of our need: *"Keep on being filled with the Holy Spirit"* (see Eph. 5:18). It's God's intent. Spirit fullness in the New Testament is emphasized as recurrently necessary. For example, see *both* Peter and Paul, who had each been Spirit-filled earlier, filled afresh for special situations. (Cf. Acts 2:4 with 4:8—Peter; and Acts 9:17 with 13:9.)

The same is true with the early church community, which was filled initially (Acts 2:4, 38) and *re*-filled later (Acts 4:31). So *keeping on* in the Spirit's fullness—opening to the Spirit's *entheos* rivers, is very scriptural.

To gain a sense of the *ways* of the Spirit in filling us, join me in a study of different verbs which occur in the Book of Acts; words which describe our being "filled" or "overflowed" or "abounded" by the Holy Spirit. He didn't simply choose these words in *the* Word to provide a variety of expressions. But they're there to show the spectrum of elements involved in the full range of experiences in the Holy Spirit.

Verb # 1: *Bapto*—Being "Baptized" in the Holy Spirit

> [Jesus said,] For John truly baptized with water, but you shall be baptized with the Holy Spirit not many days from now.
>
> (ACTS 1:5)

Bapto in ancient times was used in an interesting number of ways. It essentially described something which was immersed. Examples are: a sunken ship, a drowned person, the dipping of a morsel of bread in a drink, the dyeing of a garment.

In using *bapto* to describe our entry into the dynamic of His fullness of life and power, God's Spirit chose this word as the first to describe "living in the fullness of the Spirit." It might be said colloquially, it's as though the Lord were saying, "I want to flood all compartments!"

Further, He might well be calling for a *change*, just as a dyed garment takes on an entirely new dimension of beauty which wouldn't be present otherwise. Being filled—*baptized* in the Holy Spirit—is to bring new qualities to our life and character. So when we talk about "baptism in" (*bapto*) the Spirit, these kinds of immersions picture what is intended to be experienced.

Verb # 2: *Eperchomai*—the Holy Spirit "Coming Upon"

> [Jesus said,] But you shall receive power when the Holy Spirit has come upon you; and you shall be witnesses to Me in Jerusalem, and in all Judea and Samaria, and to the end of the earth.
>
> (ACTS 1:8)

The chief idea in *eperchomai* relates a "coming upon" of a whole new set of circumstances—as in, "these things that have 'come upon' me." In other words, the Holy Spirit wants to reshape our *perspective* (on the world), our *passion* (for the lost), our *pointedness* (in focus on human need). The Spirit's power also *clothes* (*enduo*, Luke 24:49), causing another kind of "coming upon" of His resources of enablement and power.

Verb # 3: *Ekcheo*—the Holy Spirit "Poured Out"

In Acts 2:17, Peter quotes from Joel's prophecy about the coming of the Holy Spirit: "And it shall come to pass in the last days, says God, that I will pour out of My Spirit on all flesh."

What happens when the abundance of water behind the dam courses through the generator within the dam and releases energy? A roaring sound? Perhaps. But the purpose is not the thunderous sound as the water rushes through the sluice gates, but to generate the *light* to serve cities miles away. By reason of the opening of the potential within the dam, energy is avenued unto the intended purpose of this release of power.

So, a look at this verb calls us to hear God saying, "Live in the fullness of the Spirit of enthusiasm, and let the rivers surge in and through you to light the world wherever you go, day by day."

Verb # 4: *Pleroo*—"They Were Filled"

"And they were all filled with the Holy Spirit" (Acts 2:4). In the Greek language, this verb was not used unless there was actually an *overflow*. In other words, *pleroo* means, "there's more than enough." It's a "rivers of enthusiasm" reminder of our Lord saying, "Don't ever depend upon the scanty resources of experiences past, because My *abundant* resource is always available. There always will be *more than enough* of My Spirit working in you, but you need to keep open to His renewing, refilling workings!"

Paul's call to be "Praying always with all prayer and supplication in the Spirit" (Eph. 6:18), by *continuously being* "filled with the Spirit" (Eph. 5:18) are directions to assure our keeping this *overflowing* occurring. Our wise response, praising with "psalms and hymns and spiritual songs, singing and making melody in your heart to the Lord" (Eph. 5:19) gives place to this *pleroo* overflowing fullness with the Spirit. Let every day be filled with "more than enough." For example, drive to work singing, en route praising the Lord as you let the language of praise overflow.

Verb # 5: *Epipipto*—"Falling Upon"

> While Peter was still speaking these words, the Holy Spirit fell upon all those who heard the word. And those of the circumcision who believed were astonished, as many as came with Peter, because the gift of the Holy Spirit had been poured out on the Gentiles also. For they heard them speak with tongues and magnify God.
>
> (ACTS 10:44-46)

Epipipto suggests one of the loveliest ideas I've found concerning "being filled with the Spirit." Do you remember Jesus' story of the prodigal son? When the boy returned, the father met his son with great affection—he "fell on his neck" embracing him with joyous acceptance (Luke 15:20). This "falling upon" is not a ludicrous scene of a man falling out of a tree on a bypassing boy. It is the picture of a man coming and capturing his long-lost son in a grace-filled embrace of gratitude and affection. And that's the same word (*epipipto*) which is used here in Acts 8:16. Look at that episode. "For as yet He had *fallen upon* none of them. They had only been baptized in the name of the Lord Jesus" (italics mine).

Seeing the entire context, we find believers who had been baptized in water as an action of obedience following their repentance and faith in Christ, but they had not yet received the *fullness* of the Spirit. Peter and John were sent to Samaria where Philip had ministered in evangelism, but now there needed to be follow-up work. This underscores the need for what is often called "a second work" of grace, *not* because our *salvation* is enlarged or expanded upon, but because our *enablement* for power-filled service is a distinct action in God's order of grace-works.

It's the same today. The Holy Spirit wants to "fall upon" us to capture us in the embrace of heaven, to catch us up in the fullness of God's love, so by that love He may overflow His great love to others as we touch them in His name. *Finally,* let's all *open—receive* expanding rivers of divine infilling and overflowing; opening to the Spirit of *entheos,* God filling the whole of our life.

Verb # 6: *Lambano*—"To Receive"

"Then they laid hands on them, and they received the Holy Spirit" (Acts 8:17).

Interestingly enough *lambano* conveys *both* the idea of giving and/or receiving. In short, everything ultimately relates to *our* will to be *open—*to *allow,* and then to *God's* will to pour the power, grace, and glory which will flow *all* ways—to and from us!

Dear one, I'm presuming you're like me, wanting this openness to be and continue to be manifest in your life and attitude. I've addressed you as one not needing to be convinced of the value in the fullness of the Holy Spirit; as a brother or sister who *desires everything* Christ Jesus promises His disciples.

Do you agree with me that if our Lord might say, "Open to the spirit of enthusiasm," He has a reason? Well, I knew He said it to me, and since the Bible enjoins us to "keep on being filled with the Holy Spirit," I think we can all assume it's a lifelong discipline for every earnest believer.

Let's observe it.

Chapter Sixteen

Living a Life of Submission

S everal years ago, one of America's best-known industrialists began attending our church. He had visited for several months before we met. As we conversed one day, he was very candid when he told me about laughing at himself and his early encounters and responses upon attending the services.

He'd received Christ elsewhere, and he was young in the Lord when he first arrived. God used our ushers as an instrument to touch this man's life . . . deeply! Because I serve a church that has been blessed with remarkable growth, when our ushers greet the people upon their arrival in the sanctuary they have specific instructions. Contrary to people's tendency to "sit in back," our ushers are expected to "lead" (not herd, but "persuasively invite") people to the row closest to the front of the sanctuary which is yet unfilled. This allows latecomers to be seated without distracting other worshipers who arrived early, and our people generally respond very positively to the request. So it was in this context the business leader spoke with me one day.

He said he had always cooperated out of courtesy, but added:

"Pastor, you have no idea how it rankled me. I detested being told by those people where I should sit. Everything in my life until then had always been under *my* control. Having the direction of a sizable industry, I am accustomed to having it exactly the way I *think* it should be, *when* it should be, and *how* it should be."

He laughed at himself for he said:

"But I didn't realize this wasn't the way the Lord wanted my life. He used some very ordinary men, some dear brethren, who earlier in my life I virtually would have scorned as people I could buy and sell a thousand times over. Now, the Lord used them to remind me of how much I need to learn the spirit of sub-mission."

He not only accepted sitting where ushers told him to sit while *pretending* a good attitude, but he learned what it meant to have a *genuine* spirit of loving, trusting submission to Jesus Christ, seeing the situation for what it was: a call to yield to Him, working *within.*

Bluntly put, there really aren't many of us as readily willing to acknowledge the need of this discipline. In the judgment of some, "A life of submission" sounds like a page out of a handbook for membership in a religious order; a call to a monastery. In fact, in much of today's church, many have almost sanctified the notion of autonomy, of independence, of "I can do just about whatever I want, because of my freedom in Christ." Such self-justifying claims, asserting a supposed "right" to bypass learning the practice of submission, take different forms. "God is no respecter of persons." "I am as important in God as anyone." "Submission breeds mind-control cults."

On the face of it, you can't deny the element of truth these *words* represent, but the *spirit* of submission is the issue, not par-roted words about "freedom." In terms of spiritual reality, we *are* made free. But our liberty in Christ isn't a program of per-petuating self-rule in the soul. Our "freedom" is (1) to free us from practicing sin, (2) to free us from smallness of soul, and (3) to free us from a "Lone-Ranger" order of independence which proposes *"me"* as the single-handed controller of everything in my life. The spirit of submission, lived out on biblical terms, proposes that God could, in fact, use other people to *teach* me, to *circle* me with *supporting insights,* to *help me grow;* bringing me to a *voluntary* willingness to be accountable to others; even if that means I'm exposing myself to the possibility that at times these "others" will adjust and correct me in the spirit of love. These valuable, life-building assets can only be realized if I am willing to learn the spirit of submission, and "submission" is a scary word for so many of us.

The Meaning of Submission

"Submission" sounds as though one person might be exploited, manipulated, or dominated by another. But let's clear the air with an understanding of its definition.

First, please, read with me:

Now when Jesus had entered Capernaum, a centurion came to Him, pleading with Him, saying, "Lord, my servant is lying at home paralyzed, dreadfully tormented."

And Jesus said to him, "I will come and heal him."

The centurion answered and said, "Lord, I am not worthy that You should come under my roof. But only speak a word, and my servant will be healed. For I also am a man under authority, having soldiers under me. And I say to this one, 'Go,' and he goes; and to another, 'Come,' and he comes; and to my servant, 'Do this,' and he does it."

When Jesus heard it, He marveled, and said to those who followed, "Assuredly, I say to you, I have not found such great faith, not even in Israel!" . . . Then Jesus said to the centurion, "Go your way; and as you have believed, so let it be done for you." And his servant was healed that same hour.

(MATT. 8:5-10, 13)

Here is a "beginning point in understanding the *true* idea of submittedness, not because the *word* "submission" appears but because (1) the *heart* of the concept is there in the centurion's response to Jesus, and (2) the actual *way* in which the word was originally derived is present in the setting itself.

This is a military setting. It's a captain of men who says, "Jesus, I say to my soldiers, 'Do this and they do it.'" In other words, "I am a man *under* authority and I *administer* that authority according to a specific order of *alignment*." He understood that *his* submission, or alignment with authority placed above him, was the source of that power available to manifest itself through him as he submitted to it himself. His power or authority was not self-derived. It was delegated through an appointed order (military or governmental in this case) and his acceptance of his role as a "submitted" man was what gave rise to the power or authority he exercised.

The centurion proceeds to use his position of authority to make an analogy. His observation is essentially this: "Jesus, just as I have military *authority*, I know You have authority in another realm. So all You need to do is to speak a word." Now listen to Jesus' perspective: "I have not found such great faith, not even in Israel!" Jesus not only confirms the man's faith, but is essentially commending the man's perspective, understanding, and spirit.

What follows is a beautiful story in which Jesus exercises power over affliction and brings healing to the centurion's servant. And seeing this, the thoughtful soul must inquire of what possibilities you and I have waiting to be released if we will learn God's order of alignment for our lives and voluntarily function in submission to that order.

1. Just as the centurion related to an order of authority over him, what are those points of divinely appointed order I need to accept?

2. Just as the centurion's servant was healed by reason of a release of faith born of his perspective on true humility, and Christ's power born of true authority, who or what in my life awaits healing, wholeness, or recovery—if "submission" is learned?

The meaning of the word is unquestionably related to military structures. *Hupotasso* (Greek, to submit) was literally, culturally, used to refer to an arrangement of troops *under* proper order; each private, corporal, sergeant, lieutenant, captain, etc., relating correctly right up the line through majors, colonels, and generals—to a commander-in-chief.

In such military regimentation the existence of the structure is not designed to reduce the significance of anyone or inflate the importance of another. It is designed to *assist* the effectiveness of all, to *assure* the interests of all, and to *assemble* the whole of the body to resist and overthrow the enemy.

An enormous *blessing* is available through a disciple's willingness to learn the spirit of submission. And the glorious release of *power* awaits the individual, the congregation—indeed, the whole body of Christ—if and when we would learn to "submit ourselves to one another in the fear of God" (i.e., "in reverence for His divine order"). It's overwhelming to conceive the possibilities, but our fears and fierce independence too readily crowd them aside.

The Bible is very clear: there *is* a God-ordained order for every facet of our lives. None of us are simply "stand alones." Of course, we *do* stand individually responsible before God in terms of our relationship and accountability to Him . . . *first*. But life is constituted of many other dimensions, relationships, and factors. And even in the realm of our spiritual relationships—to church, to Christians, to ministries—it is very easy to subtly arrogate to oneself a broad individualism on the supposition that "I'm a free creature under God and I'll do just what I want or see 'best.' " We can be "ever so nice a guy," keeping the laws of society, even obeying the boss at work. But get me in church? Hey, we're *all* "in charge" here!

But that leading industrialist I mentioned was willing to learn submission to *spiritual* authority too—right to the point of "submitting" to a lowly usher. He refused to retain the almost self-righteous proposition that he had his "right" to make judgment as to which realm he would or would not submit.

There are, in fact, certain realms of authority and accountability where it won't *damn* our soul if we refuse submission. But it certainly can *shrink* our souls. "Unsubmission" of heart is unlike Jesus.

> Let this mind be in you which was also in Christ Jesus, who, being in the form of God, did not consider it robbery to be equal with God, but made Himself of no reputation, taking the form of a servant, and coming in the likeness of men. And being found in appearance as a man, He humbled Himself and became obedient to the point of death, even the death of the cross. Therefore God also has highly exalted Him and given Him the name which is above every name, that at the name of Jesus every knee should bow, of those in heaven, and of those on earth, and of those under the earth, and that every tongue should confess that Jesus Christ is Lord, to the glory of God the Father.
>
> (PHIL. 2:5-11)

His example calls you and me to discover the power release and growth that will only happen in and through us if we properly learn the spirit of submission. The path *down*—submitting—is the way *up*—receiving authority, and even then, all authority in the spiritual realm is only to be exercised in the spirit and with the attitudes of a servant.

> But Jesus called them to Himself and said, "You know that the rulers of the Gentiles lord it over them, and those who are great exercise authority over them. Yet it shall not be so among you; but whoever desires to become great among you, let him be your servant. And whoever desires to be first among you, let him be your slave—just as the Son of Man did not come to be served, but to serve, and to give His life a ransom for many."
>
> (MATT. 20:25-28)

Submission to God's arrangement and order is not to rank people above others, but to serve the interests of all, so "the whole army" comes to victory. The submitted disciple learns there is a "tactical advantage," a mutual protection that takes place through (1) *committed involvement* with a church family, (2) *submitted service* as a member of the body, and (3) *acceptance* of a personal *accountability* to others in Christ.

In this response to God's order, everybody wins. It is not a matter of saying, "Who's on top, who's boss?" It's a matter of saying, "Lord, teach me my place—I humbly yield to learning, to growing. Lord, I'll even sit where the usher says!"

God's intended order calls us to a real commitment to grow in understanding as we learn and apply it to various relationships.

While society interprets "submission" to mean "subjugation," or to "dominate," it doesn't mean that at all. Subjugation and domination are what happens when one person or kingdom over-rules another: they're intimidated, plundered, mastered, then broken.

But "submission" has nothing to do with that, for there really isn't any such thing as *forced* submission. True submission can never be forced because, foremost, submission is always an inner atti-tude—a heart issue. It can never be *required:* it can only be *volun-teered*—given as a willing gift. Only I can choose whether or not I will submit.

Under Christ, we must learn the spirit of submission as it relates to others—others we serve with, others we serve under, others we don't want to serve at all. But *willingness, humility,* and *servanthood* must be kept in view. I may *say* I'll "submit," but if my heart rankles and internally resents or resists, I am not accepting or participating in the spirit of submission. And not only will I fail to garner the *power* God intends me to know through becoming a submitted person, I'll miss the *blessing.* Read the words of this marvelous hymn. The blessings awaiting the submitted disciple are beautifully set forth.

TRUST AND OBEY

When we walk with the Lord in the light of His Word,
What a glory He sheds on our way!
While we do His good will He abides with us still,
And with all who will trust and obey.

Refrain: Trust and obey, for there's no other way,
      To be happy in Jesus, But to trust and obey.

Not a shadow can rise, not a cloud in the skies,
But His smile quickly drives it away;
Not a doubt nor a fear, not a sigh nor a tear,
Can abide while we trust and obey.

Not a burden we bear, not a sorrow we share,
But our toil He doth richly repay;
Not a grief nor a loss, not a frown nor a cross,
But is blest if we trust and obey.

But we never can prove the delights of His love
Until all on the altar we lay;
For the favor He shows and the joy He bestows
Are for them who will trust and obey.

Then in fellowship sweet we will sit at His feet,
Or we'll walk by His side in the way;
What He says we will do, where He sends we will go,
Never fear, only trust and obey.

                              John H. Sammis

Such a statement places the spirit of submission "on the table." It reveals that true submission is more than learning the principle of submission in the *texts* of Scripture—it is learned in passing the *tests* of life; how we *apply* submission in the most primary or the basic situations of our lives is the real evidence of that degree to which I have become "submitted."

- As a husband, how do I relate to my wife—as a servant or as a tyrant; as a responsible leader or as a heel-dragging child?

- As a wife, how do you relate to your husband—as a supporting partner manifesting the unique sweetness and love potential in true femininity, or as a complainer, controller, or nag?

- As a parent, how do I relate to my children—as a role model, serving their need for a picture of what they can become, as an interested-in-you Dad or Mom, caring, correcting, affirming, and disciplining when necessary?

- As an employee, how do I relate to my job, my fellow workers, and my supervisor; as a trustworthy bearer of my share of the task, as a dependable, on-time "you can count on me" partner, or as a passive, disinterested, "only as much as I've gotta do" pain to have around? (Or, worse yet, as the company "religious freak" who talks a faith that has no relationship to diligence in daily duty as an employee!)

- As a Christian, how do I relate to my church—as a supporting giver, an active servant, a right-spirited member, a team player with the leadership? Or am I an "I'll give, but only to what I'm interested in." "I'll attend, but don't ask me to do anything," or an "I'll be around, but I want to keep my distance," or an "I'll join, but I'm reserving my right to murmur or criticize when I want" sort of person?

- As a disciple, how do I relate to the practical wisdom of finding a small circle of peers in Christ, to whom I make myself accountable, and with whom I stand in a willingness to be mutually corrected, assisted-toward-growth-in-grace, and bonded through a common, powerful love of God for strength; for times when I need support to face trial, temptation, or stressing circumstances?

Only by our willingness to learn and grow in these ways will we ever become all that we truly can be in Christ. Seeing our Savior is seeing the model of the submitted life, and yet He functions with more dynamic, authority, and dominion than anyone in all history. Look at Him.

He stoops to a manger on earth, though rightfully the King of the Universe.
He is baptized to serve the Father's purpose, though onlookers might have presumed it an act of repentance.
He accepts rejection without retaliating in kind.
He willingly accepts the slapping of His face, yet doesn't spit back.

He prays, "Father, not My will, but Yours be done."
He accepts the slashing and spearing of His body, and says,
"Father, forgive them, they don't understand."

Jesus submitted to misunderstanding people and tirelessly gave Himself to seek to help them come to understand. When He could have responded to disciples who said, "Let us call down fire from heaven; they wouldn't let You come into town there," Jesus in effect says, "No. That's not our style—*you don't know what spirit you are of*" (Luke 9:54-56).

He was calling His disciples to learn that the spirit of His kingdom is not to exercise power to prove you're superior or right. Rather, He calls us to learn the spirit of submission; to let a grander power manifest through us—the power of love which, given time, will beget trust and responsiveness.

- There are husbands who never win the spirit of submission from their wives, because they never lay down their own lives; instead, they lay down their own *laws*, demanding their own authority or supposed privileges.

- There are wives who never draw from their husbands the best responses, because they are unwilling to surrender to a possibility; the possibility that, were they to show the sweet spirit of volunteered submission, they might evoke something beautiful from their husbands; but they are unwilling to risk losing control in order to secure the potential of that beauty.

As the Lord grew me (I'm afraid I was a slow learner), I gradually came to see the structure of His order and respond to it. There is so much to be *gained* through a disciple's learning the biblical spirit and practical pathway of submission. And there seems to be so many lessons and points of application to open that way.

This one chapter can hardly develop what a book might fully unfold. But may I enlist your further study?

The following outline is a resource I've used in my work with *men*, and also in seminars with *couples* and *spiritual leaders*. Audio-cassettes teaching on "submission" as a dynamic lifestyle are also available.* But here, for further study, you might find use for the following, to examine the truth and path of submission.

*A catalog of Dr. Hayford's tapes and books is available from Living Way Ministries, 14480 Sherman Way, Van Nuys, California, 91405-2396.

The Concept of Submission

I. *The Semantics of Submission, Matthew 8:5-10*
  A. When Jesus declared, "I have not found such great faith," He was remarking on the comment of the Roman centurion who acknowledged his recognition of Jesus' authority over sickness because of his own understanding of the principle of being "set under authority." This is the essence of the New Testament word, *hupotasso,* which is essentially a military word denoting "order," "place," or "rank." Translated most frequently "submit" or "subject," the word occurs in fourteen books of the New Testament, a total of forty-four times.
  B. *English terms* which answer to this idea include "yielded" and "obedient." The oft-used expression "surrender to God's will" incorporates the idea of submission as an introductory act, while "walking in the will of God" conveys the idea of submission as a life-pattern.
  C. *The term "covering"* is heard much today. It is also related to the idea of order and therefore to submission. (Example: Ezek. 28:14 uses the term denoting Satan's rank before his transgression.) "Covering" implies protection by virtue of one's yielding to or acceptance of an overseeing and loving authority. Therefore in the vernacular of faith, we say we are "covered with the blood of Jesus," which affirms that we have submitted ourselves in faith to the protection that blood provides from judgment on our sins.

II. *The Significance of Submission, Hebrews 2*
  A. *All sin* is the resultant outflow of the rejection of one's place in God's order of things. First, Lucifer's "I will ascend," and second, Adam's seeking of knowledge not intended for him (Isa. 14:14; Gen. 3:5-6).
  B. *All redemption* is the resultant outflow of the submission of the Son of God to the Father's will:
    1. *To incarnation,* Hebrews 5:5-7;
    2. *To identification* with man, Matthew 3:13-17;
    3. *To suffering in life,* Hebrews 5:8; 12:3; Matthew 26:52-54; and
    4. *To death,* Philippians 2:8; Hebrews 2:9.
  C. *The highest of human destiny* in the redemptive program of God through His Son Jesus is the *restoring of man to his intended place of authority as ruler.* Hebrews 2 develops this

majestically, and shows man removed from being "subject to bondage" (v. 15) and experiencing all things "in subjection" under him. Verses 9-10 clearly display that Jesus' pathway of submission—the unquestioning life of trustful obedience—leads to this rulership.

III. *The Specifics of Submission, 1 Peter 5*

There are seven basic areas of life-relatedness which require a submissiveness on the part of mankind. Each merits a whole range of development, and bears far more Scripture support than the brief list of references given here. But this simple outline serves as a framework for further study. New Testament life, in which the fullness of God's love for man has been revealed, summons submission at these levels of relationship:

A. Submission to *God the Father*, Hebrews 12:5-9; James 4:6-7

B. Submission to *the Truth*, Romans 10:3 (Receiving God's provision of righteousness through Christ alone, without works)

C. Submission to the *body of Christ*. This refers to all three:
   1. Jesus as the Head, Ephesians 1:20-23; Colossians 2:18-19
   2. Local eldership, Hebrews 13:17; 1 Corinthians 16:16, and church government
   3. Individuals of the membership, Ephesians 5:21; 1 Peter 5:5

D. Submission to *parents*, Luke 2:51; Ephesians 6:1-3; Colossians 3:20

E. Submission to *civil authority*, 1 Peter 2:13-23; Romans 13:1-7

F. Submission to *employers*, Colossians 3:22, Ephesians 6:5-7

G. Submission to roles as *husband and wife*, Ephesians 5:22-33; Colossians 3:18-19

IV. *The Spirit of Submission, Psalm 37*

Any truth can be stretched over the rack of cold, literalistic application and made into a dried hide of demanding duty. However, New Testament life is not designed to *wrap* man in newly developed legal demands, but rather to *fill* man with new possibilities for living in the love of God by the outflow of the Holy Spirit (Rom. 5:5). The enunciating of the basic-to-life principle of submission can be responded to in fear, in doubt, in presumption, in love, in trust or in understanding. To select the wise response and avoid the foolish requires a wholehearted openness toward the Holy Spirit. Only He can lead us into the *living* of *any* truth. We need to be mindful that:

A. *The Spirit of submission is not cowardly,* 2 Timothy 1:7. He will not produce passive, insensitive saints who flop before anything in supposed "submission." We are *not* to submit to:
   1. Satan—1 Peter 5:8-9. Example: sin/sickness are resisted.
   2. Flesh—1 Corinthians 9:24-27. We are to make no provision for it.
   3. Legalism—Galatians 2:4-5. It is *always* in opposition to the gospel.
B. *The Spirit of submission is not confused,* Acts 4:15-21; 5:26-42. Deals with the question: "How does one submit to conflicting authorities?" The apostles satisfy *both* God and rulers—submitting unto both. They do *not* submit to demands of silence, but they do submit to scourging with joy.
C. *The Spirit of submission is not contentious,* 1 Corinthians 11:16
D. *The Spirit of submission is not comparatively competitive.* Second Corinthians 1:12 warns against the ugliest aspects of a spirit of competition; while Proverbs 27:17 recommends the best aspects of "sharpening" one another by interactive activity.

Conclusion: There is no earnest New Testament believer who does not want to be effective in ministry. Jesus has clearly encouraged our expectation of full ministry flow in John 14:12. But the flow of *His* kind and quality of ministry requires the preparation of His kind and quality of submissiveness. Before He became the Great Shepherd, He submitted to being the Lamb of God. The course for fulfillment of our ministries is charted by submission to that same tender walk before the Father.

Chapter Seventeen

The Practice of Solitude

T he hallmark of people who walk faithfully with the Lord for long seasons of time, who go beyond anything they had known before, who come through with faithfulness, stability, and strength of character, has been they have learned a simple way. In the last analysis, what truly brings a person to living steadfastly over the long-term in the things of the Spirit of God is not the ability to stand splendidly in glory moments. Rather, it's in the ability to find a way through difficulties, by God's grace; to ultimately stand firm, having found resources of grace in ways less obvious. I'm thinking, for example, of *quietness*, of *solitude*, of *"waiting"* as resources for dealing with the tough times in our life—at *any* time.

Let me address the practice of solitude.

I suppose all of us wish or long for times we can "get away from it all." I don't necessarily mean as a superficial escape mechanism, but as a quiet quest for God.

Of course, we do need times to literally "get away" at the surface level of recreation, and there's no fault in that. A tennis court, a golf course, or a vacation in Switzerland—they're all great. But recreation, vacation, or relaxation are not what I mean by solitude, though they may at times provide a setting for the same. Still, we need to separate these *active* recreational times from the value realized in the more *pensive* order of *re*-creating that solitude affords. By "solitude" I mean to refer to one's being *alone*—with the Lord.

In Mark 6:30-32, we see this illustrated during Jesus' ministry. It was *His* idea, and it speaks volumes to us today:

Then the apostles gathered to Jesus and told Him all things, both what they had done and what they had taught. And He said to them, "Come aside by yourselves to a deserted place and rest a while." For there were many coming and going, and they did not even have time to eat. So they departed to a deserted place in the boat by themselves.

No elaboration is needed. The text is fully self-explaining. There simply are times that we need to *stop*. And Jesus noted that and *called* His disciples to observe a "time-out" with Him.

I was interested to discover what appears to be a companion event to this, a similar "break away" in Paul's life; one that could go unnoticed unless we trace the geography referenced in Acts 20:13.

Then we went ahead to the ship and sailed to Assos, there intending to take Paul on board; for so he had given orders, intending himself to go on foot.

Luke is making a simple geographic reference that in sailing from Troas their next stop was to be at Assos. But Paul goes another way. It seems he's said, "You guys go ahead on board. I'm going to hike to Assos and I'll meet you there." The distance he would have walked is possibly twenty-five miles, while the ship would sail west, then south, then east again, and around a point. The longer route for the ship's journey would take some time, so Paul apparently chose to walk. But why?

It's perfectly logical to conclude that he wanted time to be alone. Now, "alone" probably wasn't completely without companionship, because that would have been dangerous in those times. But I doubt we can imagine the cramped quarters, the pressure of confinement in the ship's hold or even on deck on such small craft over the extended time for journeys that ancient day required. But in contrast to being shipboard, here's a chance to be out in God's creation; to breathe the refreshing air in the countryside. It would be marvelous! It seems clear that Paul is making the journey on foot because he feels he needs a *break*—a change of pace.

Other examples from the Word are readily apparent:

- God's dealing with Moses became profoundly impacting and history shaping through his extended season in his forty days atop Sinai.

- Elijah escapes from Jezebel's pursuit, and through a forty-day visit to Sinai he meets God and rediscovers, as it were, what his life is really about.

- David's flight from Saul produces some of the greatest psalms, written from his wilderness hideaway at En Gedi.

- John is exiled to Patmos, and from this place of seeming "out of commission," he finds his greatest commission yet as he meets Jesus and is told to write the Book of Revelation.

There are any number of cases—biblical and extra-biblical—where people go into times of solitude. In these times, rather than *escaping* reality, they find an *entrance* into it; they come freshly into the reality of God's presence and find there a renewal of His purpose. Such instances in the Scriptures and the lives of others teach us how to regain in quiet what we've lost in the busyness of our intensely urban, highly industrialized, and technologically complex culture.

Making Time for Solitude

To find times for solitude definitely requires our making a choice.

A businessman friend who lives in the Northwest recently told me of his experience. An almost vicious combination of factors were pressing in on him; difficulty with one of his kids, a vocational decision, plus professional pressures. He wasn't really anxious to run from any of these, but he did want to know God's will and way for dealing with each of them.

So, he spoke with his wife, and in the midst of this convergence of difficulty, he explained to her his sense of "being called *away*" for a few days. He'd said, "Would it be OK with you, honey?" Her sensitivity in response was, "OK—go for it."

He felt God was calling him to take three days, so driving to the coast of Oregon, about 100 miles from where they lived in the Willamette Valley, he found a place to be alone with God. And there, in a condo on the beach, he spent the three days, fasting, reading the Bible, and taking time to write in a journal the things God unfolded to his heart as the Lord began to unravel tension and unveil direction.

"That was all I did, Jack—read the Word and spend time with God," he said. "I have no way to tell you what happened! It was life-transformational. Quiet walks and talks on the beach became releasing in God's presence. When I came back, I don't know if the son we were having trouble with had changed or if it was my change of perspective on him, but we came 'out of the woods' with that problem. Then, business suddenly rectified itself, while I also soon received perfect clarity on the decision I was to make."

It's worth studying for emulation. Alone in solitude, God met a man because the man gave Him time. He didn't only "get away to the quiet," but to the Lord God.

That's an important point to distinguish when we talk about a Christian disciple's solitude, reflection, or meditation. Because the *general* value of meditation is understood in every tradition, and promoted by religious systems and also as a very real part of New Age philosophy, I want to be distinctly clear. When I speak of meditation or solitude, I am not relating it to any other context than *"being in the presence of God."*

The Christian disciple's practice of solitude is not about resorting to some "inner consciousness," or to some "alignment with the universe." Mystical or solely psychological self-help systems can lead a person to make himself available to abstract "energies," and end up conjuring up demonic confusion. But a Christian's prayerful solitude isn't seeking some abstract contact with "the infinite"; we're seeking *Jesus*. Those meddling in an undefined spiritual realm, however sincere the pursuers of such possibilities may be, can become tragically self-destructive. But what we're discussing has no part in any such order of confusion.

Jesus Visited Me

I've been greatly blessed in my own experience by the renewing power of solitude. Let me relate a case of my own quest.

I had been ill for a sustained period of weeks. I had still been able to keep my schedule, but the combination of maintaining my pastoral work and speaking schedule, along with the nagging physical drag the affliction had put on my body, had brought me to a devastating point of weakness, weariness, and exhaustion. Already in so extended a condition, and recognizing the next season of weeks held little reprieve, my view of the immediate future was becoming very bleak. Expectancy was low, anticipation almost absent. All work was about to become pointless as this combination of factors draining me was begetting an indifference, rather than a desire for ministry.

Still, within, I felt a longing—a hunger for "something" from God. And that's what prompted my saying to Anna, "Honey, I think I'll go up to the mountains." She replied instantly, yet gently, "You know, when I awoke this morning, I felt that's what you needed. You go ahead—go early." Her quick response wasn't due to any impact showing on our relationship, but her own sensitivity to my stressed condition confirmed my need for solitude—for being with the Lord. Alone.

I was due to speak two days later at a college's autumn retreat at a conference center in the San Bernardino Mountains. So rather than continuing to press my schedule at home that next twenty-four hours before leaving, I arranged to leave early.

I was drained of soul, exhausted in body, and thirsty in spirit.

Upon arrival, I must confess, I did little except *"be"*—I *did* almost nothing. But my *"being"* was a conscious "with Jesus."

How well I recall sitting on the porch of the small mountain cabin. Just sitting. Looking into the brush, or up at the pines or beyond to the higher elevations. And I would quietly talk—informally—to the Lord. I would weep as I sang, without gusto but with a deep sense of quest, "As the deer panteth for the water, so my soul longeth after Thee." And it was in that setting that "it" happened.

One of the most memorable encounters in my entire life came during the afternoon of that twenty-four-hour period of solitude. The sheer love of God was shown toward me in an unforgettable encounter. All I can say is, *Jesus visited me.*

I don't mean I saw an apparition. Nor am I claiming a trance-like experience. What I mean is that *that* day, as I strolled into a grove of magnificent redwoods, quietly expressing my thanks to God for His grace, goodness, and patience with me, I was suddenly, powerfully, genuinely, and humblingly aware of His presence. He made Himself known to me.

Yes, it was emotional. No, it wasn't imaginary. But in a way I will never forget, I was refreshed and reminded how infinitely gentle the love of God is and how fully His presence is available if I will give Him time, by withdrawing from other persons and pressures and let *Him* be made known to me.

Of course, we can't go to the mountains or the coast every *week* to have some time for solitude, but let me suggest something that might assist you on an *ongoing* basis. Allow me to describe how I more commonly include the discipline of solitude in my schedule.

First, it's not something that I calendar, but it comes when I know "it's time." About every week to ten days, as a general rule, I'll find I'm not sleeping well on a given night. I usually *do* — quite well; but I'll find my mind is restless, usually stirred as I think of things undone or forthcoming, and I'll wake up in midnight hours.

Now, I can lay there and think, fret, worry, or wonder wearily, "When will I go back to sleep?" But instead I'll get up, put on my bathrobe, and go in the living room.

I'll just sit in the dark . . . looking out the window into the night, simply saying to my Lord: "Jesus, I'm just here to be with You."

Does He care? Does God "count" such "non-performance" oriented behavior?

The answer is, *"Absolutely Yes!"*

I don't know what the story is of your romantic past, but I remember so well the early days of Anna's and my relationship, and the things which occurred that laid the foundation for our "togetherness" to continue so fulfillingly now for more than three decades. But we had times when just "being together" and saying very little became more permanently enriching than any verbal or physical expression could fulfill. And if that value is discoverable and verifiable in a human relationship, don't make any mistake, friend, your Lord Jesus is quite happy to have you or me just be with Him — person to person — in His presence, growing to *know* Him. Look at God's Word on this theme:

> Wait on the Lord; be of good courage, and He shall strength-en your heart; Wait, I say, on the Lord.
>
> (PS. 27:14)

> I wait for the Lord, my soul waits, and in His word I do hope. My soul waits for the Lord.
>
> (PS. 130:5-6)

There is a touching verse in the Psalms which refers to the *animals*: "These all wait upon You. That You give them their food in due season" (Ps. 104:27).

Years ago, in *Waiting on God*, Andrew Murray wrote tenderly of how this passage shows the way the animal kingdom is attended to by the Heavenly Father — faithfully, and so completely. Yet they contribute *absolutely* nothing to Him to bring about His tender response and care. They simply "wait" on Him. Murray then went on to remind of Jesus' words, and how badly we all need to be renewed in hearing that the Creator's creature-care is certainly no less for us.

> Therefore I say to you, do not worry about your life, what you will eat or what you will drink; nor about your body, what you will put on. Is not life more than food and the body more than clothing? Look at the birds of the air, for they neither sow nor reap nor gather into barns; yet your Heavenly Father feeds them. Are you not of more value than they? Which of you by worrying can add one cubit to his stature?
>
> So why do you worry about clothing? Consider the lilies of the field, how they grow: they neither toil nor spin; and yet I say to you that even Solomon in all his glory was not arrayed like one of these.
>
> Now if God so clothes the grass of the field, which today is, and tomorrow is thrown into the oven, will He not much more clothe you, O you of little faith? Therefore do not worry, saying, "What shall we eat?" or "What shall we drink?" or "What shall we wear?" For after all these things the Gentiles seek. For your Heavenly Father knows that you need all these things. But seek first the kingdom of God and His righteousness, and all these things shall be added to you. Therefore do not worry about tomorrow, for tomorrow will worry about its own things. Sufficient for the day is its own trouble.
>
> (MATT. 6:25-34)

Listen, loved one. Jesus is saying the same to us today:

- "Why do you let yourself be 'pressed' by the matters of tomorrow?"

- "Why do you try to figure out how you're going to work it out?"

- "Can you add a foot and a half to your height? Then, why do you think you can get yourself out of the hole you are in—out and up from under the pressures which weigh you down?"

- When Jesus says, "Look at the lilies of the field," I don't think He's only saying, "See how the Father cares for nature." But I think He may also be addressing our basic need to "get out and get away"—to *first* make time to be alone with Him and *then* be reminded by His creation.

As I said, we can't always go to the mountains or coast, but often in the early morning, I simply go outside. Just as at nighttime "alone in the living room," I am with the Lord, there are times I'll walk through the neighborhood before others are busily out and active. Other times, I'll just go out in the yard. These become wonderful moments of solitude. Not long ago, the Lord "touched" me there as I walked quietly communing with Him in our backyard one day. It was early, just past dawn, when He "met me" in a way that makes me think I understand something of what the writer of the song meant when he said,

> I come to the garden alone,
>   While the dew is still on the roses;
> And the voice I hear, falling on my ear;
>   The Son of God discloses.
>
> And He walks with me,
>   And He talks with me,
> And He tells me I am His own.
>   And the joy we share,
> As we tarry there,
>   None other has ever known.
>   C. Austin Miles

That hymn is a reminder of how much we need times of solitude—just *being with* God; seeking that kind of relationship that does nothing more than open to His love, through dependent, childlike "waiting."

But we live in a world which not only doesn't sing such songs very much anymore, but one where gardens are fewer—and the environment is being eaten up by the smog. And simultaneously, it seems souls are being eroded by the force and flow of duty's demands, and corroded by the pressured atmosphere of either self-inflicted or externally required circumstance. So easily, the simplicity and beauty that comes by "just being with the Lord" becomes a difficult-to-find commodity. But, loved one, solitude *can* be found. Even "waiting" at a desk.

Solitude and Journaling

Let me introduce a powerful potential which relates to times of solitude and encourage you toward the companion discipline of reflection and journaling. This aspect of *"quiet and before God"* is a dynamic that's helped multitudes in *every* era, but which I think is especially needed today to maintain sanity in a sometimes seemingly wild and weird world. Look at Philippians 4:8-9 with me:

> Finally, brethren, whatever things are true, whatever things are noble, whatever things are just, whatever things are pure, whatever things are lovely, whatever things are of good report, if there is any virtue and if there is anything praiseworthy—meditate on these things. The things which you learned and received and heard and saw in me, these do, and the God of peace will be with you.

I think these words point to *reflection* in times of quiet *with* God, just as the two verses before (4:6-7) pointed to supplication in times of prayer *before* God. The anxiety-release of impassioned, "binding and loosing" supplication is to wisely be complemented by our quiet, pensive *thinking* on God's goodness.

Logizo, the verb for "think on these things," is a mathematical or bookkeeping term. It points toward reflection as a means to take time and "tally the goodnesses of God." *Keeping score of the good things!* Why? Because we so easily become immersed in preoccupying things that so often *aren't* so good. We need to "think on" the lovely and the blessed, the beauties of God's acts of kindness, mercy, and provision.

But I've *also* found it's wise to write down the "bad things" I'm facing up to, or being troubled by. It's an amazing thing I've learned about problems. If I write them down, I've always found two things to be true. First, there weren't as many as I thought. Second, when I write them down *before the Lord,* it seems as though the mere "writing before Him" both *shrinks* their threat and *starts* their solution. Right then, I'll begin to sense direction and experience peace. There's something about defining those monsters on paper that moves them out of the fog of confusion and turmoil.

Writing of them in the presence of Jesus gives perspective on *their* true size—and *HIS!* There's great power released through reflection and meditation in Christ's presence. Give time to it.

How to Journal

Journaling simply means to write down things that occur to you when you're alone with the Lord. They don't have to be poetic or profound. But you *do* need to have a special place you write these things.

You don't need a fancy journal: A simple ringed binder can work very well. I often use a plain pad of yellow paper with lines on it. Though I have nicer journaling books, this very unimpressive pad serves me best, it seems.

Then, *what* shall we "journal"?

Journaling can involve *self-examination, interaction with God's Word,* and *recording what you "hear" the Lord speak* to your soul.

First, Self-examination

By this quest, I *don't* mean to call you to dredge up the past in order to convince God you are holier because you are feeling more guilty than ever. Still, the Bible shows the importance of coming before the Lord to let our hearts be examined in His presence. This is illustrated in the Book of Psalms, the "all-time great Journal" of history. So many of the Psalms are simply the product of people who wrote in the presence of God—describing their fears, their failures and their faith.

- In Psalm 38, David responds to the chastening and correcting of God by writing down his thoughts.

- In Psalm 51, David writes of his confession for sin before the Lord.

- In Psalm 73, David complains before God about how discouraged he is over how well the people who hate God are doing.

Think of that. A man frankly, boldly says, "God, I'm not doing well and it bothers me that the people who don't seem to care anything about You appear to be doing better!"

Ever feel that way? David did.

And apparently God not only isn't threatened by such heart cries, but when David did that, He decided to even put that in His "Big Journal"—the Eternal Word of the Holy Scriptures!

But there's a reason: David's *registering* discouragement didn't *result* in discouragement. In that same psalm, after "journaling" his discontent and his complaint, David ends by saying, "This is the sourness of soul I felt *until I came into the presence of the Lord.*" It's a beautiful, powerful, pivotal point, and that same transition will happen when any of us get alone with Him and take time to examine our hearts honestly before God.

Interacting with the Word

Journaling may also include writing down my subjective response to what I have read in my devotional use of the Bible. I don't mean the fruit of my *study,* so much as my lessons of *discovery* when I'm alone with the Lord and His Word.

In Psalm 19, David describes the preciousness of the Word to him as he responds to God's Word and expresses his delight in it. For example, listen to verses 10 and 11.

> More to be desired are they than gold, yea, than much fine gold; sweeter also than honey and the honeycomb. Moreover by them Your servant is warned, and in keeping them there is great reward.

That's a "journaled" expression of thanks for God's Law. Then, David "journals" his response to having reflected on God's Word and its intent toward him (vv. 12-14):

> Cleanse me from secret faults. Keep back Your servant also from presumptuous sins; let them not have dominion over me. Then I shall be blameless, and I shall be innocent of great transgression. Let the words of my mouth and the meditation of my heart be acceptable in Your sight, O Lord, my strength and my redeemer.

The entire 119th Psalm is very much a case study of the same thing. It is a person saying, "Lord, this is what Your Word means to me." It's more than honoring the Word of God as the "whole counsel of God," but exemplifies our personally responding to the things He says from His Word, *to me*—as I listen to the Lord speaking to me as I humble my heart before His open Book.

The Holy Spirit's Dealings

Then, in the atmosphere of solitude the Holy Spirit will often *speak* to us. He does that. Still does that today. Personally. And when He does it's good to journal it.

That's what occurred in Psalm 27:8, where the psalmist notes, "When You said, 'Seek My face,' my heart said to You, 'Your face, Lord, I will seek.'"

Can you see it? The Holy Spirit spoke to a person's heart, the person recognized it and wrote their response: "Lord, what You're saying to me by Your Spirit, I'm saying back right now. I'm going to do it."

I recently came across the thought: "A person's spirituality is the sum of their responses to what they believe to be the voice of God." That's a good definition of spiritual growth; tuning to what the Lord says to you and then responding on His terms. You'll find it happens best when you have sufficient times alone with Him to hear His voice, to record His words to you, and to live as His Holy Spirit directs, refreshes, corrects, and renews.

I've learned to read in the discipline of solitude and to depend on the renewal it can bring. I've also found great help from the discipline of journaling God's dealings with my heart.

These practices seem to converge in an account I journaled, then incorporated a couple of years ago in my book, *Moments with Majesty*. It's a compilation of about a hundred short articles, most of which were written in times I was alone with God and He would breathe a concept to my understanding or clarify a viewpoint in my mind. In one of these articles, I tell a story about one of the most pressured occasions in my life and a time of solitude worked for me by God's grace.

"Remembering Jade Cove"

Anna and I were recently coming back from Carmel, where we celebrated our wedding anniversary. Driving south on Highway 1, that famous roadway that hugs the Pacific Coast, I reminisced as we passed Jade Cove, near Big Sur. That's the place where, years ago, by the grace of God, I "turned the corner." I don't mean a curve on that twisting, perilous highway, but the turnaround at Jade Cove rescued me from something as bad as a car accident.

For several weeks I had been experiencing a horrible accumulation of pressure—mental and emotional. Work had piled up, schedule demands were burning me out. Through a combination of circumstances, I was riding the ragged edge of a nervous breakdown.

Some nights I would dream of being chased—and then crushed—by a massive object relentlessly pursuing and slowly gaining on me as I ran to escape it. Other nights I feared closing my eyes to go to sleep, feeling if I did I would not awaken again—that my heart would stop or my breath cease. I was rational enough to know this wasn't true, but weak enough in my emotionally drained condition that I was unable to break the tormenting thoughts.

Then I discovered the words of the songwriter.

Listen . . .

I will both lie down in peace, and sleep; for You alone, O Lord, make me dwell in safety.

(PS. 4:8)

And another lyric:

I lay down and slept; I awoke, for the Lord sustained me.

(PS. 3:5)

I can hardly describe the power of those words as they flowed across my weary soul. I grasped them for the reliable, eternal words of truth that they are. They were all the more meaningful to me when I remembered they were written by a very busy man—a man of accomplishment and crushing responsibilities. David was a successful king and a conquering hero, yet a man who needed release from pressures that threatened his sleep.

God's words buoyed my soul for several weeks, sustaining me until that day on Highway 1. I was driving slowly northward, hoping a break in schedule and a change of scene would take the cascading voices off my mind and the rising fear from my heart.

I had stopped at the sign. Jade Cove, it read. I went down near the water's edge to look at the beautiful seascape. To listen to the waves. To feel the sea-spray on my face. To pray.

It was there something happened—better yet, Someone. Because as surely as I knew His Word had sustained me when fear plagued my nights, I knew God's presence had drawn near to deliver my mind. Like fog burning off the coastline, the Son of God simply reached down and lifted the burden I had carried for months.

I share that with you now to urge *you* to receive His Word. "I will both lie down in peace, and sleep; for You alone, O Lord, make me dwell in safety."

Call upon His Holy Spirit to deliver you. I know He will, because He did that for me at a place called Jade Cove, and He did it through the power of a man named Jesus.

He's there for you. Right now. You don't even have to go to Jade Cove. Because . . .

Whoever calls on the name of the Lord shall be saved.

(ACTS 2:21)

Chapter Eighteen

The Life of a Worshiper

When we talk about the expanding life in God's power and blessing, there is no escape coming face-to-face with the fundamental personal discipline of worship: (1) daily, as a private, devotional practice, and (2) regularly, in assembling together with the people of God in a local congregation.

I realize I might be suspect in the second point, being a pastor of a church. "Wouldn't a pastor say that? After all, he needs people in attendance or he's out of a job!" But the gathering of the people was never man's idea. It was God's:

> From everyone who gives it willingly with his heart you shall take My offering. . . . And let them make Me a sanctuary, that I may dwell among them. . . . And there I will meet with you, and I will speak with you from above the mercy seat.
>
> (EX. 25:2, 8, 22)

The divine idea of assembly has nothing to do with attendance records, with the size of any local congregation, or to swell the coffers. The issue is that He wants to meet with His people as a *corporate* body as well as in *private* fellowship. The practice of worship with the assembly of saints is a "gathering together" which is pointedly and prophetically directed.

> Not forsaking the assembling of ourselves together, as is the manner of some, but exhorting one another, and so much the more as you see the Day approaching.
>
> (HEB. 10:25)

We have already dealt with worship at a private level, but here is worship called forth (1) in assembly, (2) at appointed times, (3) in faithfulness to God's Word, and (4) as a discipline of the believer. "Get Me to the Church on Time" might well be a theme for each of us.

The text expresses two very sobering thoughts. First, this was a discipline problem in the early church. "What? You mean people neglected church attendance back then?" There's the answer; as the writer commands, "Don't forsake assembly as the fashion of a few has become!" But a second, *more*-sobering issue than "missing church" is noted in these words, "so much the more as you see the Day approaching."

Listen. Not only were some neglectful of gathering with the saints, and told, "Don't miss church!" but the warning is cast in terms that indicate the truth that there is a power in the discipline of worship that protects against (a) giving into the spirit of the times (Rom. 12:1-2), (b) losing touch with the spirit of anticipation of Jesus' return (1 Tim. 4:8; 2 Tim. 4:8) or (c) neglecting attentiveness to our role as stewards of gifts for which we'll be accountable when He comes (Matt. 25:14-30).

Of course, the flesh has counter arguments to challenge discipline's call:

- "Perhaps I need a break—don't want to let 'religious tradition' push me to performance. If my heart's not in it, no use going—and I just don't 'feel it' today. Probably more 'honest' to stay home. God won't mind—especially since I'm being more honest by *not* going than if I went feeling like this."

- "I'm so 'beat' today, I'd be a hindrance to others. If I go, I'll only be someone whose presence siphons off the jubilation of the assembly. How could I possibly receive something from God in my condition?"

- "We had such a fight last night, and I still have such a rotten attitude, how could God take my presence seriously, or even speak to me?"

- "I have fumbled so miserably this week that if I go to church today God will know I'm coming only as a hypocrite, like I was trying to fake Him into thinking I'm a good guy 'cause I showed up at His place. I better get my act cleaned up before I go. Maybe I'll just stay home and pray—read the Word—show Him I'm sincere, first. Yeah—next week I'll be better."

Ever hear your *own* "small voice" arguing this way? Silence it, because God's Word has an overarching answer to every claim the flesh makes. If you're tired, stumbling, fumbling, or needful, He says, "OK. Assemble. For it's in the environment of your obedi-ence, and the presence of My people, that I'll be able to best deal with you, to refresh, to renew, or to restore!"

The Approaching Day

The expression "the Day approaching," of course, refers to the coming of our Lord Jesus Christ. Sound-minded faith knows any day in our lifetime is as likely a day as any, and calls us to fidelity in assembly: "Lord, when You come, You'll find me faithful. At Your appearing You'll find me *'ready'!'"*

Don't mistake my words. I'm not suggesting something so biblically insipid as the notion, "If you're not in church when Jesus comes, you'll miss the Rapture!" That isn't the issue. But neither can you nor I escape *all* the implications of the phrase, "the Day is approaching—*so much the more* be assembled!" It's simply a matter of raw obedience to God and His Word. Go to church! Dash the notions that assembling with the body is only ritual or tradition. You need to be there!

C.S. Lewis' *Screwtape Letters* focus the devious ways of subtle, satanic spirits, at whispering ideas which creep into our minds, "selling" notions that seem so momentarily logical, such as, "The church is only a historic, institutional, traditional, man-concocted idea, and going every week a human invention!" Or, "Besides, where you attend it's so 'dead,' so boorish!"

But such *dead thoughts* need to be identified as coming from the Death-Pit itself. There is *nothing* "dead" about you and me making a habit of being there. When an honest, humble soul comes to meet *Him*, Jesus can make Himself alive to us *anywhere*. Come. Sing. Love. Give. Listen. Don't criticize. Smile. Praise. Look past imperfect people to God. Worship Him. Stop analyzing the limited skills of others. Humble your heart.

If you open yourself to His love, being *willing* to be faithful in church attendance, you'll find His reward.

159

It's worthwhile to look at Jesus' own habits in this regard. Read Luke 4:16, which speaks of Jesus' "custom" of regular "church attendance":

> So He came to Nazareth, where He had been brought up. And as His custom was, He went into the synagogue on the Sabbath Day, and stood up to read.

I can't help laughing, in a sense; at any critic of church attendance who refuses to go on the grounds of "the place is too spiritually 'dead'!"

You want to argue church attendance with Jesus? Go ahead, do it!

"Well, Lord, You certainly know that things aren't as spiritual as they ought to be. You know people aren't warm, understanding, or friendly!"

And Jesus replies: "Warm and friendly? Have you ever been at Nazareth? The day I was there they tried to throw Me off the cliff!" But Jesus showed up anyway *"as His custom was"!*

Case closed.

First Corinthians 16:2 shows us the pattern of life in the early church; further indicating a continuing discipline of church gatherings.

> On the first day of the week let each one of you lay something aside, storing up as he may prosper, that there be no collections when I come.

Hear it? "When you meet together on the first day of the week." Our "Sunday appointment" isn't anything to be argued and debated. Let's never labor the issue of "which day." If anyone worships any other day, I certainly don't mind, but there's no arguing *against* Sunday.

> One person esteems one day above another; another esteems every day alike. Let each be fully convinced in his own mind. He who observes the day, observes it to the Lord; and he who does not observe the day, to the Lord he does not observe it.
>
> (ROM. 14:5-6)

The real issue is that on *some day*—each week—you gather with the saints. In the early church, the biblical evidence we've seen is that they gathered on Sunday (and don't accept the debater's argument that these early believers had submitted to a dead pagan tradition that bound them into some kind of a "carnality or pagan aberration resulting in Sunday worship." No, sir! They worshiped on Sunday because they recognized it as *the day Jesus rose from the dead!* Every weekly assembly was a re-celebration of the resurrection life of Christ! So, let's continue that "re-celebrating," in our obedience to worship at a weekly appointed time. Here are four reasons:

1. We will find that grace is released to us, because we "make room" for that grace through our obedience and acceptance of the discipline of attendance.

2. It gives us a chance to acknowledge with humility, "I need the body of Christ." We are not stand-alones; not "Lone Rangers" in today's church. We need to be with the body because we are members of a living body, and a "member" separated from the body will decay.

3. We acknowledge a distinct accountability to the body of Christ; we show a practical availability to serve; we allow a place and time for correction. *We show up;* and by our presence, thereby acknowledge we're righteously submitted to Christ's rule in and through His church.

4. We manifest a model: "In all things showing yourself to be a pattern of good works" (Titus 2:7). By our attendance, worship at an appointed time, we show a pathway for others to observe, not as a self-righteous display, but as a demonstration in the *Lord's* way, taking to heart our understanding that there is wisdom in our obedience to live as a worshiper who acknowledges "an appointed time."

Worship As an Altar

With our *appointment* to worship, let's consider worship as a time we "meet God." We need to regularly come into the *presence* of God in worship, to *encounter* through worship. We have, as I've sometimes put it, "an unalterable need of an altar."

Now, this aspect of worship often happens best when we're *alone* with the Lord; but not, of course, as a substitute for our attendance at church. The Bible doesn't give you or me that option. Both public and private times of worship are needed in a disciple's life with Christ. Along with our gathering times with the church, let's also have times that we meet the Lord at private altars of worship, encounter, and growth.

God's Word provides examples in the many altars which constitute the life of Abraham. Let me cite four instances.

After the Lord had called Abraham (still called Abram at this point), He had made clear the man's destiny was to not only realize promise for his own life, but that the influence of his life would touch the nations.

There is no way to determine exactly how all this distilled in Abraham's soul. At the very least, he had to have felt that he was into something that was well beyond his capacity to fulfill—except God help him.

It is interesting to trace Abraham's life and discover "altar moments." There are at least eight pivotal events at which he encounters the Lord in distinct ways. These four, within Genesis 12 and 13 are illustrative:

1. The Altar of Promise

> Then Abram took Sarai his wife and Lot his brother's son, and all their possessions that they had gathered, and the people whom they had acquired in Haran, and they departed to go to the land of Canaan. So they came to the land of Canaan. Abram passed through the land to the place of Shechem, as far as the terebinth tree of Moreh. And the Canaanites were then in the land.
>
> (GEN. 12:5-7)

This first "altar moment" involves two dynamics directly related to our experiences. It is an *altar of promise*—"To you I will give this land," but it is an *altar amid adversaries*—"And the Canaanites were then in the land." The picture is focused: It's a classic photograph of God's declared purpose in our lives, in immediate juxtaposition to the adversary's presence and potential to inhibit that promise being fulfilled.

Take that thought and apply it to your own life. What promises has God made alive to your heart? What potential has He indicated He intends to multiply and prosper through you? And in contrast, have you found obstacles, opposition, oppression? Of course we do. And the answer is to *seal* the promise at God's altar—securing it in faith. What is fixed in place at an altar with

God will find solidity when it later comes under attack. The adversary's resistance is real, but what is sealed at the Father's throne will survive and triumph:

> For this reason I also suffer these things; nevertheless I am not ashamed, for I know whom I have believed and am persuaded that He is able to keep what I have committed to Him until that Day.
>
> (2 TIM. 1:12)

2. The Altar of Intimacy

Abraham's second altar is equally demonstrative of a stabilizing step in faith's progress. It took place at an *altar of increased familiarity, of growth in intimacy.*

> And he moved from there to the mountain east of Bethel, and he pitched his tent with Bethel on the west and Ai on the east; there he built an altar to the Lord and called on the name of the Lord.
>
> (GEN. 12:8)

Abraham's "calling on the NAME of the Lord" (emphasis mine) is a direct reference to a distinct dimensional grasp of something more of the Lord's nature, character, and fullness of person. The Bible speaks of "name" as more than merely a title or label.

> The name of the Lord is a strong tower; the righteous run to it and are safe.
>
> (PROV. 18:10)

The name of the Lord represents the fullness of His person, and in this mention of "the Lord," we are introduced to the evidence that Abraham was coming to know the Lord as more than merely the God of all creation and power. He is finding a more intimate familiarity with the Lord in His readiness to meet us in a personally caring, sustaining friendship.

Receiving God's *promise* for our lives and *power* over the adversary is never a substitute for our growing in intimacy with Him as a Person. Abraham's faith was not the fruit of formulas and slogans. It was born of a growing relationship at a personal level with the Lord—the sustaining, personally caring One.

3. The Altar of No Return

Genesis 13:3-4 is a moving testimony to God's grace in retrieving us from the subtle snares of confusion by which even the most faithful of us will sometimes be set back.

> And he went on his journey from the South as far as Bethel, to the place where his tent had been at the beginning, between Bethel and Ai, to the place of the altar which he had made there at first. And there Abram called on the name of the Lord.

Abraham had made a trip to Egypt. Why? We're not told. The Lord had promised him the land where he was; he was growing in a closer knowledge of the Lord, personally—but then, the trip to Egypt.

Except for the marvelous grace of God the trip was a sad commentary on Abraham's fear and weakness. But the Lord retrieves him through a show of intervening mercy (read 12:10-20), and when it's over he's not only come *through,* he's come *out*—magnificently!

This altar is an *altar of no return;* it's the time and place that Abraham puts down a stake—"I'm here where God means me to be, and there's no wandering, ever again!" It's an altar all of us must come to at some time. It doesn't mean there will never be trial, test, or even stumbling. But once the stake is driven—once the altar of no return is built in God's presence—there is something that will transpire in the soul that never again leaves the assigned purposes of God ("this is your land"); that never drifts away for anything of other interest or human speculation.

- It needs to happen in a person's *belief:* doubt will never again be given a place to question God's will and purpose for me.

- It needs to happen in a person's *sense* of mission: I know what God wants me to do and I'm not only going to *do* nothing less, but I have come to know I'm *good* for nothing else!

164

● It needs to happen in a person's marriage: There is no other one for me—God has given me one partner for my one lifetime!

Apply the principle where it needs to be applied: Build *your* altar(s) of no return!

Finally, there is a fourth altar—

4. The Altar of Possession

Arise, walk in the land through its length and its width, for I give it to you. Then Abram moved his tent, and went and dwelt by the terebinth trees of Mamre, which are in Hebron, and built an altar there to the Lord.

(GEN. 13:17-18)

Abraham had earlier been given the promise that the land would be his, but now the Lord calls him to actually pace it off—measure the dimensions of God's promise.

This *altar of possession* is that action by which Abraham is coming to real and practical terms with a general-until-now promise. It is one thing to have a *given* promise and to have a *possessed* promise. Abraham's actually walking through the land evidences God's practical ways of bringing any of us to terms with the *details* of His will.

Imagination is a wonderful thing, and when God captures our imaginations with His promises, a vision may well become our treasured hope. But there comes a time when the Lord will bring us to the *reality* of the promise—its dimensions, its demands—the *time* it will take to fully realize all the promise entails. So it is He will bring us to an altar at which we (1) confirm our acceptance of the *implications* of the promise, and (2) commit our life to the *pursuit* of the promise's full outworking.

Such altars are essential. And as we trace the life of faith's father, we learn the potential that flows from a life of private worship—walking with God in the secret places of encounter and growth; coming to know Him in ever-expanding intimacy and ever-broadening mission. Abraham's building of altars is laden with lessons for us. The unalterable need of an altar is for learning the wisdom of bringing life's difficult things and turning them into stepping-stones of worship presented before God.

Hebrews 13:10 says, "we have an altar," unlike any other altar, referring to what we have through the New Covenant: an intimate approach with the Living God. It affords a boldness of access, for we do not have a High Priest who cannot be touched with the feelings of our weaknesses, but One who, feeling sensitized to all we feel, readily hears us and invites us: "Come boldly before the throne of grace."

An old hymn asks, "Is Your All on the Altar?"

> You have longed for sweet peace, and for faith to increase,
> And have earnestly, fervently prayed;
> But you cannot have rest or be perfectly blest,
> Until all on the altar is laid.
>
> Would you walk with the Lord in the light of His Word,
> And have peace and contentment always;
> You must do His sweet will to be free from all ill,
> On the altar your all you must lay.
>
> Oh, we never can know what the Lord will bestow
> Of the blessings for which we have prayed,
> Till our body and soul He doth fully control,
> And our all on the altar is laid.
>
> Who can tell all the love He will send from above,
> And how happy our hearts will be made,
> Of the fellowship sweet we shall share at His feet,
> When our all on the altar is laid.
>
> Refrain:
> Is your all on the altar of sacrifice laid?
> Your heart, does the Spirit control?
> You can only be blest and have peace and sweet rest,
> As you yield Him your body and soul.

Elisha A. Hoffman

This summons of the old hymn is a healthy remembrance for us. As we think of the disciplines of worship, always remember they not only involve high ecstasy and joyous praise in public assembly, but worship also calls us to plain, private moments of disciplines, *simply being with God.* And in every circumstance, especially when hard times come, to build an altar of life's rock-hard circumstances—and meet God.

Worship and Stewardship

Finally, let me mention one other thing about worship.

Worship also involves the stewardship of what God has blessed us with materially. The Bible makes very clear that the giving and bringing of tithes and offerings is not simply an Old Covenant proposition. I realize the vulnerability of any Bible teacher being criticized if he or she teaches the contemporary practice of tithes and offerings.

I've heard the arguments. Every one. From every aspect. And I don't want to seem contentious or obstinate. But let me simply mention two things in answer to the possibility you might have had that order of input.

First, 2 Corinthians 3 summarily teaches that the glory of the New Covenant will always exceed the glory of the Old. Then if "tithing" is made an Old Testament practice, how can a New Testament believer ever do less? Answer: We can't, if we grasp the spirit of New Testament giving. "Well," someone says, "I'll accept that, but I'm not going to call it a tithe."

Fine. That's all right. But let the principle be understood, that the giving patterns of the New Covenant can't retreat to less than what was the practice under the Old Covenant. Oh, not because we're saved by it, but because our stewardship in worship and giving should manifest the spirit of the New Testament which transcends the Old.

Second, Jesus confirmed and approved the practice of tithing. As you will recall, in Matthew 23:23, He was faulting the Pharisees for their attentiveness to the smallest detail of tithing and their inattentiveness to great issues of loving, justice, and graciousness. He ridiculed them, almost fiercely, for their smallness of soul in overlooking great issues of the Law. But He went on to say, "These [tithing] you ought to have done, without leaving the others [justice and mercy] undone." Christ clearly approved that they tithed, and disapproved that they didn't do *more* than that.

Our giving and generosity are taught elsewhere in the Scriptures:

- Paul writes to confirm and approve the generosity of the Philippians in chapter 4 of that epistle.

- He calls the Corinthians to liberal giving notwithstanding hard economic times (2 Cor. 8–9).

- Luke 6:38 calls us to give. These are Jesus' words. "Give, and it will be given to you: good measure, pressed down, shaken together, and running over will be put into your bosom."

That expression, "put into your bosom" refers to clothing which had an apron on the front, and He's saying, "You hold that out and it'll hold more than your hand could ever give." God will abound back to you as you learn His way of giving.

I know there are people who take exception and say, "You shouldn't teach giving because God is going to give back." But listen, dear one. Let's just face it. We can't get away from the proposition. I admit that ideally it would be wonderful if the reward promised was never on our minds. But nonetheless, if we give, God is going to give back to us. He has built the order of our world; it can't be reversed because it's as much His will as any other of His natural laws. Giving rebounds with blessing. It's not even as though God has to make an independent decision because we give; as though He watches and says, "Oh, they gave, so now I'll give." No! Rather, the blessing returns because something is released in the invisible realm according to God's reciprocal law of giving. When we live as people who worship with faithful stewardship, there is a release, an outflowing, and overflowing of God's abundance because we have aligned with the order of His ways.

Once you do so, you'll find it works. If a person were to leap off a tall building, they wouldn't have to call into action the law of gravity. It just works. And when you come to give, you don't have to call into action some law of reciprocity. It just works. God responds to those who align with His ways, because He has built it into His system. As we worship Him with fidelity in tithes and offerings, watch Him abound grace to you—not because we bought it, and not because we earned it. But because we are *learning to give* in obedience as we worship; whether it's gathering together with the saints as a discipline, walking with Him and learning altar-building, or being faithful in stewardship. We have learned the way of God's people who function in all the facets of worship with obedience, which has always its rich reward.

III

PRAYER
DISCIPLINES

"And Above and Beneath It All..."

The aged apostle came to the conclusion of one of his letters, and in giving a series of short, concise commands summarizing essentials for disciples he wrote, *"Pray without ceasing"* (1 Thes. 5:17).

Whatever else may be said about either *living* as a disciple of Jesus Christ or *walking* with Him by faith, in love, through trial and in power, prayer is the one discipline above and beneath all others.

It has been said that more books have been written on prayer than any other worthwhile theme occupying human inquiry or aspiration. No thinking person denies there is "something" in this practice. This is often true even when they've denied there's even "Someone" *there* to whom prayer may be offered. Prayer is a word or idea used by the materialist or Eastern mystic to describe quiet creative reasoning or "transcendent" meditation. Still others will refer to prayer as anything from describing a "good feeling" (toward a cause, a person, or a memory) to "an impassioned cry" for Help! from "whoever's out there."

At a fuller, deeper dimension, for the disciple of Jesus, prayer is person-to-Person communication. It is a combination of

worship—through adoration, praise, and thanksgiving *to* God;

fellowship—through devotion, communion, and conversation *with* God; and *intercession* — through supplication, fasting, and spiritual warfare *before* God.

"Praying always with all prayer and supplication in the Spirit" is a phrase inclusively covering this triad of prayer, as Paul enunciates it in his concluding appeal to the Ephesians (6:18). Some translations make "all prayer" to read "all *kinds* of prayer," and it's a worthy translation pointing us to a learning path of applied growth in understanding the *means* and *methods* of prayer.

The Bible's call to prayer is not a call to the mystical or to the theoretical. The pathway of prayer is preeminently *learnable,* not intended to be *mysterious,* and always intended to be practical. This section is designed to provide a grid of understanding regarding the basic disciplines included in prayer.

Starting with the seven basic "steps in prayer" which Jesus outlines in instructing His disciples on *how* to pray, we'll follow with three other keys to effective "asking *in* prayer," and "attacking *through* prayer." In all, we are moving toward applying the *one constant* the Bible teaches the earnest disciple: "Pray without ceasing." To learn to *live* in the spirit of prayer is to learn to *walk* in the presence of Jesus. Always.

Confident Faith

"OUR FATHER IN HEAVEN . . ."

> In this manner, therefore, pray: Our Father in heaven, Hallowed be Your name. Your kingdom come. Your will be done on earth as it is in heaven. Give us this day our daily bread. And forgive us our debts, as we forgive our debtors. And do not lead us into temptation, but deliver us from the evil one. For Yours is the kingdom and the power and the glory forever. Amen.
>
> (MATT. 6:9-13)

Jesus opens His teaching with an emphasis on our relationship with God as "Father." In doing so, He lays the foundational truth that we are given grounds for confidence in prayer on the strength of that "Father-child" relationship, which the Bible says is established and secured through Christ.

> Now this is the confidence that we have in Him, that if we ask anything according to His will, He hears us. And if we know that He hears us, whatever we ask, we know that we have the petitions that we have asked of Him.
>
> (1 JOHN 5:14-15)

There is nothing more crippling to effective prayer than not having confidence in our relationship with God. When Jesus refers to God as the "Father," He helps us to understand the glorious relationship we are intended to have with Him.

Unfortunately, the concept of "father" has been marred for many through disappointing earthly relationships with parents or authority figures. Because of this common human fact, Jesus made a point to show us the Father in a way no one else ever could. For in Christ Himself we see that God is a Father who transcends even the finest earthly father; He is able to redeem us from the broken images or painful memories of our lives. As we follow Christ's teachings about the Father and see Him show us the Father in His life, we come to understand the power of His words to Philip: "He who has seen Me has seen the Father" (John 14:9).

In Luke 15, Jesus uses the story of the prodigal son to paint a magnificent picture of what our Father God is really like.

Here is a young man who wasted everything he'd been given—his inheritance, his opportunities, and his father's trust. He ended up working in a pigpen. But in unfolding this story, Jesus unveils God's heart toward each of us through five essential phrases. He shows that, regardless of what we have wasted, God's arms are still reaching toward us, openly and lovingly.

The first thing we learn about is God's *quest* for us. We see this in the phrase that says the father saw the prodigal son when he was still "a great way off" (v. 20). This shows us something unique and precious about the longing heart of God. For, as the father watched for his wayward son, so God's heart yearns and watches for each of us, even when we are far away from Him. In other words, regardless of what we have done or where we are, *God loves us.*

Second, we see that when the father saw the son on his way home, he "had compassion, and ran and fell on his neck and kissed him" (v. 20); he *received* his son.

I have often reflected on this story, thinking about the reluctance that son must have felt as he drew closer and closer to home. He must have been uneasy about his return, feeling very unworthy. He knew he had squandered his resources, had wasted his entire inheritance, and had nearly lost his life! He had every reason to doubt his father's acceptance.

But Jesus describes God's open heart toward us by showing how the young man's father welcomed him. The verb tense used here to say, "he embraced him and kissed him" literally translates "he kissed him repeatedly." The father must have received his wandering son with much the same joy that he'd had when he first embraced him at his birth. It was as though a brand-new son was being born all over again! "For this my son was dead and is alive again; he was lost and is found" (v. 24). And in this same way, it is with joy that *God receives us.*

Third, after this loving reception the Father called for "the finest robe" to be given to his son. The particular style of robe referred to was full-length in cut; in those days, a garment reserved only for those who held a position of honor and prestige. So it is clear that this fallen son was being *restored* to his former position as an heir in the household. The privileges of relationship with his father were returned to him, even though he had lost the inheritance he'd been given. Likewise, God not only *receives* us as forgiven sons, but He *restores* us from the loss our past has caused us. Although we may have abandoned the life-gifts He first gave us, He welcomes us back with a loving embrace and brings us again to our intended place in His will and purposes.

Fourth, the father had a "jeweled ring" put on his son's finger. How the hearts of those listening to this story for the first time must have leapt when Jesus related this part! They would have recognized instantly the significance of this action, for in ancient times the giving of such a ring indicated the son's *full return to partnership* with his father in the family's business. The ring gave him the right to exercise authority in all commercial or legal matters, for it represented the full weight of whatever authority or power that family's name carried.

Thus, in calling us to pray "Our Father," Jesus has shown us how God invites us to let Him *authorize us as His partner.* Our prayer in the "family name" of Jesus is authoritative prayer. And that name is given to us freely and fully, carrying with it all the rights and privileges granted to us as members of God's eternal family.

Fifth, the Father had shoes or sandals placed on his son's feet. These shoes were more than mere clothing. Old Testament imagery teaches that people in mourning or grief commonly removed their shoes as a symbol of their sorrow. By placing shoes on his son's feet, the father was making an announcement to his son: "The time of mourning and the days of separation are over! The time of rejoicing has come!" And in this we see the final teaching of God's heart toward us: *"God rejoices over us!"* He rejoices at our return, and at the restored relationship we share with Him.

Through the story of the prodigal son, Jesus illustrates our standing before God: We are welcomed to a place of confidence through the forgiveness given to us through Christ. Our Father offers us an authoritative right to be sons (John 1:12), to function in partnership with Him and extend His dominion over all the earth. No matter what we fight, whether the powers of hell or our own weaknesses, eventual victory will be ours.

This is what Jesus wants to teach us when He instructs us to pray, "Our Father in heaven." He is founding all prayer on a growing relationship with a loving God. And as the truth of God's reception and our restoration fills us, we will discover yet another benefit: *We will learn to receive each other.* We begin, with Christ's help, to see one another as brothers and sisters who have been received by a loving Father. And in that light, we can join together in harmony, lifting up a concert of powerful, effective prayer as people who have discovered God's love and are learning to pray confidently in Him.

Transforming Faith

"HALLOWED BE YOUR NAME."

The frequently intoned word "hallowed," literally means, "Holy be Your name." In these words we are invited to experience the transforming power of prayer as Jesus introduces us to life's mightiest action: Worship. "Holy be Your name" is a call to *worship* at the throne of God.

It will better help us to understand worship when we realize that the throne of God is an actual place. We are not just offering our worship "up there somewhere." In Revelation 4:8, John describes his glorious vision of God's throne and the mighty angelic beings around it. An innumerable host is seen worshiping God, saying,

> Holy, holy, holy,
> Lord God Almighty,
> who was and is and is to come!

It is to this place that Jesus invites us, not just in an imaginary sense but in a living, dynamic sense of worship. We are called to gather before our Father and to bring Him our own offerings of praise.

Psalm 22:3 helps explain why worship is so important and so potentially transforming of our life and circumstance. The text teaches that through their worship, God's people may literally make an earthly place for Him to be enthroned in the midst of them:

Yet Thou art holy, O Thou who art enthroned upon the praises of Israel. (NASB)

Through this insight, we can see the dynamic objective of worship: it isn't simply an exercise in religious forms, but worship is God's assigned way to bring His presence and power to His people. In other words, just as *we* enter into God's presence with worship, so *He* responds by coming into our presence. Our worship invites Him to *rule* in our midst. When our hearts are opened wide in worship, God will respond. His presence and power will come to *transform;* to change us and our circumstances.

So we see a dual objective of worship: (1) To declare God's *transcendent* greatness, and (2) To receive His *transforming* power in our lives, situations, and needs.

In a dynamic sense, the words "Holy be Your name" are both an exalting of God and a humbling of ourselves. When we use those words, we are inviting the Holy Spirit to make God's presence and Person real in our midst. Such encounters on a regular basis can only bring transformation — the conforming of our wills to God's, the shaping of our lives into His likeness.

But we all, with unveiled face, beholding as in a mirror the glory of the Lord, are being transformed into the same image from glory to glory, just as by the Spirit of the Lord.

(2 COR. 3:18)

Worship is not the only means to this transformation — we need to respond to the Word, obey the Holy Spirit, and walk in obedience daily — but worship *can* bring it about faster. To better understand transformation through worshiping, let's first examine the meaning of holiness, since that is the trait of God's nature that Jesus focuses on in this section of the Lord's Prayer.

As often as "holy" is used as a worship expression, it too is seldom understood. We tend to only think of holiness as an external characteristic, a meditative expression, an organ-like tone of speech, a certain style of garments. The problem with this restrictive view is that we too easily may end in feeling intimidated or disqualified because we feel we haven't the needed external traits of holiness to earn God's pleasure.

On the other hand, some consider holiness to be a stern,

forbidding trait of God's nature, a sort of attitudinal barrier on God's part—an obstacle created by His flaunting His perfection in the face of our weaknesses and sins. This too is wrong.

But in contrast, and simply stated, holiness is shown in the Bible as something relating to God's *completeness.* That is, God's holiness essentially acknowledges that *as* He is complete; there is nothing lacking in His person, and nothing needs to be added to make Him "enough." This insight into the meaning of God's holiness holds a promise: *Because* His holiness is complete, and *because* it is God's nature to give, He wants to share His holiness with us to complete *us!* His holiness, then, is not an *obstacle* to our acceptance, but a resource for our completion and fulfillment as persons. God is ready to pour Himself into us, to complete those areas of our lives that are lacking or "unholy" because of our sin.

As we open ourselves through worship to this desire of God's, we will find His holiness and wholeness overtaking our *un*holiness. His personal power, responding to our worship, will begin to sweep away whatever residue remains from the destruction caused by our past sins.

In worship-filled prayer, a spiritual genetic begins to take effect. The traits and characteristics "born" into us when we became a part of God's family will begin to grow, making us more and more like Him. Just as surely as physical traits are transmitted to us by our earthly parents, so the nature and likeness of our Heavenly Father will grow in us as we learn and grow more in worshiping Him.

This truth is reflected in the command, "You must be holy, for I am holy" (Lev. 11:45; 1 Peter 1:16). Those verses hold a promise of holiness and completeness. They are not so much a demand that we stretch ourselves through self-produced devices of "holiness" as they are God's guarantee that His life in us will become increasingly evident and powerfully transforming. So in teaching us this prayer, Jesus calls us into the Father's presence to give the Father the opportunity to remake us in His likeness.

That's transformation!—a transformation that allows God to extend His kingdom through us. And this personal dimension of transformation is only the beginning.

Beyond the power of worship-filled prayer to change *us,* it can also achieve a remarkable impact on *others.* In instructing us to enter the Father's presence with worship, Jesus points the way to a faith that can transform all of our lives and the lives of those we encounter. He says, "Since God is your Father, let your worship in

His presence make you more like Him; and as you do, His working in you will affect those around you."

So, let us enter His presence with worship! Let's take the faith-step that moves us to experience the transforming power of God's rule in our lives and character, and through our faithful prayers.

So take a new stance. Move your posture in worship beyond one of passive *reflection* to one of a power-filled potential for *transformation*. The *Holy* One we "hallow" in prayer is ready to invade each situation we address with His *completing* presence and power.

Responsible Faith

"YOUR KINGDOM COME. YOUR WILL BE DONE ON EARTH AS IT IS IN HEAVEN."

The Lord's Prayer further shows us how Christ intends us to effectively discharge our *responsibility* in prayer. "Your kingdom come. Your will be done on earth as it is in heaven." Jesus' counsel on how to pray illuminates a truth that we often ignore: People need to invite God's rule and power into the affairs of their lives through prayer, for if humans won't pray, God's rule in their circumstance is forfeited.

That thought runs counter to the common supposition, "Well, if God wants to do something, He'll just *do* it." This sorry strain of fatalism infests most minds. But the idea of man as a pawn moved by the Almighty at His whim is *totally* removed from the truth revealed in Scripture. Jesus shows us that mankind—each human being—is responsible for inviting God's rule—i.e., His benevolent purpose, presence, and power—into this world. Rather than demonstrating man as a hopeless, helpless victim of circumstance, the Bible declares that *redeemed* man is hopeful and capable of expecting victory when he prays in faith. The grounds for this understanding can be found in the beginning of the Bible. It explains why Jesus teaches us to pray for the reinstatement of God's rule "on earth as in heaven."

Man's Loss. In Genesis 1, the Bible states that dominion over this planet was given by God to man. That assignment under God's rule was not only one of great privilege, but one which essentially made mankind responsible for what would happen on earth (Gen. 1:28). Unless we understand this fact, we will never really understand that most of the confusion, agony, and distress in our world today exists as a direct result of our having betrayed God's initial entrusting of earth to us. As a race, we have violated the responsibility God gave us.

This betrayal began at the fall of man. Through that tragedy we have suffered inestimable loss. Man not only lost his *relationship* with God, but he lost his ability to *rule* responsibly as well. Man's ability and authority to successfully administrate God's rule over the earth is completely frustrated—whether the issue is environmental pollution or home and family management. And further, this lost capacity for a peaceful, healthful life has an added complication.

According to the Bible, "the whole world lies under the sway of the wicked one" (1 John 5:19). Man's fall not only lost an administration intended for us as humankind under God's rule, it also betrayed our God-given trust of ruling earth into the hands of the devil, Satan, the "Evil One." Since the Fall, mankind has not only been vulnerable to satanic deceptions, but by our own sin and rebellion we have contributed to the confused mess our world has become. Between man's sinning and Satan's hateful quest to destroy, death and destruction have invaded every part of life as we know it—breaking relationships, dashing hopes and dreams, and ruining destinies.

God's Restoration. But when man's betrayal of God's trust turned this world over to the powers of death and hell, God lovingly provided us with hope—a living option in the person of His Son. God sent Jesus, whose ministry announced the possibility of man's restoration to God's kingdom: "Repent, for the kingdom of heaven is at hand" (Matt. 4:17). In that statement, Jesus made it clear that the rule of God was once again being made available to mankind. No longer did any member of the race need to remain a hopeless victim of sin and hell!

In His ministry, both then and now, Jesus manifests every aspect of the kingdom He offers. When Jesus heals, He is showing what can happen when the rule of God enters a situation. When He answers need at any dimension, He is putting into action the power of God's rule available for our lives. As Jesus teaches, His objective has always been to help straighten out our thinking ("repent"), to help us see what Father God is really like, so that we might respond correctly to Him and His kingdom.

But at the same time that Jesus ministers, hell seeks to level its hostile devices against the Messiah King and the kingdom He offers. Consequently, Jesus demonstrates a warlike *opposition* to the invisible powers of darkness. He is well known for demonstrating God's love, but He is equally well known for the way He confronts the demonic powers of hell. Colossians 2:15 says that in the climactic act of His crucifixion, Christ smashed these powers, (1) making possible the offer of reentry into divine life with God, and (2) paving the way for us, His followers, to also strike down satanic powers we encounter (Mark 16:17-20).

Man's Responsibility. In light of these truths, each person must decide whether or not he or she will draw on the resources of Christ's triumph through the cross and learn to live to advance God's kingdom in this world. Acceptance of Christ *begins* our participation in His kingdom (John 3:3-5), and we are then called to *advance* it, as we share the gospel of Christ with the world around us (Matt. 28:19; Acts 1:8). There is no more effective way to accelerate this advance than for believers to pray together!

Our *first steps* in faith are made on the feet of prayer, whether we are moving into victory or into witness. Our ongoing growth in prayer is in our recognizing that faith and victory are *not* achieved merely through the zeal of human programs, but by power-prayer that acknowledges Calvary's triumph as a release for God's presence and power.

This is why Jesus instructs us to pray "Your kingdom come." By this prayer we are taking on our role as members of a race who once betrayed the King and forfeited His intended purposes into the claws of the adversary. But now, as His redeemed sons and daughters, He has endowed us with restored "kingdom authority," through prayer to welcome His entry into every need and pain of this planet.

The power is God's, but the privilege *and* responsibility to pray are ours. So, let us hear and understand Jesus' words and come together at His throne, expecting and receiving the flow of the Holy Spirit's power. By His anointing we will find prayer enablement to see God's purposes being accomplished through us.

This is what it means to pray, "Thy kingdom come"; to see the rule and power of the kingdom of God as present and practical, to see the personal possibilities for power-prayer in every dimension of our daily lives. Never let the promise of Christ's future kingdom keep us from possessing the dimensions of victory that God has for us *now*. Jesus is coming again to establish His kingdom over all the earth! But that should not cause us to neglect our present prayer or ministry responsibilities for advancing the Gospel.

Until He comes again, Jesus directed us to "occupy" (Luke 19:13, KJV). That "occupation" entails drawing on the resources of God's kingdom and power, reaching into the realm of the invisible through prayer, and changing one circumstance after another.

"Your kingdom come. Your will be done on earth as it is in heaven." It is our privilege to pray this, and our responsibility thereby to exercise the beginning of our reinstatement to partnership with God, in seeing the tangled affairs of this planet reversed from the fallen order to God's intended order.

Dependent Faith

"GIVE US THIS DAY OUR DAILY BREAD."

In these words, Jesus is talking about more than our having enough food or having our physical needs met. He is issuing an invitation for us to come to the Father daily for refreshing, for renewal and nourishment for both our souls and our bodies. This phrase, "Give us this day our daily bread," registers a specific command for us to recognize our *dependency* on the Lord for *all* nourishment, and to realize that this provision for our needs flows out of the discipline of daily prayer.

James 4:2 makes a strong statement regarding the necessity of prayer: "Yet you do not have because you do not ask." These words show that the Lord is ready to release many things to us — but His readiness doesn't remove our place or need of asking. In other words, the promises or prophecies of God's care for us do not bypass our need for prayerful, acknowledged dependence. The Lord Jesus teaches us to willingly turn to the Father and call out in prayer for Him to work in our lives. Rather than relying on our own strength (chin up, teeth clenched: "I'm going to get this done."), we need to come to the Father in prayer. Daily. Dependently. And gratefully.

Dependent prayer is not desperate or demeaning prayer. It is neither frantic (as though we only resorted to turning to God in a crisis) nor depersonalizing (as though God required us to grovel in order to escape His wrath). In contrast to these distorted views, dependent prayer is both the *way* we gain a personal realization of God's unswerving commitment *to* us, and *how* we participate in God's promised provision *for* us.

Psalm 90:12 says, "So teach us to number our days, that we may gain a heart of wisdom." It's a soundminded request for wisdom to recognize how *few* days we have, and how much we need to employ them wisely. In the words, "Give us today," Jesus is showing our need to learn an accountability for each day's hours and events, as surely as our need for having adequacy of food and other needs. Dependent prayer can help us do this. Jesus is not merely teaching us to request "bread" at morning, noon, and night. He is teaching us to ask for the Father's direction and provision in every event and during each hour of our day.

Committing each day's details to God in prayer—requesting "today's bread"—can deliver us from pointless pursuits and wasted time. Such prayer paves the way to victorious days. "My times are in Your hand; deliver me from the hand of my enemies" (Ps. 31:15).

What wisdom! When we put our day in God's hands, any enemy we face can be conquered. Whether our enemy is ourselves—procrastination, sloth, or other weaknesses—or the enemy is a demonic conspiracy Satan has plotted against us, *our Lord is able to deliver us!* "Daily bread" praying is "daily victory" and "daily overcoming" praying, because it enters into drawing on God's full provision for our sufficiency. He will help us overcome anything that might wrench our lives from His purpose, or cause valuable time to slip through our fingers.

Submit your day to the Lord and ask Him to provide for your needs. Whether your need is food or counsel for the day's activities, you will find that it *will* be provided. He will faithfully and abundantly respond as we set our "times" in His hands.

And when we learn to pray this way we will find another wonderful promise being fulfilled: "As your days, so shall your strength be" (Deut. 33:25). Learning to pray, "Give us this day our daily bread," finds in the Lord a strength proportionate to each day's needs. Whatever challenges a day holds—confrontations, difficulties, even tragedies—we will receive the strength to face it. Just as we derive physical strength and nourishment from eating daily bread, so we will gain spiritual strength and nourishment when we learn the wisdom of acknowledging our dependency upon the Father—and pray His way.

Releasing Faith

"AND FORGIVE US OUR DEBTS, AS WE FORGIVE OUR DEBTORS."

The next point in the Lord's Prayer addresses our need for forgiveness. Some people use the phrase "trespass against us," while others use the word "debts" for this section of the prayer. Both expressions are accurate and uniquely significant. In fact, we need to pray *both* ways, for in these two expressions Jesus shows us the two sides of human disobedience: sins of *commission* and sins of *omission*, wrong things we have done and right things we neglected to do.

"Forgive us our trespasses" speaks to our need of asking the Lord to forgive us for having "stepped over the line." God is concerned about trespassing because He wants to keep us from the things which will damage or destroy us. In His Word He sets clear, protective guidelines—territorial boundaries, if you will—that say, "Do not trespass here." When we violate these commands intended to help us avoid what becomes self-destructive, we are guilty of "sins of commission."

On the other hand, "Forgive us our debts" relates to our failures; to cases where it might be said that we "owed it" to the situation to do differently than we did. But in failing to act rightly, we have become debtors. And such indebtedness can hang like a cloud over the soul, hindering our sense of freedom and faith for the future.

With this phrase of asking forgiveness, Christ fashions this dual dimension of release into our regular pattern of prayer: a request for release from (1) the shame of guilt, or (2) the pain of neglect.

To grasp the power potential in this prayer for forgiveness, we need to see that both of the phrases are conditionally linked. In saying, "as we forgive," Jesus specifically teaches that the degree of our forgiveness—our willingness to release others—establishes a standard of measurement. He gives back to us that measure of release and forgiveness that we show others. And this fact brings us to the heart of life's most practical truth: *If I do not move in God's dimension of release and forgiveness toward others, I will inevitably become an obstruction to my own life, growth, and fruitfulness.*

See it, dear one. There are dual dimensions. We need to see that "forgiving faith" goes both ways: (1) We must confess our own sinning; and (2) We must forgive others whom we feel violate us.

Notice also, that by emphasizing our need for forgiveness of sin, Jesus isn't shaking a stick of condemnation in our faces. This isn't the issue. The real problem is that we are all somewhat warped and need to be *taught* to pray for forgiveness. We are all people *bent* from God's original design and purpose. Not one of us is flawless, no one without selfishness and pride. Sin is an inherited inclination in us all, and it needs to be forgiven. The call to pray this prayer is the promise it will be answered. We *need* to pray, "Forgive me, Father," and we need to pray, it often. But the prayer is *not* to level a focus on guilt, but on grace.

Jesus taught us to pray for forgiveness on a regular basis not to remind us of our sinfulness but to keep us from becoming sloppy in our ideas about the grace of God. Too often, we distort God's grace and give in to the deception that "I can do anything I want as long as God's grace encompasses me." But in Romans 6:1-2, the Word demands pointedly: "What shall we say then? Shall we continue in sin that grace may abound? Certainly not! How shall we who died to sin live any longer in it?" In calling us to pray, "Forgive us our trespasses," Jesus isn't seeking to remind us of our failures, but He *does* want to sensitize us to sin, and to the fact that this sin hinders our growth in Him.

God's forgiveness is graciously offered and abundantly available. He warmly invites us to pardon, cleansing, and release in the Scriptures:

- As far as the east is from the west, so far has He removed our transgressions from us.

  (PS. 103:12)

- He will again have compassion on us, and will subdue our iniquities.

  (MICAH 7:19)

- Their sins and their lawless deeds I will remember no more.

  (HEB. 10:17)

- If we confess our sins, He is faithful and just to forgive us our sins and to cleanse us from all unrighteousness.

  (1 JOHN 1:9)

Forgiveness can be counted on. The condition — *confession* — is presented clearly, and the availability is promised: "He can be depended on to forgive us."

Second, Jesus describes forgiveness as being relayed *through* us to others. God's Word expands and applies the truth that we who have received forgiveness need to be forgiving. Jesus directs us to go to anyone who has something against us and, in an attitude of humility and forgiveness, rectify our relationship with them. And He says this must be done before we can make any serious, honest approach to Him in worship.

Therefore if you bring your gift to the altar, and there remember that your brother has something against you, leave your gift there before the altar and go your way. First be reconciled to your brother, and then come and offer your gift.

  (MATT. 5:23-24)

And whenever you stand praying, if you have anything against anyone, forgive him, that your Father in heaven may also forgive you your trespasses.

  (MARK 11:25)

When we go to another for reconciliation, we must be certain we are not doing so in an attempt to justify ourselves. If someone has a difference of opinion or some problem with me, regardless of whose fault it is, God will not allow me to make any charge against that person. Christ desires that we be willing to go the extra mile and assume the role of reconciler — just as He did for us in reconciling us to the Father.

Understanding that people often perceive a situation opposite of how it really is will help us to act as Christ commands. For example, if you have been offended, you may be completely unaware of the viewpoint of the one you feel has hurt you. To the other person, it will often seem as though *he or she* were the one violated, and that *you* are at fault. The effects of sin and Satan's discord in our lives makes us all *so* terribly vulnerable to natural misunderstandings, we need to learn this point of human understanding. We must acknowledge it in order to open up the reconciling process. Then when we become willing to go to others, recognizing that their attitudes toward us are likely based on something they perceive as being *our* fault—when *we* accept the burden of the misunderstanding (as Jesus did to bring peace between God and us), a real release *will be realized*. Let's learn to accept the responsibility for whatever has breached our relationships with others. Restored relationships can become possible when this Christlike lifestyle lives out the meaning in His prayer-lesson: "Forgive *me* . . . as I forgive others."

Naturally, there may be times when the most loving, scriptural stand we can take is to confront others with their wrong. Jesus did so, and the Holy Spirit will show us when we are to do so. But the Spirit of forgiveness never does this in a self-defensive way; rather it operates in a spirit of reconciliation.

This kingdom order of forgiveness will not always be easy.

By nature we all prefer to be "in the driver's seat," so to speak, and the ministry of "reconciliation" always puts us at the mercy of the *other's* responses instead. But this is exactly where Jesus put Himself when He laid down His life to offer forgiveness to us. Though God hasn't called us to be someone's doormat, we *are* called to learn Christ's pathway to dominion. To do so is to see that this kingdom path to power is in the Spirit of the Lamb, and never in one of self-defense.

There is no greater step upward in faith than the one we take when we learn to forgive—and *do it*. It blesses people who need our love and acceptance, and it releases us to bright horizons of joy, health, and dynamic faith in prayer.

Obedient Faith

"AND DO NOT LEAD US NOT INTO TEMPTATION, BUT DE-LIVER US FROM THE EVIL ONE."

Our sixth step brings us to the most paradoxical part of the Lord's Prayer: "And do not lead us into temptation, but deliver us from the evil one." At first these words seem confusing in light of other Scriptures which assure us that God does not tempt anyone. James 1:13-14 makes this clear: "God tempts no man, but when we are tempted we are drawn away of our own lusts and enticed." Seeing this, then, we know that in teaching us to pray, "Lead us not into temptation," Jesus is not teaching us that we have to beg God not to trick us into sinning. Nor is Jesus teaching us a prayer for escaping the demands of growth that come through God's leading us—and He *does* lead us—into *trial*.

To understand what Jesus *is* teaching we must first gain a clear understanding of the word "temptation"; a word that carries a two-sided meaning. First, temptation essentially has to do with the desire of an adversary to test and break through our defenses. Second, temptation deals with the strength gained through encountering an adversary; that is, when the one who is tested overcomes the test, the resulting victory builds strength. Temptation, therefore, is both positive and negative, depending on our viewpoint and response.

In that light, Jesus isn't suggesting that we should ask or expect to avoid the kind of confrontation He faced with Satan. In fact, the Bible tells us that the Holy Spirit *led* Christ into that experience of conflict with the devil (Matt. 4:1). As a direct result of overcoming this time of temptation, Jesus was brought to a place of victory and dominion over the enemy (John 14:30). So this section of the Lord's Prayer holds a promise of victory, rather than a plea for relief from struggle.

We are not asking God, "Please don't play with us as pawns on a chessboard, risking our loss by 'leading us' into questionable situations." Rather, to examine various translations of this challenging verse and noting the tense and mood of the Greek verb *lead* or *bring unto,* is to discover the phrase "Lead us not into temptation" is *a guarantee of victory*—if we'll take it!

A clear translation of these words shows Jesus is actually directing us to pray: "Father, should we at any point be led into temptation, test, or trial, we want to come out delivered and victorious."

So the issue in this portion of the Lord's Prayer is not a questioning of God's character, but *ours.* Such praying is saying, "Lord, *You* won't lead or introduce me into any situations but those for my refinement, growth, and victory. Therefore, when *I* encounter circumstances designed to lead me astray, I *will* recognize that it *isn't* Your will for me to walk that way. By the words of this prayer, God, I am committing myself in advance to *wanting* victory, to *seeking* deliverance, and to *taking* the way of escape You have promised me."

> No temptation has overtaken you except such as is common to man; but God is faithful, who will not allow you to be tempted beyond what you are able, but with the temptation will also make the way of escape, that you may be able to bear it.
>
> (1 COR. 10:13)

Here, then, is obedient faith confronting the reality of our vulnerability to temptation. It's sometimes so quick in its rise and so subtle in its approach that Jesus' prayer lesson teaches us our need to have established our steps in advance through regular prayer. With these words, "Lead us not," we come to the Lord, in advance, and commit ourselves to receive His deliverances, rather than to allow temptation to entrangle us in its snares. This prayer doesn't question God's nature or leading, but declares we are casting ourselves on Him.

Once again, it's important to understand the intent of this

prayer because man is so easily deluded by temptation. Jesus isn't suggesting it is God's nature to trick or corrupt us by tempting us. Instead He's emphasizing it is God's nature to "deliver us from evil." The prayer simply establishes a commitment on our part to receive the triumphant life Christ offers us in dominion over evil. Living becomes more effective when we avoid being neutralized by hell's manipulations or by our flesh's cry for self-indulgence.

This prayer doesn't remove temptation's challenge, but it does help us understand that we aren't evil simply because we're tempted. Furthermore, we have a certain promise: God has a doorway of exit for us! When temptation comes, the prayer "deliver us from evil" insures us a way out.

What a great certainty this is. What a beautiful climax to this lesson in the Lord's Prayer.

> And the Lord will deliver me from every evil work and preserve me for His heavenly kingdom. To Him be glory forever and ever. Amen!
>
> (2 TIM. 4:18)

> Then the Lord knows how to deliver the godly out of temptations and to reserve the unjust under punishment for the day of judgment.
>
> (2 PETER 2:9)

If we seek Him, God *will* deliver us out of temptation! Thus, when we pray "deliver us from evil" we are committing ourselves to walk in triumph and dominion over the things that would seek to conquer us: to live in obedient faith. And to live this way is to count on God's deliverance, for "He is able!"

Chapter Twenty-Five
Prayerpath: Step 7

Trusting Faith

"FOR YOURS IS THE KINGDOM AND THE POWER AND THE
GLORY FOREVER. AMEN."

Our study of the Lord's Prayer is climaxed in examining these words of trusting faith: "For Yours is the *kingdom* and the *power* and the *glory* forever." Here is the active expression of a heart that has found the absolute assurance of the complete triumph of God . . . in *His* time.

Turn with me to Acts 1:6-7. I think the words of Jesus to His disciples will give us additional insight into this section of the Lord's Prayer:

> Therefore, when they had come together, they asked Him, saying, "Lord, will You at this time restore the kingdom to Israel?"
>
> And He said to them, "It is not for you to know times or seasons which the Father has put in His own authority."

Jesus spoke these words following His resurrection, as He was giving His final instructions to His men before His ascension. He had been explaining principles of the kingdom of God, and the disciples had gotten confused (Acts 1:3-5). In light of what He was teaching, and with the facts of the Crucifixion and the Resurrection behind them, Jesus' disciples inquired: "Just when will this kingdom finally come?" They must have felt sure ("Surely, now!") since Jesus was continuing to speak of the kingdom now (Acts 1:3) *after* His death as He had *before* His death, that the time *must* be ripe for the messianic kingdom to be established. Surely now was the time for Israel to be liberated from Roman oppression!

But Jesus patiently replied that it wasn't for them to know when it would take place (v. 7). He wasn't stalling them. Nor was He denying the ultimate kingdom someday. But He was redirecting their understanding. The issue of the kingdom's "coming with power" is asserted in the very next verse:

> But you shall receive power when the Holy Spirit has come upon you; and you shall be witnesses to Me in Jerusalem, and in all Judea and Samaria, and to the end of the earth.
>
> (ACTS 1:8)

He was showing them the Holy Spirit's coming was a mission to work the *spread* of the kingdom *through* them, not the *finish* of the kingdom *for* them. This conversation between Jesus and His disciples, with Jesus' promise of the Holy Spirit's power in relation to the timing of His kingdom, can help us understand the meaning of the concluding phrase of the Lord's Prayer. We can see that Jesus was teaching the pathway to *trust*—to the knowledge that when we have prayed in faith, we can rest firm in our confidence God has heard—He *will* attend to all issues, and even when we don't see *our* timing in the answer, *His* purposes aren't being lost.

Consider the words, "Thine is the kingdom."

For many, these words seem to point to the future. But Jesus taught very clearly that in certain respects the presence and power of His kingdom are given to us *now:* "Do not fear, little flock, for it is your Father's good pleasure to give you the kingdom" (Luke 12:32). Although we will only experience the *fullest* expression of His kingdom when He comes again, we mustn't diminish the fact that this prayer is dealing with God's rule and power impacting situations *now.* Wherever the Spirit is given room and allowed to work, the kingdom "comes."

So here, at prayer, Jesus is reminding us that such privileged participation in the power of His kingdom life has terms: We are called to submit to God's rule in our lives.

> Therefore submit to God. Resist the devil and he will flee from you.
>
> (JAMES 4:7)

Therefore humble yourselves under the mighty hand of God, that He may exalt you in due time.

(1 PETER 5:6)

The Power and the Glory

The first factor in developing a trusting faith is learning that the rule, the power, and the glory *are* God's. He allows us to share with Him, but He is Lord. He gives us power, but only He is omnipotent. He teaches us, but He alone is all-knowing. And the submitting and humbling spoken of in James and 1 Peter are prerequisites to sharing God's authority. Satan flees the believer who has learned the truth of *"Yours* is the power."

Faith is ever and always challenging the status quo where evil reigns, where pain and sickness prevail, where hatred and hellishness rule, or where human failure breeds confusion. As we learn to live under the Holy Spirit's rule, we will be able to take a bold, confrontive stance against all in opposition to that rule—whether demon, flesh, or earthly circumstance. Such a stance says, "I rely upon the One who claims ultimate and final rule everywhere. I won't give way to any lie which attempts to cast doubt on God's ultimate, complete victory." And when we do this, we will often see results which would not have been realized without "kingdom praying."

But what about when we don't see any results?

What then?

The disciples' inquiry echoes from our lips too: "Will the kingdom be now?"

To this question, Jesus teaches us to pray, *"Yours is the kingdom."* In these words He's leading us to realize that even though answers may not fully appear yet, two things come from trusting faith: (1) The knowledge that the ultimate triumph of God's manifest power shall come *in His time;* and (2) The assurance that, *until that time,* He has given us His Spirit to enable us to do His will.

Here is our fortress of confidence. Although time may pass without our always seeing "victory" as we would interpret it, we know—and pray with praise—we have not been deserted! God's Holy Spirit brings us His presence and power right now, for whatever circumstances we encounter.

There will be times we will see God's kingdom power in action—in healings and miracles in our lives. And there will also be

195

times the Lord simply says, "Trust Me—the time is not yet, but in the meantime the power of My Spirit will sustain you."

Great power and privilege *are* given to the church. "Nothing will be impossible for you," Jesus says (Matt. 17:20). Yet, as certain as the promise and possibilities are, we must humbly and honestly acknowledge there are some times when we seem unable to "possess" the promise. Such acknowledgments should not seem to be statements of doubt. Nor are they cases of God's refusing to grant us an answer or fulfill His Word.

God's promises *are* true and His Word *is* faithful! But the "kingdom timing" is His too! And so are the ultimate power and glory.

When we conclude the Lord's Prayer with, "Thine is the kingdom and the power and the glory," we aren't being either passive or poetic. We are reflecting the power of trusting faith: faith which stands in firm confidence, regardless of circumstances. This faith declares, "Lord, to You belongs all kingdom authority, You are the possessor of all! And as I gain that kingdom, a portion at a time, I trust You—for the kingdom is Yours."

There are no greater grounds for rest and contentment in life than the certainty wrapped in these words:

"Yours is the kingdom"—all rule *belongs* to God.

"Yours is the power"—all mightiness *flows* from Him.

"Yours is the glory"—His victory *shall be* complete.

With this kind of prayer comes boldness, confidence, and rest. For when all is said and done, our greatest resource is to rest in God's greatness. In Him we find confidence that our every need will be met, our ultimate victory realized; and in His time, by His purpose, and for His glory, all things will resolve unto His wisest, richest, and best.

So let us, now and ever, join the angelic throng around His throne, uniting our concert of prayer and praise with theirs, saying, "Holy, holy, holy . . .

Who was.

Who is.

And Who is to come—

THE ALMIGHTY!

Chapter Twenty-Six

Jesus' Lessons on Bold Faith

A s is my usual habit, I awoke early for the purpose of prayer. But when I sat on the edge of the bed, I heard a whisper to my heart, "You have forgotten the discipline of daily devotional habit."

Immediately I knew what the Holy Spirit was dealing with me about. And though the prompting to some might have seemed a rebuke, I didn't protest. Because I understood He was speaking to me about my personal walk with Jesus. The issue was *"quiet* and *with* Him" as compared to my passionate praying about issues and asking for answers. There is a difference between these two.

Daily Devotional Habit

It was as though God were saying, "I am not just looking, Jack, for your petitions and power prayer with passion. I will honor your seeking to see My kingdom enter the world, as you pray for the invasion of My power into hell's darkness. And I do welcome your worship as you extol My name. But child, I wish you would simply spend more time with *Me;* to know My heart and let Me deal with yours; to give you instructions in the personal matters of your own private life, as you learn to *wait* on Me."

Now, I had *not* been totally closed off to "simply being in His presence." But I *had* become so excited, indeed zealous, in the application of great principles of supplication, intercession, and faith's confession (things I'd begun to learn and practice) that the *power* potential in prayer was distracting me from the *devotional* aspect of a personal walk with Jesus. But now, the Lord was reminding me of His desire for *me:* "I just want *you* to be with Me."

Daybreak is a small booklet I wrote following that encounter; a handbook outlining details for one's daily devotional habit. It points to a more personal and intimate walk with the Lord, to bring *our days* to Him, to allow Him to order *our steps*, as we learn to function in the wisdom of "daily devotions in the presence of Jesus."

By reason of that small book's abundant availability and inexpensive price (published by Tyndale, and available through your Christian bookstore), I have not elaborated the patterns for my daily devotional habit here. However, let me still give you the following outline. It provides a grid; a simple structure to prompt your private, personal *walk* with Jesus — your "talk-time" with the Savior. While I will pursue other aspects of personal prayer in detail, let me first establish one thing: *all prayer is best cultivated on the foundation of a Quiet Time.* In a regular "QT" with the Savior, deepening *relationship* becomes established at a personal dimension. A fundamental pattern for such a regular Quiet Time with Jesus is in this outline from *Daybreak.*

I. *Enter His Presence*
   Begin by presenting yourself, with thanksgiving and praise, placing your whole being before God — Mark 12:30.
   A. You can find a new reason every day to do this — Psalms 100:4; 118:24
   B. Present your body in worship to Him — Romans 12:1; Psalm 63:3-4
   C. Sing a new song to the Lord — Psalm 96:1-2; Colossians 3:16
   D. Allow the Holy Spirit to assist your praise — 1 Corinthians 14:15; Jude 20

II. *Open Your Heart*
   Present your heart to God with confession for cleansing, and diligently seek purity — Proverbs 4:23.
   A. Invite the Lord to search your heart — Psalm 139:23-24
   B. Recognize the danger of deception — Jeremiah 17:9; 1 John 1:6-10
   C. Set a monitor on your mouth and heart — Psalms 19:14; 49:3
   D. Keep Christ's purposes and goal in view — Psalm 90:12; Philippians 3:13-14

III. *Order Your Day*

In obedience to our Lord, present your day and submit to His ways and rule in your life—1 Peter 5:6-11.

A. Surrender your day to God—Deuteronomy 33:25b; Psalms 37:4-5; 31:14-15
B. Indicate your dependence on Him—Psalm 131:1-3; Proverbs 3:5-7
C. Request specific direction for today—Psalm 25:4-5; Isaiah 30:21
D. Obey Jesus' explicit instructions—Matthew 6:11; 7:7-8

Taking these simple pointers, allow *regular* times to "be up and early with the Lord." NEVER let the adversary condemn you because you miss a day or days. Let every time you *are* with the Savior be as precious to you as He wants it to be. You *will* find that early morning hours are usually the best to find unbroken, undisturbed occasions for quiet in His presence. It was Jesus' pattern, and it deserves emulation (Mark 1:35). And remember, use the outline for a guideline, not a regimented requirement. I've found it helps to target HIM (His presence), MY HEART (and purity) and MY DAYS (His counsel about the details of my life).

In the environment of this kind of walk with Christ, boldness of faith and expanding intercessory prayer will grow. *Petitionary* requests—however simple or complex—become *confident* requests, when we simply come to "know Jesus." So with this "starter" resource in hand, and "intimacy as priority" in focus, the beginning of prayer's discipline is in place.

Perseverance in Prayer

Moving forward on this foundation, a disciple's growth in prayer will broaden in its dimensions. Ephesians 6:18 says, "Praying always with all prayer and supplication in the Spirit, being watchful to this end with all perseverance and supplication." Because of the importance of the *idea,* and because of the false *images* surrounding a key word to understanding this passage, let's study the matter of "perseverance."

In this text, the word means *"steadfastness, constancy, continuing much time in"* prayer. The idea is clear and should be readily understood. But though "continuance" is clear and to be obeyed, the concept of "perseverance" is still often twisted in some people's thinking to mean something other than "keeping at it." The image somehow has evolved that "perseverance" is needed in prayer in order either to gain God's approval or somehow to win His interest. Curiously, two stories from Jesus' parable-lessons have been used to deepen this distorted idea. So without removing the importance of our learning "all kinds of prayer" and to apply what we learn "with persevering, steadfast constancy" and "much-time-at-it" *prayer*, look with me at these two stories. Both have been used to preach "persistence" or "perseverance" in prayer, when to draw that idea from these stories is to violate the text. The lessons intended are to beget *boldness* and *assurance* when we pray; to ask freely and expect greatly.

The concept of "perseverance" is vital to understand, because if we think in human terms, we will mistakenly view "persevering in prayer" as a gutsy, grit your teeth "I'll hang tough 'til God finally hears me and does something!" At best it's *"works"* praying, not *grace*. Misunderstanding "perseverance/persistence" can breed a sense that it is a complaint about our state of affairs: "God, I've been prayin' for a long time—can't see where things are? I need help, I need it now, and I am tired of waiting!" Our view supposes *earning* an answer; the other supposes we can or ought to "bully" God. But heaven really doesn't need this exhortation from us. God is never passive.

What does "perseverance" mean? Two classic passages can help us.

In Luke 11:5-8, Jesus follows up His teaching on the Lord's Prayer (vv. 2-4) by explaining the liberty one has in seeking help from a friend.

> And He said to them, "Which of you shall have a friend, and go to him at midnight and say to him, 'Friend, lend me three loaves; for a friend of mine has come to me on his journey, and I have nothing to set before him'; and he will answer from within and say, 'Do not trouble me; the door is now shut, and my children are with me in bed; I cannot rise and give to you'? I say to you, though he will not rise and give to him because he is his friend, yet because of his persistence he will rise and give him as many as he needs."
>
> (LUKE 11:5-8)

This lesson has been strangely turned around and I don't really understand why. Now, Jesus *didn't* intend what I'm about to describe, but I *have* heard it read and explained as though He meant to say: "Who of you are in bed at night, when a friend comes and beats on the door until broad daylight? Finally, you stumble out of bed, and say, 'OK if you are gonna beat on the door all night, then I'll get up and come down.' So beat on God's door until you get what you want!" The distortion suggests a picture of God, *bothered until He blesses.* But the persistence as Jesus taught it *doesn't* have to do with an unrelenting "beating on the door in prayer until God is awakened to your need."

Here's the picture He gives instead.

Jesus says, "Who of you has a friend, whose relatives unexpectedly arrive in the night. There is no food sufficient to feed them after their journey, and now they're at your door; knocking at a late hour, asking for your help. If this happened, would you say to your friend: 'Just keep beating on the door . . . I'm really not interested in you, but I'll wait and see. If you keep pounding long enough, I might help?' Of course not!"

Jesus is teaching by contrast; showing what *doesn't* happen with us or with God. If a person knocks on your door at 3 A.M., you may not appreciate being awakened, but you're not going to get up and say: "Bug off, I don't need your wake up call at this hour." Instead, as the Scripture says, you "will get up and give him as many as he needs."

Here, our Savior is saying something we all need to know about God . . . and about how He feels when we ask Him for things we need. *He doesn't mind!* It's that simple. It's the lesson Jesus means us to hear, so we'll persist in asking—continuously. To reenforce this, Jesus presents a picture precisely the opposite of our human tendency to feel, "My problems are too small to bother the Almighty." To counter this hesitancy, Jesus uses this story.

In the Greek language, "persistence" is *anaideia.* The first part of the word, "an" is the negating of the related word, *"aidos,"* which means "modesty, courtesy, reserve, or propriety." In other words, the person's "persistence" is a kind of *"un*-reserve, a challenging of social propriety," as when waking somebody up in the middle of the night. The "asker" *didn't* get his answer because he beat on the door until his fists were bloody, but because he had the boldness to ask a friend—at night—and to directly relate a need. The nature of their relationship—friends—is what emboldened him to go and say, "Hey, I need help and I need it now!" So, Jesus is saying, "You have a Friend in heaven and you don't need to be hesitant about asking."

You don't need to be bashful about asking God, or worry about being "appropriately reverent." Just ask. You don't need to be hesitant if there's a need: Get at it! You don't need to be cautious in your approach to Almightiness!

Loved one, be done with the idea that God is nervous that you might ask something outside His will, and with such energy that you will force Him into something He doesn't really want to do. He is saying. "Be bold. Don't be afraid to ask. Anything!"

Jesus presents a parallel concept in Luke 18:1-5.

> Then He spoke a parable to them, that men always ought to pray and not lose heart, saying: "There was in a certain city a judge who did not fear God nor regard man. Now there was a widow in that city; and she came to him, saying, 'Avenge me of my adversary.' And he would not for a while; but afterward he said within himself, 'Though I do not fear God nor regard man, yet because this widow troubles me I will avenge her, lest by her continual coming she weary me.'"

Now, before we read Jesus' conclusion, let's get a clear picture of the setting.

—This was a corrupt judge.
—He didn't care about God or man.
—He had no respect for either divine justice or earthly justice.
—But he still takes action in the interest of this widow, because she keeps coming to him asking her case be handled.
—His motive is not her justice.
—His motive (hardly noble) is that he is tired of being bothered by the woman.

Now, is Jesus making the judge a parallel to the Father? No. Obviously not.

This is *not* a parable which teaches by *comparison* (as the other story, saying, "Be bold like this"). Instead, this *is* a parable which teaches by *contrast*. Jesus is showing the *opposite* of the way it is with God, yet how many times I have heard otherwise. I've seen people look at this story and interpret it as though the bride of Christ is like the widow, a woman with a tough case who can only get God (the judge) to act by persistent complaint. But Jesus is showing God's *readiness*, not His reluctance. With the lesson in Luke 11, *"to ask boldly,"* Christ's prayer message in Luke 18 is that we should expect God to *take action quickly*.

Here is Jesus' conclusion, verses 6-8:

Then the Lord said, "Hear what the unjust judge said. And shall God not avenge His own elect who cry out day and night to Him, though He bears long with them? I tell you that He will avenge them speedily. Nevertheless, when the Son of Man comes, will He really find faith on the earth?"

Jesus makes the contrast between our Father in heaven—The *Just Judge*—and a disgustingly inconsiderate *unjust* human judge.

So where is the concept of persistence? Well, we're seeing it. Persistence is *not* the desperate extension of human energy as though we're to "labor long" in an attempt to see heaven disposed in our interest. Nor is it as though God were "waiting in the wings" to see if we were really sincere, and after we had squeezed blood from the bedposts in frantic prayer, He would finally say, "All right, now that you have proven yourself sincere, I'll do something."

That isn't God's way.

Instead, *the essence of persistence is in recognizing that there is no situation to which you need surrender.* You can always ask your Friend in heaven. He'll hear. You have a Just Judge on your case. He'll act quickly.

Yet, listen dear friend. Sometimes the answers *do* seem long in coming. And when that happens, *know* it isn't heaven's disinterest.

Sometimes "a long labor"—a period of travail—is required before we see the "birth" of what we have been anticipating. But be certain: the promise will be born. What may seem *long* on the earthside of things is often but a moment in glory. So take patience.

Persistence is needed. But not as a humanly energized insistence that God "see our sincerity" or that we try and "move God" to action. He doesn't act on the basis of our zeal but on the basis of our simple faith and His changeless love.

God *doesn't* need to be moved to action. He's ready *now!* But to move mountains in *this* world often takes a season, so wait while heaven's bulldozers are at work, and find that the mountain *is* disappearing—a truckload at a time!

And as with the birthing process, so prayer's travail often involves a time of contractions. During that season, don't give up.

Hold forth boldly and praisefully to see heaven break through with new life and victory in this world.

Even if time transpires, the mountain will move.

And even though "hard labor" may continue for a night— with tears, *joy* will come forth in the morning!

Chapter Twenty-Seven

Prayer that Intervenes and Reverses

The disciples' call to prayer is to a life of expanding dimensions—from worship to petition, from thanksgiving to warfare. As we've noted, Ephesians 6:18 points the way to *"all prayer and supplication in the Spirit."*

- *"Praying always with all prayer"* (that is by every means of prayer)

- *"and supplication"* (literally, persevering for the promises, as contained in the text)

- *"in the Spirit"* (with supernatural assistance from Him)

Let me invite you—no, let me *urge you*—toward what's at hand. I want to discuss three grand words of prayer—*supplication, intercession,* and *thanksgiving.* But I especially want us to see them in their relationship to "intercession"—that order of prayer I call "the prayer that intervenes and reverses."

Supplication

In writing the Philippians, the Apostle Paul registered one of the broadest, most inclusive and practical calls to prayer in the Bible.

> Be anxious for nothing, but in everything by prayer and supplication, with thanksgiving, let your requests be made known to God; and the peace of God, which surpasses all under-

standing, will guard your hearts and minds through Christ Jesus.

(PHIL. 4:6-7)

Philippi was a Roman colony, an outpost of Rome's authority, and therefore secured with a special contingent of Imperial troops. Paul's choice of terms, noting the *promise* of prayer, takes on special meaning in this light. He says: "the peace of God will guard your hearts and minds"; the word *"guard"* describing the garrisoning of Roman troops to secure a colony. In other words, he was saying, "If you will take a specific stance in prayer, God will establish a stronghold in your mind, bracing you against the adversary so that you will never be cast into tumult or confusion, whatever your trial or need."

This text points the way for our entry into this place of secured confidence following prayer. But it involves more than simple petition—ordinary "give us this day our daily bread" asking. It calls us to *supplication,* an interesting word in the Greek language (*deomai*) which essentially has to do with "asking," but extends further. We'll best understand if we make a brief word study.

There are three words which *Strong's Concordance* has linked in alphabetical sequence: *deomai, deo,* and *dei.* When I looked up the first, my discovery of these words in their natural *lexical* order helped me to see them in their *logical* order. First, their definitions:

Deomai—"to supplicate or to make supplication; to beg; to pray earnestly."

Deo—"to bind something up or to tie something up."

Dei—"a Greek particle, "ought"; used to express the moral imperative.

As we've noted earlier the "moral imperative" refers to that which in the order of things "ought" to be. For example, if there's a need we *ought* to help; if there's a fire, we *ought* to do something—help, warn, get water, put it out. To "ought" is "in the order of things" do what's necessary and right.

Now, it was almost by accident that in finding the linguistic relationship of these words, I was assisted to grasp the concept of *supplication*—the pivotal difference between simply "asking" and "supplicating."

"To ask" is to simply make our request, and we've dealt with that already. But "supplication" answers to those times when a focused point of *passion* in prayer is needed. And when this need is joined to our recognition of the privileges we have been given in prayer, a distinct dimension of prayer is approached.

I had always been puzzled by *deomai* being translated "to beg" where prayer was involved, since Jesus does not *ever* teach prayer as "begging." It doesn't reflect our relationship with God. But when we look at the cognate, *deo* — "to bind," the concept of prayer and spiritual authority is clearly in view. It ties to Jesus' teaching regarding the authority His church shall be given over the dark powers of hell. Listen:

> And I will give you the keys of the kingdom of heaven, and whatever you bind on earth will be bound in heaven, and whatever you loose on earth will be loosed in heaven.
>
> (MATT. 16:19)

Thus, it appears that *deomai* as a prayer exercise called "supplicate" has more to it than earnest begging. The evidence is that we are to see supplication (*deomai*) as involving the Christ-authorized action of "binding up" certain things. Understandably, then, we ask, "What things do I have the *right* to bind up"?

The answer, I believe, is in our seeing the cognate relationship of *dei* to *deomai*. It would seem to show we are assigned to "bind up" things that are *not* what "ought to be," *unto* what "ought to be." Supplication, thus seen is prayer which can return things to their intended order; to what is proper or ought to be.

Look at our world, created under a divine order now long since violated. We understand that so much of our world is as it is because the "order" intended has fallen into confusion, chaos, and disarray, due to the fall of man, human sinning, and satanic activity. Now, seeing things "out of order," God has ordained a "mission possible" for we who have come under *His* order. We not only have the privilege of *fellowship* in prayer, but an invitation to *partnership* in prayer; to learn a dimension of "binding" by prayer, unto the reconstitution of His original order and intent for peoples' lives and circumstances.

Supplication (*deomai*) moves into the confusion of the fallen order of things (a broken heart, a broken home, someone's broken health) and begins through supplication to "bind up" broken things, drawing the strands of such "binding" back to what "ought to be" — God's intent and God's will.

In short, the praying church has been capacitated by Christ's promise, to pray in ways that *stop* what hell's councils are trying to *advance*.

This is what is meant by prayers that "bind and loose." The "binding" is not only as we often may conceive something being "tied up," but is based on the concept of "binding" as it is used when a contract has been made. For example, when a property is being developed, an architect will regularly visit the site, meeting with the contractor to assure the details of the contract are fulfilled. Holding the contractor to the contract is legally possible because the terms of a contract are "binding." But possible only as the architect or his representative insist on the "binding" clauses of the contract, that contested or neglected features of the project will be finished as they *ought* to be, and as the owner *wills*.

The analogy is obvious. In this world, Satan is trying to construct things that are totally out of line with God's blueprint. You and I are on-site observers of what is taking place in human lives and earthly circumstances we're aware of. When what *ought* to be *isn't*, our role in supplication is to say "Lord, what You contracted for at the cross—for Your purpose and power to save (*name*) or deliver (*name*), isn't being done 'on earth': Let *Your* ruling power— Your kingdom *come!* Let *Your* will be done *on earth* as it is in heaven. As Your agent assigned to this case in prayer, Lord, I say, *stop* the adversary's advance. According to Calvary's terms I 'bind' the enemy from success; according to Your will through the power of Jesus' blood, I loose on earth what You have already willed in heaven."

Please notice: In "binding and loosing," the grammar of the Greek phrase, "whatever you bind will be bound—whatever you loose, will be loosed," makes one thing clear that is sometimes unnoted. It is important that we understand this fact: Our binding only accomplishes on earth what has *already been* accomplished in heaven. In other words, we don't *make* things happen; prayer *releases* their happening. God has ordained the intended order so we are *not* "creators" of what occurs, but "releasers" of what He has desired to be, but which flesh or devil oppose. So when we "bind" or "loose," remember His is the power and the provision; ours is the privilege of participation. Further, let us always be wise and praiseful, knowing the source of the power we exercise. Where does it flow from?

The Cross! Never forget it, loved one. What Jesus did at the Cross was once and forever to break the capacity of the Adversary to sustain his rule over mankind. Apart from Calvary's power, we're no different. You and I have no defense in our own power. We're all helpless against Satan's strategies or contrivances, except . . . except that when we have the resources of Calvary, we not only have a sure defense for our own soul, but a point of appeal in calling for heaven's best in the face of hell's worst.

Because of Jesus' victory through the Blood of His Cross, prayers of supplication can "bind" — we can contract for heaven's "ought to be" deliverance, and rejoice in seeing God's will done.

In this light, then, it's unsurprising Paul said when we pray that way, "the peace of God will guard your heart." Prayer (asking) and supplication (binding and loosing) lay the groundwork for a deep peace to possess the soul, *if,* as Philippians 4:6 says, praises of thanksgiving are offered with them. Faith brings peace and anxiety will cease. Prayer has found a place of confidence by *calling* on heaven's resource and victory, by *applying* it in simple faith. Then "with thanksgiving," we *rest in praise* as heaven's power moves to actuate the holy will and purpose of God's intended order "on earth as in heaven." The things we've addressed in prayer are set forward in Calvary's power of "release," for God's glory and in Jesus' name. Amen.

Intercession

Continuing with "all prayer" as our goal, let us look at intercession. Seeing the Apostle Paul's admonition in 1 Timothy 2:1-3, it's important and impressive to see the *priority* this order of prayer is given along with supplication.

> Therefore I exhort first of all that supplications, prayers, intercessions, and giving of thanks be made for all men, for kings and all who are in authority, that we may lead a quiet and peaceable life in all godliness and reverence. For this is good and acceptable in the sight of God our Savior.

Of particular significance is the *place* and the *scope;* the priority — *"first of all"*; and the aegis of influence *"for kings and all who are in authority."* In this foundational New Testament call to intercession, we have what I believe is the Bible's fundamental realm of assignment with regard to civic and political affairs. The directive is to pray for civic issues that are grander and broader than our own immediate points of personal concern or involvement. Obedience to this call will disallow any notion or practice of prayer as a preoccupying, self-centered concern. We are promised influence that can affect the climate of a culture; "That we may lead a quiet life."

It would be understandably tempting to say, "Who am I to suppose when I kneel I can decide the moral, the spiritual, or the political, military, or economic circumstances in my country—in my *world?*" But the Word of God not only says intercession has that capacity, it specifically says it's one of our *first* assignments: a priority which, if observed, can reveal the living church's *real* role in determining government. (While I believe a Christian in a free society *should* vote and be as politically active or involved as he or she feels called, the Bible says *little* about direct political control, yet *much* about the intercessor's role.)

In James 5:16, the writer notes, "the effective, fervent prayer of a righteous man avails much," and then provides an illustration of such prayer. The text, freely translated, reads, *"the spiritually energized prayer of an impassioned person seeking God, will count for more than they can imagine:* look *how!"* Then the case of Elijah is described.

> Elijah was a man with a nature like ours, and he prayed earnestly that it would not rain; and it did not rain on the land for three years and six months. And he prayed again, and the heaven gave rain, and the earth produced its fruit.
>
> (JAMES 5:17-18)

A study of the Old Testament text being referenced reveals a dramatic story of social, spiritual, economic, and meteorological impact through one man's intercession. Meteorologically speaking, the climate of the culture was *literally* changed from drought to rain. The same passage shows Elijah's victory over the prophets of Baal—a spiritual triumph—and the breaking of a drought, which would have obvious economic/social impact. God's judgment on the people was reversed; and this magnificent passage says that same potential is available today if we will leave what intercession can accomplish.

The broad sweeping possibilities of "intercession" are unfolded in an examination of the Greek and Hebrew words used: *entynchano* (Greek) and *paga* (Hebrew) hold essentially the same meaning; a definition that, in fact, seems peculiar to most when first heard: both mean to "light upon," "come upon by accident" or "strike" (as lightning, unpredictably). Maybe you're like me, and your first exposure to those definitions evokes a bit of bewilderment: "Prayer—by accident?" Let me give some examples of the use of *paga* in the Old Testament to demonstrate the awesome truth in this word.

In Genesis 28, Jacob is in flight running from Esau, his brother. He comes to a place that will eventually be named Bethel. But as he arrives there, he looks for a place to rest. During the night of sleep, he had the vision called, "Jacob's ladder." When he awakened the next morning after God met him in a dynamically powerful way, giving him a promise for his whole future, Jacob says, "Surely the Lord is in this place, and I did not know it" (v. 16). However, the day before when he stopped at that site, the Scripture says, "He lit upon a certain place" (KJV). In other words, to Jacob's eye, this was a random place of stopping, but in God's plan, it would become the milestone of his life.

There is the idea of intercession. What seems random in catching us in time, circumstance, or attention-commanding is *not accidental but providential.*

Dear one, almost every day of our lives, you and I come into apparently random situations. If we perceive they are ordained of the Spirit, we will learn to respond to them, knowing God has brought us to them. There will be occasions when we will have "a seemingly random thought" or a "signaling" which might seem accidental, but wisdom will teach us to seize these moments as intended by God to cause us to intercede.

The issue of intercession does not only have to do with grand, national, and international issues as we have already reflected upon, but anything that the Lord places before us as a point intersecting our daily life. Perhaps you are driving along and see an accident in the roadway. Recognize that in God's providence, He has you present to intercede.

Please capture the divine significance of this for a moment. In many cases, you and I are the only people He has on the scene who has sufficient spiritual sensitivity to know we can make a difference. The Lord wants to "salt" all of society with people who have this understanding; recognize that as intercessors, they are present for the purpose of travailing in prayer for a world which otherwise would experience only tragic consequences of life's problems, without the hope of divine entry to their circumstance through intercession.

Intercession occurs when people realize God has ordained boundaries of blessing for human experiences, and unless there is someone who prays, Satan will try to violate the boundary line. He will try to make it less than it would have been in God's counsel and covenant. Intercession sees that God's purposes reach all the way unto what He wills. You see, there is a passivity that possesses much of the mind-set of so many of us. It's kind of a spiritual sloth that goes this way: "Well, God is all powerful. He can do whatever He wants and I'll sort of agree to it. Isn't that what 'Thy kingdom come, Thy will be done' means?" No, dear one.

Jesus taught us to pray, "Thy kingdom come, Thy will be done," on this earthside of things; therefore, we, the redeemed troops, are here to fight the good fight and to see heaven's covenant established and extended in the name of the King. We are not praying, "Oh, well, I guess 'Thy kingdom come and Thy will be done.' " Instead, we are praying, *"I stand as heaven's ambassador on this planet and say in this setting, God's kingdom come here, God's will be done."*

Intercession is insisting on the extension of heaven's covenanted boundaries, which hell will encroach upon and try to push back to less than what God has intended. We are the ones appointed to monitor the situation; and in prayer, we represent heaven's *purposes,* by heaven's *power,* speaking heaven's *covenant* into the situation and watch God actuate it according to our calling upon Him.

Paga occurs another place (1 Sam. 22). Saul, during the time of his backsliding as King of Israel, was offended by some of the priests of Israel. He ordered his own troops to fall on them and kill them. His troops respected God's priests too much to obey their own king. It was an embarrassment to him, so Saul turned to a pagan man, Docg, the Edomite, who had joined his entourage, and said, "Turn thou, and fall upon the priests" (v. 18, KJV). This hateful, pagan Edomite took advantage of the moment, grabbed the sword, and began to slash off the heads of some of the priesthood of God's people. The Bible says that Doeg, "fell upon [*paga*] the priests" (v. 18, KJV).

Now I admit that the scene is tragic—the slaying of God's priests. But the verb, objectively used in this setting, represents a person who goes on the attack, falling upon the perceived adversary of his king. It's a lesson in intercession, except in our case the very clear adversary is our adversary the devil, "who walks about like a roaring lion, seeking whom he may devour" (1 Peter 5:8). In intercessory prayer, you and I are taking the sword of the Spirit and at the direction of our King, falling upon the adversary, slashing off his efforts of attack, and stopping his advance.

Intercession is such a dynamic form of prayer. It involves our ensuring on earth the boundaries of God's heavenly purposes, defending against the enemy's encroachment, recognizing our privilege to take action at apparently random encounters, and "controlling the climate" of societies and nations.

So, how do we exercise the role of intercessor? In Romans 8:26-27, we read how the Holy Spirit is available to help us in this prayer dimension:

> Likewise the Spirit also helps in our weaknesses. For we do not know what we should pray for as we ought, but the Spirit Himself makes intercession for us, with groanings which cannot be uttered. Now He who searches the hearts knows what the mind of the Spirit is, because He makes intercession for the saints according to the will of God.

Also, note the relationship of these two verses to the oft-quoted Romans 8:28: "And we know that all things work together for good to those who love God, to those who are the called according to His purpose." This verse we love to quote so much must never be removed from its context.

Listen to me, dear one: "all things *don't* work together for good in this world": not automatically! *Nothing* works together for good in this world on its own.

Romans 8:26-28 needs to be kept clustered together, for it shows how when intercessions, energized by the Holy Spirit, are brought to bear upon situations we don't understand, *then* there comes the entry of God's purpose and "all things work together for good." But intercession is the pivot point determining *if* God's "good" will penetrates "all things."

As that occurs, and we partner with Him in understanding our prayer role, we allow the likeness of His Son to be developed in us.

Jesus' likeness is not only one of character, it is one of spiritual authority. Jesus not only walked in purity of conduct, He walked about setting straight things which were corrupted by the works of darkness. Remember Acts 10:38, "How God anointed Jesus of Nazareth . . . who went about doing good and healing all who were oppressed by the devil." Jesus was not just a good man . . . He was *God's* man. So, as the Lord calls us to be conformed to the image of Christ (Rom. 8:29), learning Holy Spirit-assisted intercession is a part of our character growth in Christ; a part of being conformed to His image as disciples.

Thanksgiving

Finally, learn the power of thanksgiving!

> Rejoice always, pray without ceasing, in everything give thanks; for this is the will of God in Christ Jesus for you.
>
> (1 THES. 5:16-18)

The Bible doesn't say "everything" is a "thank-worthy thing." It says, in everything you "see" be thankful. For example, if a person sees flames threatening your home because of burning brush, you wouldn't stand there and say, "Thank God." You would grab a rug to beat it out or spray water to drench it. Now, when hell's fire begins to draw near through whatever circumstance, the Bible says, use praise and thanksgiving—to God for His almightiness—to strike down the blaze. In other words a situation seems tough, painful, flesh-produced, or hell-spawned. I'm not told *"for* everything give thanks," but *"in"*—that is, "in the middle of everything, however desperate, GIVE THANKS!"

Why? How? Go out and begin slapping down hell's flames with praise to God; shout to the high heavens that God is able to master this situation by His dominion, which you welcome with your worship. Say:

I thank God this situation can't master us.

I thank God He is bigger than what is happening right now.

I thank God that though I had this accident, He is going to move into this scene and assist me.

I thank God that though my sister has been diagnosed with cancer, that we have a Living Lord who is going to see us through.

I thank God that though I seem to be weak in my body today, He has promised me His strength and resource.

In everything, give thanks!

This is what the Bible is saying when it states, "for this is the will of God." Are cancer, difficulties, accidents, etc., the will of God? No. But the *spirit of thanksgiving* is the will of God concerning you.

As we look at worship, petition, supplication, intercession, and thanksgiving, we are seeing some of the exceeding wonders of prayer for application in our personal life as we live in the power of the Spirit, as growing disciples of Christ's.

Chapter Twenty-Eight

The Practice of Fasting

We certainly shouldn't leave the subject of the exceeding wonders of prayer without dealing with the remarkable power of prayer joined to fasting. When we deal with the subject of fasting, we at once encounter not only its unusual potential for spiritual dynamic, but an unusual problem raises its head.

First, fasting can become confused, as though it were done to generate an energy born of our own exercise, as though fasting were a means of earning something from God. But the dedication and devotion that is involved in *any* exercise of prayer, including fasting, never has anything to do with our *getting* from God or "forcing" God's action. Rather, all prayer habits are a means of aligning ourselves with His possibilities of power through our application of His principles of obedience to participate in His promises.

Second, the subject of fasting raises the problematic question for some people as to whether it is even relevant, necessary, or important today. Some suggest that it isn't; seeming to relegate fasting to the archaic, as though it is a residue of some medieval form of legalistic church tradition; people doing some order of penance in an effort to purge themselves before God's eyes by punishing their bodies through fasting.

But notwithstanding these points of misunderstanding, the Bible speaks very clearly and pointedly about fasting as a part of a Christian disciple's practice. Hear these words from Jesus' own lips:

> Then the disciples of John came to Him, saying, "Why do we and the Pharisees fast often, but Your disciples do not fast?"
>
> And Jesus said to them, "Can the friends of the bridegroom mourn as long as the bridegroom is with them? But

the days will come when the bridegroom will be taken away
from them, and then they will fast."

(MATT. 9:14-15)

Notice how Jesus said, "As long as I'm here, this isn't the time
for fasting, but when I am gone . . . Yes." He's referring to the
season from His ascension until He returns again, and thus in
plain words, Jesus not only *allows,* but seems to *appoint* fasting as a
Christian discipline.

Further, Paul enunciates fasting as a vital part of the life of a
servant of Christ. In describing his own practices "in fastings often" (2 Cor. 11:27), he verifies two things. First, that he makes
frequent application of fasting; second, he doesn't give a calendar.
Thereby we have both, the *rightness* of the discipline, without a
ritual of requirement. In short, the Holy Spirit can and will direct
us to times of fasting.

There are seasons of fasting which are observed in some
church traditions, and I certainly don't mean to devalue that or
think it unwise. It simply isn't something a person need fear failing
if they don't do. However, the discipline does recommend a need
for decision. When *might* I fast?

In our congregation's life, many of us choose to fast at least
two meals every Wednesday. In Wesleyan tradition, John Wesley
and his followers fasted every Wednesday and Friday, from morning until 4 o'clock tea.

A Biblical Discipline

When fasting is applied as a discipline, it isn't to simply demand
obedience of my body to submit to this "affliction of no food."
Rather, it's done as an active response to the revelation of the
Scriptures on the subject.

The Bible shows fasting as having played a powerful role in
some very dramatic and dynamic situations. The fact these are Old
Testament examples shouldn't in any way discourage our taking
them seriously for today.

For whatever things were written before were written for our
learning, that we through the patience and comfort of the
Scriptures might have hope.

(ROM. 15:4)

So clearly, then, we're told in the *New* Testament that *Old* Testament principles are for our instruction, and we're wise to see those which apply to our life as Jesus' disciples.

Let me give you four examples of fasting in the Old Testament which were instances of this action being taken in situations applicable to our circumstances today.

Four Lessons Taught for Today

> And they mourned and wept and fasted until evening for Saul and for Jonathan his son, for the people of the Lord and for the house of Israel, because they had fallen by the sword.
>
> (2 SAM. 1:12)

1. *Fasting at transition.*

Saul and Jonathan had just been slain. Now, in the wake of the confusion potential throughout the land, for they had lost their leader and their heir to the throne, David exercises a time of fasting and seeking the Lord. As a result, David eventually became ruler over all the tribes of Israel. The significance?

First, see the wisdom of people humbling themselves in the face of a successful attack by their adversary. Second, see the way you could apply a fast at a personal level or group dimension when such destructive events assail. As you do, seek the Lord, expect the same thing to be manifest; except *now* it will be *the Son of David* who will rise to rule over the circumstance.

2. *Fasting for survival.*

In Esther 4:16, the Queen called her own people to fast. In essence, Esther tells Mordecai, "Go to the Jewish community and tell them to fast, and I'll go before the king and plead their case." The story is a crucial one in Jewish history. The life of the nation was on the line, and as we study the flow of human history, we understand that such moments are more than simply political affairs. They are deadly, satanic attacks; any effort at destroying a people is that! So here, Esther took her place in fasting and her posture in intercession. As she goes before the king, behind her approach was a people who were fasting and seeking God.

Similarly, there are times when we face situations where "everything's at stake." But to seek the Lord with fasting and intercessory supplication, we can discover His way to reverse the situation and see God's rule and grace enter.

3. *Fasting for the future.*

Read Ezra 8:21-23, and see how great projects are best undertaken by the preparation of fasting and prayer.

The exiled Jews were preparing to return to Jerusalem with a large contingent of families and their valuables, including precious implements for reinstating worship in the temple. Ezra, their leader, says, "I didn't have the nerve to go to the rulers who were releasing us and ask for soldiers to accompany and protect us on our journey." He knew the pagan onlookers were already marveling at how God was working on their behalf (Ps. 126:1-3), so to request human protection would seem to suggest that God couldn't do the job. But Ezra does do something: "I called the people to fast, and to seek the face of the Lord that we might find the right way for ourselves and for our little ones." Listen to it! There is something tender in those words, as a man describes a people seeking to find God's protection for and guidance into the future. They were transitioning the time from where they were to where God was taking them.

Sound familiar? Are you seeking a new time of your life? Are you looking for God's protection and leading as you navigate a present opportunity? Seek Him with fasting and prayer! And as well, remember Ezra's focus not only on today's need, but on the way this action also serves the future generations—"our little ones."

4. *Fasting and spiritual warfare.*

Daniel 7–9 unfolds great prophetic promises which God had given to him.

The Lord had revealed grand disclosures of His purpose, but Daniel says in 10:1, "They were a long time in coming about." (The message was true but the appointed time was long.) The prophecy wasn't coming to full realization, it says. And that's why Daniel describes how he began to seek God with fasting and prayer.

Please notice that fasting is not something that is exercised apart from "impassioned prayer." We've spoken about supplication, intercession, thanksgiving, petition, and worship. You'll discover that most of those practices are evidenced in Daniel's prayer in 9:1-19. It's an extensive, intensive prayer, but please notice also: it's joined to a fast.

Fasting and prayer go together. Fasting without prayer is simply going without food. Prayer—seeking God—is what makes fasting powerful, not "food-less-ness." We're not on a hunger strike, protesting God's inactivity. As we'll shortly see, dark spiritual powers are resisted and broken through fasting. But here, as Daniel sought the Lord, God's purpose was released and a prophetic promise fulfilled; the prophetic promise of the termination of Israel's Babylonian Exile!

Can you imagine how many situations today are simply awaiting someone who will recognize God's time for deliverance has come? How many people "exiled from God's purpose" might be released as *we* fast and pray unto that objective?

Nothing but Prayer and Fasting

In Mark 9:29, Jesus is speaking to His disciples about a circumstance they had found themselves incapable of handling. When Jesus, with Peter, James, and John, returned from the Mount of Transfiguration, He found the other disciples frustrated with their unsuccessful efforts at casting out a demon from a boy. They asked, "Lord, why couldn't we do it?"

> So He said to them, "This kind can come out by nothing but prayer and fasting."
>
> (MARK 9:29)

Please note this text in your Bible, because I regret to tell you that some contemporary translations do not contain the whole verse. Some scholars have judged it to be insufficiently supported by manuscript evidence to retain it. However, the fact of the matter is, there is virtually as much manuscript evidence to support the phrase "and fasting" as to omit it!

In the *Expositors Greek Testament,* Dr. O. Morrison notes: "The authorization for omitting 'and fasting' with prayer because of its absence in some ancient manuscripts, really is not sufficient. But even if it were overwhelmingly so, fasting would, in its essence be implied in this text." In other words, this scholar says, "*Really* it

221

should not be omitted, but in any case 'fasting' is implied." I press this point because I fear some may feel that its omission in some translations suggests fasting isn't important (even though Jesus said His disciples would exercise fasting as an abiding discipline until He comes again). Could it be the choice to omit a phrase, when near-equal evidence would recommend its inclusion, reflects more a cultural bias against the history or ritual of fasting, or a subconscious desire to avoid the discipline itself? But most important of all is to not only see the *place* of fasting, but its *power* for breaking yokes of spiritual darkness.

Remember: Fasting is never *earning* things from God but is for *learning* things from Him. And specifically, through fasting we can learn a realm of spiritual authority over the adversary which I don't think we will be able to explain until someday when we are on the heavenside of things. But Jesus does make clear that fasting—with prayer—holds a dynamic which breaks evil power: "This kind only comes out this way!"

I don't know why, but somehow, while I seek God, fasting drains hellish powers of their capacity to withstand the entry of God's kingdom. Jesus has said it, and that's enough to know, so let's learn from this event—as well as the other pivotal and practical illustrations the Scriptures give—of the power of fasting as a discipline.

Practical Guidelines

Now a few words of counsel on how to observe the fast. To begin, simply stated, it requires just plain, good sense; and as I have already said, it involves frequent prayer. But people often ask very practical questions; for example, "How long shall I fast?"

Only the Holy Spirit can direct you regarding the length, but practical considerations ought to be kept in view. Begin by asking the Lord to lead you as to how long your fast should continue. Some people's work is of such a heavy energy expenditure it may disallow a total fast. Remember, Jesus' forty-day fast wasn't carried on while He was keeping office hours or working at the plant every day. He went into the wilderness and was completely away during that season of fasting. A day's fast as a regular discipline is the practice of many, with regularity. The three-day "Believer's Fast" has a long history in the church.

When Daniel goes on his twenty-one-day fast, the Bible says he took "no pleasant food" (Dan. 10:3). The concept is that he didn't satisfy his appetite: He only ate enough to sustain himself; a voluntary reduction of intake, denying himself delicacies yet still answering the basic need for energy. This is an acceptable fast . . . observed with a perfect spirit.

Further, because we are not trying to convince God of our worthiness but rather are simply observing a biblically taught discipline, it is not unspiritual to recognize there will be functional, practical considerations to make at the physical level and they ought to be understood. Here are a few.

First, don't fast if there are medical or dietary reasons which prohibit it. One of my dearest mentors, a man now in his eighties, is a diabetic, yet Dr. Vincent Bird, my first bishop and lifetime friend, has said to me a number of times: "When the congregation fasts, I've learned how to be in *the spirit of a fast*." He means, he applies it with his heart, seeking God in a special way that only he can describe. By reason of his diabetes, he obviously needs to keep eating, but he still moves into the ministry of prayer with a special "spirit"—both in power, but also in practical wisdom. Don't anyone ever be so foolish as to violate medically directed dietary requirements and claim some spiritual pursuit brought you to such folly.

Second, understand your body needs water. As a normal requirement, you should drink at least eight glasses of water daily and especially when you are fasting. Water is not a violation of your fast. When Jesus fasted the forty days, the Bible states, He "was without meat." This specific mention indicates no abstinence of water. So, keep in mind: even our miracle-working Savior needed water. (Incidentally, some of the most spiritual people I have known have suggested this to me—a squeeze of lemon in the water when fasting is helpful; assisting the body in casting off impurities during the fast, assisting the body's cleansing.)

Third, some individuals, whose regimen can't tolerate a complete fast, may find drinking fruit juice will help them remain in the spirit of the fast. I'm not suggesting this procedure as an escape if the Lord calls you to a more complete fast, but to recognize this as one way to diminish your food intake of an appropriate pursuit of a fast. And in this vein, when there are those who for some reason may be unable to participate at all, but a partner is fasting, they can still sustain a partnership in the fast by giving regular times of prayer beyond their usual pattern. No condemnation should be felt by one for not fasting as their spouse or prayer partner is.

Fourth, as we've said, fasting should be joined to special times of prayer, praise, and intercession. For example, during a fasting time, why not set five-minute prayer breaks each hour, or an entire lunchtime. Seek out brothers and sisters in Christ who will feel a partnership with your seeking God in such a fashion, but only if they feel it's their desire, and not the imposition of some religious pushiness on your part.

Finally, take extra time in the Word of God, when fasting. David said, Your Word is "sweeter . . . than . . . the honeycomb" (Ps. 19:10). Jesus also said the Word of God is nourishment to the soul (Matt. 4:4), so feed on it. And as you fast, be further nourished in knowing the pleasure of obedience to God as you fast: "My food is to do the will of Him who sent Me" (John 4:34). Those simple words spoken by Jesus express a concept of nourishment that we can find; especially at times of fasting, as we seek the release of the power that comes through this basic Christian discipline joined with prayer.

IV

BEYOND
DISCIPLINES

"When All Else Fails..."

There is a subtle presumption that tempts us all at times. We're especially vulnerable to its proposition since we're so surrounded by management and technologically sophisticated systems. The tendency is to suppose that if we cultivate sufficient "systems" of discipline we can master Christian living. For some, it's the idea that "faith-formulas" will achieve answers on demand; for others, the sacraments are exercised mechanically presuming they "work" without a warm, personal faith being joined to them. Any number of "sure-fire" systems have proposed themselves over the years, but the wise disciple won't be duped.

In the last analysis, our spiritual life is one of simple, moment to moment dependency upon Jesus. *Alone!* However beneficent acquired disciplines will become, settling and advancing your walk with Him, no method, system, or discipline will *ever* substitute for *just being His.*

Nothing brings this to the foreground more dramatically than life's "tough" or "dry" times. No degree of discipleship will remove you or me from the unexpected or the undesired encounter with trial, temptation, warfare, or soul-weariness.

Beyond discipline there needs to be a resignation of transcendent principles: stepping-stones for slippery times; a road map for those surprising turns that put you in a temporary desert.

Don't fear such prospects. They happen to us all.

And even in the desert God has promised the possibilities of His presence, and the promise includes a transforming of the desert into a beautiful experience.

> The wilderness and the wasteland shall be glad for them, And the desert shall rejoice and blossom as the rose.
>
> (ISA. 35:1)

To capstone our look at healthy disciplines, let me share with you two more chapters—the content of which possibly becoming most important of all we've studied together.

Chapter Twenty-Nine

Seasons of Travail

Nearly 500 pastors had gathered for a conference on the Island of Mindanao, in the south of the Philippines. My denomination had invited me to be the speaker; and as the first evening's service began, I was deeply moved by a prompting of the Holy Spirit. I knew I needed to share with those dear men and women, who so devotedly carried on the work of Christ. I feared their misunderstanding . . . for the Lord had shown me their hearts were "hardened."

However, it was not "hardened hearts" as though they were rebels or stiff-necked people, but hearts which were hardened by reason of the fires of circumstances. The juices of their souls were dried up . . . become cracked; as soil without moisture; dried, as a pond where the sun evaporated the water.

I saw these lovely people, who had labored faithfully in the heat of the day, showing the signs of dryness as a result of their service to Christ. They had faced the fires of hell in battle conflict, and dryness in such circumstances can bring a hardness or a crustiness to any of us. It doesn't necessarily mean a person has been neglectful of their commitment to Christ and His service.

Dryness is an occupational hazard of a disciple. As David said, "As the deer pants for the water brooks, so pants my soul for You, O God" (Ps. 42:1). David was a man who understood the weariness of battle and of long labor without opportunity for refreshing. At such a time he comes to a desperate sense of his need of God.

Having been in public leadership for so many years, I have ministered to hosts of thousands of believers who became just as dry as their leaders. It's easy to become perplexed, confused, disoriented, and feel that something is so wrong with you (or you

227

wouldn't be this way) that you begin to despair. In this environment, we become vulnerable to self-condemnation, failure, bondage, or affliction. In those dark nights of the soul, recognize what has happened to you.

> O God, You are my God; early will I seek You; my soul thirsts for You; my flesh longs for You in a dry and thirsty land where there is no water. So I have looked for You in the sanctuary, to see Your power and Your glory.
>
> (PS. 63:1-2)

> Hungry and thirsty, their soul fainted in them. Then they cried out to the Lord in their trouble, and He delivered them out of their distresses.
>
> (PS. 107:5-6)

> For the enemy has persecuted my soul; he has crushed my life to the ground; he has made me dwell in darkness, Like those who have long been dead. Therefore my spirit is overwhelmed within me; my heart within me is distressed. I remember the days of old; I meditate on all Your works; I muse on the work of Your hands. I spread out my hands to You; my soul longs for You like a thirsty land.
>
> (PS. 143:3-6)

In times like these, how can I find the fountain—be renewed in the blessing of the Lord? The answer is in Revelation 22:17, as the Scripture calls forth to us all: "And the Spirit and the bride say, 'Come!' And let him who hears say, 'Come!' And let him who thirsts come. And whoever desires, let him take the water of life freely."

Dear friend, I can't wait until the end of this chapter to say these remarks. I want you to notice it right now: We're being invited to drink by the One who Himself is the Fountain of Living Water, but who also is the One who, while on the cross, cried out, "I thirst."

Let that sink in, dear one. Jesus understands those times, when in the midst of such thirstiness, you also cry out, "My God, why have You forsaken me?" Our Savior is very akin to our times of travail—when our sense of aloneness and dryness cries for refreshing.

Avoiding a Mistaken Idea

I've wanted to close with these thoughts, because there is a mistaken notion in a few minds that to learn a disciplined life is to attain an exalted, almost euphoric state of accomplished spirituality. The corollary to this supposition is that struggles, trials, or dry seasons become former things of the past. But this isn't so. And *"travail"* — those dry, in-between seasons of the soul — are certain to happen to the most mature among us. Recognizing how they happen can help us deal with these when they come. So let me give eight reasons why or how soul-dryness occurs.

1. *No reprieve from sustained seasons of demanding duty.*

For example, sometime ago I was speaking with a friend who resigned his pastorate. In the midst of very real demands of a building program, personal extenuating circumstances, and a physical affliction, he recognized his burned-out condition and knew it would be best for all involved.

When there's been no reprieve from sustained seasons of demanding duty, anybody dries out. It's not just true of busy pastors. I've seen women so drained by the demands of pregnancy — then post-pregnancy emotions, and the new baby in the house — that their spiritual life absolutely goes to seed. Business people go through economic fires that sap life's juices. In such times, there can come a certain cynicism which threatens to take over. "Does anybody know, or does God know or care — about my situation?"

Take time to read Genesis 21 sometime.

Hagar had been driven out by Sarah. She was lost in the desert with a baby, the beginning of the reason for her being driven out. She's looking around, wondering if it's all over for her and the child. Then, the Bible says, "God opened her eyes, and she saw a well of water" (Gen. 21:19).

The Lord has the same hope awaiting you too. Whether your labor is as a worker serving in the name of the Lord, or your wearying labor was in having a baby, that dryness came from sustained, demanding duty. It doesn't mean you're unspiritual, but the dryness does need to be answered by God's "opening your eyes."

2. *Tireless assault of unrelenting temptation.*

A second source of dryness is *long* temptation.

One of the most demanding times in my life was a season

when the adversary bombarded my mind with an unceasing fear of failure. It lasted for a period of nearly four months. I didn't do and hadn't done anything wrong; not yielding to any order of temptation. I was steadfastly faithful to the Lord all that time. But I kept fearing the relentless barrage coming on my mind was somehow eventually going to take over and dominate, and the vicious attack seemed never to go away. But *then!*

The day came that the enemy was defeated as the Lord showed me these ferocious assaults were actually fashioning for me a great reward. "Blessed is the man who endures temptation; for when he has been proved, he will receive the crown of life" (James 1:12).

I can hardly describe the joy I felt: "Praise God—this struggle isn't all for nothing. There's a *crown* of reward I'm about to receive!" That rich promise became *so* releasing to me! Let it be so to you too when your soul is drained by long assault.

3. *Bewilderment over personal tragedy or reversal.*

How many times do our minds ask questions when something upsetting, tragic, or overwhelming has happened? "Blessing" seems absent due to such "invasions" into our lives or our circumstances. At such times, it's so easy to conclude it happened because "there's something wrong between God and me."

Oh, how the adversary loves to steal from us and then to slap at us; to strike us in the face as though we were the ones guilty for creating the environment for his hateful invasion. Such bewilderment that follows is another thing that can dry us out. Learn to lay before the Lord any personal disappointment, any crushing sense of failure, or any "thing" which has caused you the dryness born of reversal and the condemning questions that so often ensue.

4. *Attempting too long to "be strong" without partnership.*

There is a certain nobility in devotion when we seek to carry a load on our own. The Bible *does* say, "Everyone shall bear their own burden." But it also says "Bear one another's burdens, and so fulfill the law of Christ." This strikes to the heart of the way some sincere people try to live: "Oh, I don't want to bother anybody with my problems." They talk as though there is a certain noble quality in their single-handed stalwartness, "going to go it alone."

But not so, dear one. If we attempt too long to be strong

without partnering with one another, we are not only violating the Scripture, we're destined for dryness. The words, "Each one shall bear their own burden" refers to our personal responsibilities, but the word *"burdens"* in "bear one another's burdens" is the word for *"overload."* So, whenever you're "on overload," *say so!* Don't wait until you're so mad that you scream it to somebody or you're ready to break some other way.

About a year ago I spoke with a small group of men with whom I meet regularly, and said, "Guys, I need to tell you—I'm just about numb: I've gone on *overload*." I was becoming nit-picking and irritable, and my wife pointed it out—nicely, but accurately. I needed people to pray for me—to partner with me for a *breakthrough*, not just an excuse ("You'll have to understand me . . . I'm *so* busy.") Excuses don't make it. Honesty in saying, "I need help" *does*.

Within days I experienced an amazing turnaround, as the numbness and dryness were gone which I had accumulated through the raw demands of duty.

5. *Attacks of antagonism, hostility, and criticism.*

There will always be people who are quick to pass judgment, to criticize, to complain. Their "ministry" can bake any soul dry!

Several years ago when God had broken forth with unique revival in the place I was serving, one of my most beloved teachers from Bible college training days turned against me. Though not mentioning my name, he publicly attacked certain things which were happening to me as the blessing of God swept through our church.

Bitterness began to enter my heart. The sense of love for a man I had always respected, now was being betrayed, and instead of my being *watered* by that love, I found myself being *scorched* by criticism. I was beginning to respond in a way that betrayed dryness until I found another fountain of God's grace to compensate for what had been taken from me. Forgiveness followed, but I learned the danger of dryness when you are unjustly attacked.

6. *Serving a sensory level rather than the spiritual level.*

When you're weary, it's wise to learn that relaxation alone won't completely minister to your need. *Both* the spiritual *and* the physical dimensions need resting, and the soul only finds it in God.

I had gone on vacation, and I needed it! I remember how delightful it was to get to the beach with Anna and the kids, enjoying a condo loaned to us for a week.

They were great days. But about the fourth day, when everything seemed to be so relaxing, out from under pressure, I found I was feeling *empty* inside. As I thought about my good *external* feeling, I wondered about the hollowness I felt inside. Then, it occurred to me.

For four days, I hadn't read a word of Scripture; I hadn't prayed a prayer; I hadn't once sung a song of praise. It was just kind of, "Let's get away from it all." Without planning or saying as much, it was as though we were so involved with church, the Bible, and prayer that we didn't want to do anything especially "godly" for a while.

Does that sound *awful* to you? Sure it does, but forgive me — it's the way I felt. And it *wasn't* because I didn't love the Lord. It's simply that I was exhausted beyond feeling.

But I was "called back" by the inner "hollowness" that I felt. And through that experience I learned the impracticality of trying to recover at the physical/emotional level of my life if I neglect the spiritual level of my life.

If the lesson speaks to you, accept it. It's not a plea for *religious* action when vacationing, but a remembrance of our need of *Him — relationship*. He's the Fountain that answers to our dry times.

7. *Experiencing doubts without bringing them to Jesus.*

How many suffer sieges when prayers seem unanswered, problems seem unsolved, a prophecy unrealized — "things" which create questions. We begin to doubt if God is hearing our prayers, we back away from promises, and we discard the prophecies of promise He's given us.

Don't wallow in doubt. Renounce it by taking every question to the Lord. He isn't offended by our doubts. Say, "Jesus, I want to talk to You about this. I don't understand."

You might not find an instant answer, but I think you *will* find the refreshing of His presence. "In Your presence is fullness of joy; at Your right hand are pleasures evermore" (Ps. 16:11). It is impossible to remain dry for long — however doubt-ridden — when we choose to abide in the presence of the One from whom the springs of living water flow.

8. *Neglect of basic disciplines of spiritual sustenance, or known disobedi-*

ence to understood directives of the Holy Spirit.

We'll go dry if we don't pray, if we don't drink the water of the Word, if we don't praise, and if we don't lift our voices in song. Dryness is generated if I consciously pursue a path of disobeying.

One day not long ago, I was walking through the living room at the house and looked over at the piano. I happened to be feeling kind of weary at the time. (As you may know, I play the piano and have written some songs of Christian worship.) As I glanced at the keyboard, the Holy Spirit whispered to me, "You haven't been there for several weeks, have you?"

I immediately realized He was addressing the reason for my dryness and weariness: I hadn't taken time as I usually did in coming before the Lord in Spirit-refreshing praise. I accepted the prompting, turned to a time of worship, and shortly was renewed and refreshed.

The neglect of basic disciplines of spiritual sustenance—prayer, the Word, praise—has a way of drying out any of us. It may not be a very profound observation, but the answer to the very frequently asked question, "What's happening to me?" is simply—"You can't neglect the basics."

Times of travail come to every believer. They weary the body, dry the soul, taunt the spirit, exhaust the emotions, beget doubts in the mind, breed despair in the heart. All those things seldom happen at once, but the variety of points at which we're vulnerable are enough to bring us all to times of questioning: "How'd I get here? How can I get out?" or, "What's wrong, God? Why can't things be different?"

When dryness besieges the soul, it can touch areas of our life so that it seems God's presence has evaporated. And when that happens, (1) don't think you're strange, and (2) don't accept the Liar's accusations; but (3) do turn to the Fountain of Living Water—Jesus, and (4) do remember that *seasons of travail mean something is about to be born!*

"Sing, O barren, you who have not borne! Break forth into singing, and cry aloud, you who have not travailed with child! For more are the children of the desolate than the children of the married woman," says the Lord. "Enlarge the place of your tent, and let them stretch out the curtains of your habitations; do not spare; lengthen your cords, and strengthen your stakes. For you shall expand to the right and to the left, and your descendants will inherit the nations, and make the desolate cities inhabited. Do not fear, for you will not be ashamed."

(ISA. 54:1-4)

And to that great promise of "new life" where there's been "barrenness," add one more promise from Isaiah's prophetic message:

Ho! Everyone who thirsts, come to the waters; and you who have no money, come, buy and eat.

(ISA. 55:1)

For as the rain comes down, and the snow from heaven, and do not return there, but water the earth, and make it bring forth and bud, that it may give seed to the sower and bread to the eater, So shall My word be that goes forth from My mouth; it shall not return to Me void, but it shall accomplish what I please, and it shall prosper in the thing for which I sent it. For you shall go out with joy, and be led out with peace; the mountains and the hills shall break forth into singing before you, and all the trees of the field shall clap their hands.

(ISA. 55:10-12)

Chapter Thirty

The Child and the Lamb

I want to bring a brief postscript to these many hours that we have spent together around the Word of God studying about our life in Jesus Christ our Savior and opening to the ministry of the Holy Spirit.

I trust these printed words have inspired you toward Spirit-filled living.

As I've focused on the keys to a growing, expanding walk with the Lord, we've explored

the prospects of discipleship;

the fundamental disciplines for servants of Jesus;

the exceeding wonders of prayer; and

how to face obstacles which appear.

We've hoped to secure the principles for living a growing life in God's power and purpose. But as we finish, one thought remains — which is to my mind as fundamental and essential as any I know.

Especially when "power" and "blessing" are mentioned, you've doubtless heard the verse quoted many times, "Not by might nor by power, but by My Spirit, says the Lord of Hosts" (Zech. 4:6). It's usually quoted in some dramatic or sensational way.

Naturally, I joyously praise God for those dramatic or sensational ways in which His power sometimes works. But, dear friend, the very quotation of that verse, when accompanied by a thunderous demonstration of praise for God's visitation and might, somehow misses the essential setting and the point of that promise.

- The man who is being given the promise was at a time of real difficulty: his name was Zerubbabel.

- The building project that he was seeking to lead — the rebuilding of the temple in Jerusalem — was not going well at all.

That's when the Prophet Zechariah came to him and said, "Zerubbabel, this is God's word to you . . . 'Not by might nor by power, but by My Spirit, says the Lord of Hosts.' " I frankly think the Lord was *not* saying, "Watch Me whip this thing together in one glorious miracle moment." Rather, it appears instead that He was saying to Zerubbabel, "I have a way that transcends what you can do. Just call upon Me for My grace to bring it about." (See Zech. 4:7 also.)

God's *grace,* available *for all our need for all our lifetime,* is the grandest promise of all, and it's joined to and it flows from the moment of our forgiveness of sin and beginning of eternal life. Just as grace is the means by which we receive salvation, grace is the means for letting God work in His might and power for all our walk with Him. The heart that learns this will grow to learn *the spirit of the love of God* in Jesus Christ.

Do you remember when Jesus spoke to His disciples and said, "You don't know what spirit you are of." It was because they were looking for a visitation of God to do a powerful thing, when He was wanting them to learn to have a *tender* heart.

That tender, teachable, touchable way is the path to true power; to lasting, miracle-expecting, Christ-exalting power and blessing. And in that understanding, I want to leave you with two words: the *child* and *the Lamb.*

The Child

In Matthew 18:3, Jesus said, "Unless you . . . become as little children, you will in no means enter the kingdom of heaven." In these words He was *not* so much talking about receiving new birth and going to heaven, as much as learning a childlikeness of heart, so we enter into the dimensions of God's *rule* — His kingdom power and blessing in our living.

He was saying that childlikeness is the way to maturity.

Does that seem a paradox of terms — becoming a child and mature? Let me tell you quite simply what I've come to believe very deeply about spiritual "maturity."

There is no such thing as "adulthood" in spiritual life.

I've become convinced we only learn how to be "more of a child" if we're really growing; more of a child in tenderness, responsiveness, teachability, shapeability, and correctability by the Father through His Spirit and His Word. And as we humble ourselves like children before the Ancient of Days, though we might attain 80, 90, or 100 years of life, our wisdom is small at best, and our "maturity of years" but a fleck of dust on the face of all eternity. In number of years, we will all be *forever* but children, however wise life's lessons may seem to have taught us to become.

The Lamb

Finally, as we come before the Lord in childlikeness, let us learn the second word: The *Lamb*.

In Luke 12:32, Jesus said, "Do not fear little flock, for it is your Father's good pleasure to give you the kingdom." Hear Jesus say, "It's lambs 'who take the kingdom.' "

And He should know.

For it is in His dying as "the Lamb of God" that He ultimately gained possession of all authority in earth and heaven, and over all death and hell. Jesus knew that even as He became a *child* in Bethlehem, redemption would be revealed through a *lamb* on a cross. So we who follow in His pathways as disciples are wise to ever and always let this fact dominate our lives: childlikeness and lamblikeness.

And as we conclude in the intimacy of this insight, may our integrity with the Child who became the Lamb work these things in our lives. And may God always grant, until the day we see Him face-to-face, that we live as *His* sheep, who will one day stand before Him with praise saying,

Worthy is the Lamb to receive blessing and honor and glory and power, forever and ever unto the ages of the ages. Amen!

(SEE REV. 6:12)